Drugs, Law, People, Place and the State

Though any psychoactive substance can be revered or reviled as a drug, as people's cultural norms shift, ultimately its status is determined in law by the state. This publication explores the regulation of drugs – alcohol and cannabis to heroin and cocaine – and practices such as social drinking and public injecting under political regimes. Drugs are discussed in their geographical contexts: the colonial legacy of cannabis prohibition for bioprospecting in Africa, the veracity of the persistent notion of the narco-state, Turkey's governance of drinking amid civil unrest and alcohol's place in the neoliberal political economy of Ireland. In addition, drug policies are examined: from problems in managing drug-related litter in the United Kingdom to supervised injecting facility provision in Australia, harm reduction in Canada and the global network of drug policy activists. Place is significant, but porous borders, territorial overlaps and multi-scalar linkages are influential in remaking the world through current challenges to the 'war on drugs'. This book was originally published as a special issue of *Space & Polity*.

Stewart Williams is a Senior Lecturer in the School of Land and Food, University of Tasmania, Australia. He is interested in matters of risk, regulation and resilience from the perspective of public policy and spatial planning. He has combined critical social theory with mixed research methods to analyse housing and homelessness, climate change and disaster management, community decline and regeneration, and drug production and consumption.

Barney Warf is a Professor at the Department of Geography and Atmospheric Science, University of Kansas, USA. His research concerns producer services and telecommunications, particularly the geographies of the Internet, including the digital divide, e-government and Internet censorship. He examines these topics, and others such as political geography, religion, cosmopolitanism and corruption, through the lens of political economy and social theory.

Drugs, Law, People, Place and the State

Ongoing Regulation, Resistance and Change

Edited by
Stewart Williams and Barney Warf

Routledge
Taylor & Francis Group
LONDON AND NEW YORK

First published 2017
by Routledge
2 Park Square, Milton Park, Abingdon, Oxon, OX14 4RN, UK

and by Routledge
711 Third Avenue, New York, NY 10017, USA

Routledge is an imprint of the Taylor & Francis Group, an informa business

British Library Cataloguing in Publication Data
A catalogue record for this book is available from the British Library

ISBN 13: 978-1-138-70045-1

Typeset in TimesNewRomanPS
by diacriTech, Chennai

Publisher's Note
The publisher accepts responsibility for any inconsistencies that may have arisen during the conversion of this book from journal articles to book chapters, namely the possible inclusion of journal terminology.

Disclaimer
Every effort has been made to contact copyright holders for their permission to reprint material in this book. The publishers would be grateful to hear from any copyright holder who is not here acknowledged and will undertake to rectify any errors or omissions in future editions of this book.

Contents

Citation Information

The following chapters were originally published in *Space & Polity*, volume 20, issue 1 (April 2016). When citing this material, please use the original page numbering for each article, as follows:

Chapter 1
Drugs, law, people, place and the state: ongoing regulation, resistance and change
Stewart Williams and Barney Warf
Space & Polity, volume 20, issue 1 (April 2016) pp. 1–9

Chapter 2
Drug laws, bioprospecting and the agricultural heritage of Cannabis *in Africa*
Chris S. Duvall
Space & Polity, volume 20, issue 1 (April 2016) pp. 10–25

Chapter 3
The myth of the narco-state
Pierre-Arnaud Chouvy
Space & Polity, volume 20, issue 1 (April 2016) pp. 26–38

Chapter 4
From rakı *to* ayran*: regulating the place and practice of drinking in Turkey*
Emine Ö. Evered and Kyle T. Evered
Space & Polity, volume 20, issue 1 (April 2016) pp. 39–58

Chapter 5
Neoliberalism and the alcohol industry in Ireland
Julien Mercille
Space & Polity, volume 20, issue 1 (April 2016) pp. 59–74

Chapter 6
Colliding intervention in the spatial management of street-based injecting and drug-related litter within settings of public convenience (UK)
Stephen Parkin
Space & Polity, volume 20, issue 1 (April 2016) pp. 75–94

Chapter 7

Space, scale and jurisdiction in health service provision for drug users: the legal geography of a supervised injecting facility
Stewart Williams
Space & Polity, volume 20, issue 1 (April 2016) pp. 95–108

Chapter 8

Political struggles on a frontier of harm reduction drug policy: geographies of constrained policy mobility
Andrew Longhurst and Eugene McCann
Space & Polity, volume 20, issue 1 (April 2016) pp. 109–123

Chapter 9

Mobilizing drug policy activism: conferences, convergence spaces and ephemeral fixtures in social movement mobilization
Cristina Temenos
Space & Polity, volume 20, issue 1 (April 2016) pp. 124–141

Notes on Contributors

Pierre-Arnaud Chouvy is a geographer and specialist in the (geo)politics of illegal drug production in Asia. He is currently a research fellow with the French National Centre for Scientific Research (CNRS) in Paris, France. His work can be consulted on www.geopium.org and includes such books as *Opium: Uncovering the Politics of the Poppy* (2010).

Chris S. Duvall is an Associate Professor in the Department of Geography and Environmental Studies, University of New Mexico, USA. His research focuses on human–plant interactions, primarily in Africa and amongst the African Atlantic Diaspora. His current work focuses on the historical geography of cannabis. Dr. Duvall's publications on the topic include the book *Cannabis* (2015), and one forthcoming on the historical geography of cannabis in Africa (expected 2018).

Emine Ö. Evered is an Associate Professor in the Department of History, Michigan State University, USA. A historian of the modern Middle East, she focuses on late Ottoman and early republican Turkey. Her *Empire and Education Under the Ottomans* (2012) examined educational policy and schooling in terms of society–state relations, identity politics and international affairs. Her research interests extend to public health, disease, sexuality and sex work, and intoxicants. A second book will address the rise and fall of prohibition in the early Turkish republic.

Kyle T. Evered is an Associate Professor in the Department of Geography, Environment, and Spatial Sciences, Michigan State University, USA. Trained in geographies of the Middle East, North Africa and the former Soviet states of Eurasia, his research concerns the cultural and historical geographies, political geographies and cultural ecologies of Turkey and its neighbouring states and wider regions. Specific interests include geographies of the opium poppy, health and well-being, and identity–place constructs such as nationalism, territoriality and regionalism.

Andrew Longhurst is a researcher and policy analyst at the Health Sciences Association of British Columbia and a research associate with the British Columbia Office of the Canadian Centre for Policy Alternatives in Vancouver, Canada. His research focuses on the spatial and political–economic dimensions of health and social policy, poverty and inequality, and labour market change.

Eugene McCann is University Professor of Geography at Simon Fraser University, Canada. He is an urban political geographer who researches policy mobilities, urban policy-making, planning, social and health policy, and urban politics. He has co-edited and co-authored three books on these and related topics and has published numerous journal articles. He is managing editor of *Environment and Planning C: Politics and Space*.

Julien Mercille is an Associate Professor at the School of Geography, University College Dublin, Ireland. In addition to drugs and alcohol issues, his interests include the media, health care, the European economic crisis, US foreign policy and geopolitics. He addresses these topics primarily through a critical political economy approach. In addition to his academic publishing, he writes and appears regularly in the media.

Stephen Parkin is a Qualitative Researcher in the Nuffield Department of Primary Care Health Sciences, University of Oxford, UK. He has been involved in drug-related research since 1995 and has worked extensively throughout the United Kingdom on a number of different studies. His previous work has included topics such as 'black market' methadone, peer education and recreational drug use.

Cristina Temenos is a postdoctoral research fellow in Urban Studies at the Manchester Urban Institute and Geography, University of Manchester, UK. She is an urban geographer studying the relationships between social justice and the mobilisation of social, health and drug policies across cities in the Global North and Global South. Her work on urban policy mobilities has been published in various journals as well as *The Routledge Handbook of Mobilities* (2013).

Barney Warf is a Professor at the Department of Geography and Atmospheric Science, University of Kansas, USA. His research concerns producer services and telecommunications, particularly the geographies of the Internet, including the digital divide, e-government and Internet censorship. He examines these topics, and others such as political geography, religion, cosmopolitanism and corruption, through the lens of political economy and social theory.

Stewart Williams is a Senior Lecturer in the School of Land and Food, University of Tasmania, Australia. He is interested in matters of risk, regulation and resilience from the perspective of public policy and spatial planning. He has combined critical social theory with mixed research methods to analyse housing and homelessness, climate change and disaster management, community decline and regeneration, and drug production and consumption.

Drugs, law, people, place and the state: ongoing regulation, resistance and change

Stewart Williams[a] and Barney Warf[b]

[a]*School of Land and Food (Geography and Spatial Sciences Discipline), University of Tasmania, Hobart, Australia;* [b] *Department of Geography, University of Kansas, Lawrence, USA*

We introduce this special issue firstly by tracing drugs from their traditional, cultural and religious uses through to their roles as commodities in colonial relations and now the global economy. We secondly explore the shifting nature of drugs and drug use in different places and times as shaped by politics, especially state regulation and the law. Thirdly, given the complexity as well as contingency of drugs, we survey a wide range of relevant theoretical approaches, but suggest that a critical analysis attend to their spatial framing and geography. Fourthly, and finally, we summarize the eight papers comprising this collection.

Introduction

Drugs are variously perceived by people, and can therefore be valued in very different ways both within and among communities, institutions and nation-states. Yet they have been a significant element of social and political relations for eons. The tea plant, for example, was probably encountered first by prehistoric humans (*Homo erectus*) foraging for food, but its domestication was progressed across China and beyond by Buddhist, Confucian and Daoist monks discovering, as a result of their necessary participation in all-night meditation sessions, that beverages made from an infusion of tea leaves helps with concentration (Heiss & Heiss, 2007). Traditional drug use has often been religious in nature. The ingestion of coca leaves among the Inca, peyote buttons among many Native Americans, and cannabis flowers and resin among Hindu and Sufi holy men are longstanding and deeply enculturated practices (Schaefer & Furst, 1997; Warf, 2014).

Colonialism and the industrial revolution opened a dramatic new chapter in this story, however, as drug plants that once had meanings and uses associated with particular peoples and places were re-made as novel, exotic commodities for consumption by others elsewhere. Tobacco, introduced to the British by Native Americans, was simultaneously denounced as a "demonic vegetable" and embraced enthusiastically in the new custom of smoking. By the seventeenth century, write Kenneth Pomeranz and Steven Topik, it was "as if all the tobacco in the world was roaring in a great, brown tsunami up the Thames toward London" (1999, p. 99). Opium, then also being imported into Europe from afar, similarly became a commodity in high demand. It was increasingly used over the course of the nineteenth century and not just in the form traditionally smoked in the infamous dens encountered first in the East and later in the metropolitan West. Modern industrial chemistry, manufacturing, transportation, advertising and retailing made it possible for opium to be processed into array of medicinal tinctures, soothing elixirs, cough syrups and the like, which had substantial markets at home and abroad. Opium provided profits and pleasures (as well as pain relief, if required) to the individual importers and exporters as well as producers and consumers of such goods, but the greatest beneficiaries were the colonizing nation-states' governments, which received significant revenues from its taxation. Indeed, these monies were so central to imperial coffers that British confrontations with the Chinese over their attempts to limit imports of this drug from India culminated in the Opium Wars of the 1840s and 1850s (Booth, 1996).

Today, of course, alcohol remains the most widely used drug in the world even though it is forbidden in some parts and known to have harmful effects (World Health Organization, 2014). Familiarity and accessibility can obscure the fact that it is a drug, but even relatively ubiquitous and seemingly benign commodities, including foodstuffs such as cocoa, chocolate and coffee, are also drugs (Goodman, 2007). Some drugs are synthetic, unlike these naturally occurring ones, and new psychoactive substances are constantly being invented. Their manufacture for illicit purposes is appealing because when first synthesized they have not yet been officially identified as drugs and there is a time lag often of several years before they might be made subject to any legal designation or regulatory measure. So-called legal highs or designer drugs have been promoted with vernacular names such as kronic, fantasy, grievous bodily harm and meow-meow, among others, and are sold on to recreational drug users in innovative ways, including via the Internet (especially the deep web) and using "bitcoin" type virtual currencies (Power, 2013; Taylor, 2015). These most recent of developments, enabled by new technologies, have arisen through individuals' efforts to avoid detection and/or defer prosecution by the state, but then the structural processes behind once-familiar patterns of drug production, distribution and consumption, and their impacts and the societal responses to them, are subsequently now also reconfigured.

Drugs and drug use practices with longer histories and cultural associations can also be unsettled, and some are now turning up in expected places. Thus, for example, the importation, cultivation and use of khat by migrants from the Middle East and Africa are not necessarily illicit or intentionally clandestine activities but they certainly are controversial in this drug plant's new homelands (Anderson, Beckerleg, Hailu, & Klein, 2007). Similarly, in Africa, there are cities that are now operating as major transit points in an ever-shifting, frequently re-routed global drugs trade; and some rural regions there have started to cultivate drug plants such as poppy and coca, which are otherwise endemic to and still primarily grown on continents other than Africa (Carrier & Klantschnig, 2012). Indeed, Courtwright (2002) charts a 500-year-long "psychoactive revolution" in which the diversity, availability, potency and popularity of drugs have all steadily increased. Such observations, above all, hint at the social and spatial unevenness and ever-changing nature of drugs and drug use. Especially relevant, as we explain further below, is the fact that drugs are invariably tied to cultural perceptions and misperceptions, reflecting contemporary social values and mores, while also being profoundly imbricated in the politics of institutionalized control as well as moral regulation.

What exactly constitutes a "drug" as something distinct from a food or medicine is largely a matter of historical and geographic context. The word is often taken to refer only to cultivated plant materials and manufactured products containing psychoactive chemicals which have been made illegal since deemed harmful to the individual and to society. The outlawing of any drug tends to happen quite haphazardly, but it is then also politically charged, and variously capricious or contradictory. As the social acceptance of any one particular drug or type of drug waxes and wanes over time, its legal status can shift accordingly. When this sort of change does occur, sometimes slowly, other times abruptly, it is often the result of political opportunism as much as any concern for public health. Irrespectively, however, the impacts are usually profound and extend far beyond the interests of the law and those authorities administering it.

The law, people, place and the state

The legality or illegality of drugs is a key factor in their constitution, but it varies among countries, and sometimes within them. Again, however, the distinction is a contingent one. Take, for example, the drug plant cannabis, also known as marijuana and in processed form as hashish. It was legal in most parts of the world until included in the League of Nations' 1925 Geneva Convention on Opium and Other Drugs. International agreements of this type have continued ever since to make cannabis a globally prohibited drug, but the nation-states signatory to them must then pass their own laws which can then be interpreted and enforced in the specific contexts of those peoples and places over which they pertain.

In the USA, for example, the end of (alcohol's) Prohibition in 1933 led to the demonization of cannabis as it was effectively criminalized with the Marijuana Stamp Act of 1936 and became the new *raison d'être* for drug enforcement agencies that had previously focused on alcohol. That nation-state's regulation of cannabis and many other drugs throughout the twentieth century was an interdictory one, punctuated with "War on Drugs", "Zero tolerance" and "Just say No" styles of policy campaign. Prohibition, illegality, criminalization and deterrence have similarly characterized the drug control regimes of most other nation-states (but not all of them or always; see, for example, McCann, 2008 on the more liberal alternatives of harm reduction). This is because they, like the USA, happen to be signatories to the three main international drug control treaties administered by the United Nations (UN) since 1961, 1971 and 1988, respectively. These international treaties are used to direct and frame (but can then also constrain) the approaches to drug control adopted by their signatory nation-states.

Establishing new drug laws and policies, and challenging extant ones, in any country must usually engage the national or federal legislature and judiciary as they hold supreme authority. However, change is still possible at the sub-national level. In the USA, cannabis is illegal under federal law, but its possession (in quantities of one ounce or less) has been progressively decriminalized in 24 states, starting with Oregon in 1973. A further advance was made in 2012 when both Colorado and Washington State legalized the drug for recreational use; they have since been joined by Alaska and Oregon. The use of cannabis for medical reasons is also legalized in the USA, with this reform extending to 23 states and the District of Columbia (Warf, 2014).

That a drug and its use on particular grounds is officially sanctioned inside the borders of the nation-state in one jurisdiction but not in another is an expression of the law's power and constitutive force. It is similarly exemplified by the manufacture of opioids or narcotics, which is licit when conducted under license from the UN and generating revenue for the pharmaceutical industry's powerful transnational corporations and their shareholders. These corporations gain recognition and legitimacy as they work with the government approval and support of licensed nation-states found mostly in the global North, but they also distinguish themselves from others in the global South, including millions of rural peasants whose livelihoods depend on cultivating poppy for the illegal drugs trade (Williams, 2010, 2013). On this basis, drugs such as codeine are differentiated and distanced from others such as heroin, even though heroin is legally available for hospital procedures in Australia and the UK, for example, whereas the possession and use of codeine suddenly becomes illegal in the hands of someone for whom it was not prescribed. Indeed, both of these drugs are derivatives of morphine, which is obtained from poppies, and therefore highly addictive; either one can be as problematic when irregularly obtained and used as it is effective when administered in a medical setting.

One might well wonder, in light of the above and regards drugs generally, as Goodman and Lovejoy (2007, p. 258) ask,

> why is it that at certain times and in certain places, some substances have become illicit while others remain acceptable, both legally and socially? What explains the shifts in attitudes that affect political and cultural decisions? The boundary between licit and illicit has been permeable, as opium and tobacco both demonstrate, but how can we analyse the space for negotiation in the signification of substances as one type or the other?

Drugs have been at the centre of enormous political controversies for decades, and raise numerous important issues and thus questions that bear directly on policy. Why, for example, does the federal government of the USA subsidize tobacco, which kills 480,000 people in the country annually, but make cannabis a Schedule I drug comparable to heroin even though there is no evidence that it has ever killed anyone? Prescription drugs harm far more people than all illegal ones do worldwide, and yet their abuse is only weakly deterred because it is hard both to detect and to prove, cases do not always make it to court and those prosecutions that do succeed tend still only to see relatively minor penalties applied, perhaps due to the political power of pharmaceutical companies? Why did the neo-liberal "War on Drugs" backfire so miserably, filling jails and ruining lives? Do coca eradication efforts in Latin America help to stem the tide of cocaine? How are the geopolitics of Afghanistan's Taliban and the global opium and heroin trade intertwined?

The authors of the papers presented here, like the collection's editors, have long been concerned with such matters and therefore consider the legality of drugs in nuanced ways that progress beyond just looking at the vagaries of whether or not different societies simply accept the possession, use, manufacture and supply or trafficking of drugs. There is a need to probe the regulation of drugs more deeply because some of them can be subject to excessive controls due to moral panics, for example, whereas others might be much more readily overlooked because of the increasingly available options for discretion in policing. Some drugs and drug use, if riding a wave of social acceptance, will get to be decriminalized if not perhaps even legalized. Similarly, the blanket bans on drugs imposed by nation-states over their territories and citizens can provide exemptions in particular situations. At the same time, the nature of drugs and drug use continues to change. Any understanding of them and their impacts, and likewise of how they might best be managed, can therefore soon become anachronistic and out of place. Moreover, the drug trade, like so many other domains of social life, has become thoroughly globalized, with far-reaching effects.

Theoretical approaches to understanding drugs

The topic of drugs has been theorized from diverse conceptual perspectives. Beyond the neoclassical economic fantasy of explaining drug phenomena in terms of simplistic supply and demand models, it is evident that drug production, distribution and consumption have all been enfolded within wider understandings of class, gender, ethnicity and power. The Foucauldian sense of biopower, in which drugs may be seen as integral to the production and regulation of modern subjects, is a useful point of departure (Bergschmidt, 2004; Keane, 2009). Drug regulation has become an essential part of the neo-liberal state, and the policing of bodies – especially young, male, minority ones – is an integral part of attempts to control illegal drug use. Drugs and drug use are deeply political, and their legality or illegality is as much a matter of class and ethnicity as it is a public health concern.

A different view of drugs and drug use embeds them within the context of cultural ecology, notably attempts to bridge the once-solid divide between humans and plants and portray them as a seamlessly integrated totality (Hall & Hargrove, 2009; Head & Atchison, 2008). This approach, in line with broader reconceptualizations of the social production of nature as made, not given, has drawn on actor–network theory as inspired by Latour, Delanda and others. Drugs thus easily cross once-solid dichotomies such as natural/cultural, and are discursively repositioned as hybrids that defy such boundaries. Finally, given the poststructuralist emphasis on fluidity, drugs have been seen in light of globalized networks and assemblages that inseparably link actors as diverse as Peruvian coca farmers, heroin producers in Myanmar and Thailand, or cannabis growers in California and British Colombia with users in diverse locales around the world (Marez, 2004; Neilson & Bamyeh, 2009). This line of thought calls attention to the power relations that shape drug cultivation, manufacture and consumption, firmly uniting producers and users in a manner akin to commodity chain analysis. It also points to the differential geographies embedded within and produced by such linkages.

There is an inevitable spatiality to the drug phenomena noted above. It ranges from the setting of any one location, each with its own unique physical environment as well as proximities and distances relative to elsewhere, through to the symbolically and materially powerful spaces created through the territorial demarcations maybe of jurisdiction or, alternatively, arising from the affective experience associated with a more personal sense of place. A small but informative body of literature has therefore examined drugs from an explicitly geographic perspective (for overviews, see Taylor, Jasparro, & Mattson, 2013; Williams, 2014). This corpus ostensibly started with the influential research of Rengert (1996). It has since grown to comprise work examining many of the different landscapes of drug production (Hobbs, 1998; Steinberg, Hobbs, & Mathewson, 2004); the variously socio-cultural and political economic geographies of assorted drugs including opium, coca and amphetamines (Allen, 2005; Chouvy, 2009; Chouvy & Meissonnier, 2004); and drug addiction and its treatment and prevention (DeVerteuil & Wilton, 2009; Rengert, Ratcliffe, & Chakravorty, 2005; Thomas, Richardson, & Cheung, 2008). In addressing the public health aspects of drug use, geographers have collaborated with epidemiologists, ethnographers, statisticians, lawyers and policy-makers among others (see, for example, Tempalski & Cooper, 2014).

Geographers along with scholars from many other disciplines, including anthropology, political science, sociology, economics and criminology, have exhibited growing interest in drugs for several reasons. The globalization of drug production and consumption, including the horrific associated mass violence in Mexico, is one good reason (Reuter, 2009). The Taliban's successful hijacking of the opium trade in Afghanistan is another (Piazza, 2012). In addition, as the costs of the disastrous "war on drugs" accumulate, including mass incarceration and millions of ruined lives, the constitution of drugs and drug use and how they are regulated, especially in terms of their legality or not, have drawn increased scrutiny. In the USA, for example, with the highest incarceration rate in the world, drugs are the leading cause of imprisonment – 700,000 people are arrested annually for marijuana alone – creating a burden that falls overwhelmingly on impoverished black and Latino communities (Lynch, Omori, Russell, & Valasik, 2013). The war on drugs in many ways has been a war on young men of colour.

Given the enormous inequalities that surround drugs, it is not surprising that geographers have started to take a critically analytic stance toward the subject (see, for example, Wilton & Moreno, 2012). More remarkable, however, is that their interest appears to have mostly been concentrated on aspects of drugs and drug use other than regulatory, legal ones (for exceptions, see DeVerteuil & Wilton, 2009, and select articles in both Wilton & Moreno, 2012 and Banister, Boyce, & Slack,

2015). The papers presented together here go some small way towards addressing our perceived shortfall in this area of scholarship.

Encounters with ongoing regulation, resistance and change

There are eight research papers comprising this edited collection. The first four explore the regulation of drugs (including cannabis, opium and alcohol), which has predominantly been defined in law at the national or federal scale. They critically analyse the nation-state in relation to drugs and drug control as it has manifested historically and contemporarily, bringing together public and private realms, and in the process blurring different expectations, understandings and responsibilities.

In the opening paper, Chris Duvall examines the cultivation of cannabis in Africa, long overlooked in the literature although it is apparently the most widely used drug on the continent. His argument starts with the observation that the plant's illegal status has contributed to its marginalization in agricultural policy as much as elsewhere in Africa, yet it remains a preferred crop at times for some farmers. If one views cannabis as an agricultural issue rather than as a drug-related one, it is clear that it provides an important source of revenue for many farmers, one well suited to survive uncertain climatic and financial environments. The long history of African cannabis cultivation, which predates European colonialism, led to numerous seed types, local varieties and rich deposits of knowledge. However, this agricultural heritage is little recognized beyond African farming communities other than by bioprospectors based in the global North, and the opportunities that it might afford are continually undermined by laws which criminalize cannabis and thus devalue its significance and worth.

Next, Pierre-Arnaud Chouvy analyses data on several, different so-called narco-states in order to disrupt this term's use in prevailing narratives on the global political economy of drug production, distribution and consumption. Of course, there are countries with economies and polities that are overwhelmingly dependent on illicit drug exports, but they are perhaps far too readily described as narco-states. Many of these entities (including Afghanistan, North Korea and Myanmar), however, are hardly states at all. So Chouvy, rather than accept what he suggests is an inaccurate and overused stereotype, offers a more subtle and sophisticated interpretation in its stead. In this respect, he calls attention to the complex socio-cultural and political economic forces that underpin international drug supply and demand, including the nodes, networks and interconnections through which these forces are geographically expressed.

Emine Evered and Kyle Evered focus on alcohol consumption in Turkey with their paper. Despite Koranic prohibitions, drinking has a long and varied history in that country. Thus these contributors explore the uneven topography of regulation, in which restrictions on the times and places in which public alcohol consumption was legally permitted are seen to have fluctuated in the context of a changing political environment. The hegemony here of Erdogan's Justice and Development Party (the AKP) is identified as the main reason for a steady narrowing of alcohol consumers' options in Turkey. This outcome resulted from policy decisions that were advocated by the party ostensibly out of concerns for health and youth, but a key objective and technology of neo-liberal governance is reflected in its regulation of places and bodies.

In the same vein, Julien Mercille takes us to Ireland, famed for its Guiness stout and whiskeys, and demonstrates how global, European and national neo-liberalisms have converged there with particular forms and configurations of free trade, capital mobility and deregulation subsequently reshaping the production and consumption of alcohol in that country. Thus trade liberalization (via, for example, the World Trade Organization) opened the door for expanded imports and exports of alcohol at the same time, for example, that the deterrent effect of excise taxes was declining because their value had been eroded by inflation. The Irish industry itself, lobbying in the face of growing awareness of the health costs of heavy drinking, promoted discourses in which alcoholism was portrayed as the fault of individuals rather than any sort of socially constructed phenomenon. In this way alcohol consumption has become more privately regulated, resisting the purview of the state.

The last four papers presented in this collection engage with the dynamically complex politics of drugs, and specifically explore those efforts made in the name of "harm reduction" to minimize the negative impacts of drug use. Common to all four papers is a concern with the multiple scales or levels of governance and jurisdiction structuring any one place and how they influence the regulation of drugs and drug use there to varying effect. A notable finding with several authors is the collision between the concerns and policy decisions of public health and those of the law and police.

Stephen Parkin's contribution provides ethnographic insights into some of the latest initiatives developed in response to street-based injecting drug use and the problem of discarded needles in the UK. He shows that the provision there of needle disposal facilities in public conveniences is viewed ambiguously by drug users since they see it as being good for their health and well-being but then also worrisome in terms of the criminality and policing of drug use. Parkin refers to "a collision of interventions" involving public health policy and regulatory practice, notably because the success of the health initiative examined in this paper was impeded by the law and its enforcement especially by local authorities, which contradicts the UK's much espoused national harm reduction policy.

Safe or supervised injecting facilities, which are investigated in the paper by Stewart Williams, are likewise an instance of public health services designed and delivered in the interests of harm reduction. A legal geography framework is used in this paper to analyse the juridico-political contest that shaped the establishment in Sydney, Australia, of the only one such facility officially allowed to operate in the southern hemisphere. The author demonstrates how jurisdiction has variously influenced several ongoing attempts to introduce these facilities into Australia, and he subsequently challenges the law's traditional geographical imaginary of a scaled ordering of nested spatial units. New opportunities and potential for expanding the delivery of harm reduction are also identified specifically in relation to the institutions, actors and technologies of municipal governance, which are so often overlooked in this context because they are deemed quite inaccurately to be inferior to national entities and powers.

Eugene McCann and Andy Longhurst, in their contribution, present an overdue addition to the mobile policy literature with substantial empirical evidence drawn from their research on shifting drug policy in Canada. The authors examine the movement of policy across city-regions in terms of the frequently gradual, incremental change that can result from political struggles occurring at what they call "the policy frontier". The negotiation of harm reduction is shown in the paper to contribute to the making of city-regions, and explained there in terms of how local policies and practices are uniquely produced, reproduced, challenged and/or jettisoned often in quite arbitrary ways. In fact, policies and practices can differ substantively from each other, depending on their assemblage within any one city-region's scalar politics and institutional architecture.

Finally, Cristina Temenos in her paper considers local drug activism at harm reduction conferences as an aspect of international drug policy mobility. Her investigation reveals such conferences to be important sites for the construction of relationships involving a multiple, overlapping material and discursive territorializations through which policy advocacy networks are formed and maintained and political opportunities for drug policy reform might be harnessed. However, rather than just illustrate how hosting a harm reduction conference somewhere might possibly effect a policy shift there, Temenos also shows that such conferences are "ephemeral fixtures", loosely held together in a particular place at any one moment in time. These ephemeral fixtures arise contingently in the unfolding assemblage of international drug policy and advocacy networks, and understanding them can help to explain further the spatialities of policy mobilities and social movements.

Conclusion

In sum, the collection of papers presented here investigates a range of drugs that have variously been made legal or illegal at particular times and in different parts of the world. All of the papers elucidate, in one way or another, how those plants and manufactured products that contain psychoactive substances have been and will no doubt always continue to be shaped by ongoing efforts at regulation. In this respect, the multifaceted phenomenon of drugs, ranging across drug production, distribution and consumption, and thereby implicating many, different peoples, places and practices, cannot be understood without paying attention to their legal status.

The key point made throughout this collection is that the regulation of drugs and drug use is at the same time subject to inevitable resistance as well as revision or reinforcement. The law is neither a transcendental abstraction nor a fixed monolith (albeit often reified) as it only gains full meaning and force in the instance of its practical application. Occasionally a change can ensue – if its time has come. The geographical context is critically important here, too, because the socio-cultural and political economic relationships in which any drug is embedded will determine how it might (or might not) be constituted as such and to what effect.

Disclosure statement

No potential conflict of interest was reported by the authors.

References

Allen, C. M. (2005). *An industrial geography of cocaine*. New York, NY: Routledge.

Anderson, D., Beckerleg, S., Hailu, D., & Klein, A. (2007). *The khat controversy: Stimulating the debate on drugs*. Oxford: Berg.

Banister, J. M., Boyce, G. A., & Slack, J. (2015). Illicit economies and state(less) geographies: The politics of illegality. *Territory, Politics, Governance*, *3*, 365–368.

Bergschmidt, V. (2004). Pleasure, power and dangerous substances: Applying Foucault to the study of 'heroin dependence' in Germany. *Anthropology and Medicine*, *11*, 59–73.

Booth, M. (1996). *Opium: A history*. London: Simon and Schuster.

Carrier, N., & Klantschnig, G. (2012). *Africa and the war on drugs*. London: Zed Books.

Chouvy, P.-A. (2009). *Opium. Uncovering the politics of the poppy*. London: I.B. Tauris.

Chouvy, P.-A., & Meissonnier, J. (2004). *Yaa Baa: Production, traffic, and consumption of methamphetamine in mainland Southeast Asia*. Singapore: Singapore University Press.

Courtwright, D. (2002). *Forces of habit: Drugs and the making of the modern world*. Cambridge, MA: Harvard University Press.

DeVerteuil, G., & Wilton, R. (2009). The geographies of intoxicants: From production and consumption to regulation, treatment and prevention. *Geography Compass*, *3*, 478–494.

Goodman, J. (2007). Excitantia, or how enlightenment Europe took to soft drugs. In J. Goodman, P. Lovejoy, & A. Sherratt (Eds.), *Consuming habits: Global and historical perspectives on how cultures define drugs* (2nd ed., pp. 255–260). Abingdon: Routledge.

Goodman, J., & Lovejoy, P. (2007). Afterword. In J. Goodman, P. Lovejoy, & A. Sherratt (Eds.), *Consuming habits: Global and historical perspectives on how cultures define drugs* (2nd ed., pp. 255–260). Abingdon: Routledge.

Hall, M., & Hargrove, E. C. (2009). Plant autonomy and human-plant ethics. *Environmental Ethics*, *31*(2), 169–181.

Head, L., & Atchison, J. (2008). Cultural ecology: Emerging human-plant geographies. *Progress in Human Geography*, *33*, 236–245.

Heiss, M.L., & Heiss, R.J. (2007). *The story of tea: A cultural history and drinking guide*. New York, NY: Random House.

Hobbs, J. (1998). Troubling fields: The opium poppy in Egypt. *Geographical Review*, *88*, 64–85.

Keane, H. (2009). Foucault on methadone: Beyond biopower. *International Journal of Drug Policy*, *20*, 450–452.

Lynch, M., Omori, M., Russell, A. & Valasik, M. (2013). Policing the 'progressive' city: The racialized geography of drug law enforcement. *Theoretical Criminology*, *17*(3), 335–357.

Marez, C. (2004). *Drug wars: The political economy of networks*. Minneapolis: University of Minnesota Press.

McCann, E. (2008). Expertise, truth, and urban policy mobilities: Global circuits of knowledge in the development of Vancouver, Canada's 'four pillar' drug strategy. *Environment and Planning A*, *40*, 885–904.

Neilson, B., & Bamyeh, M. (2009). Drugs in motion: Toward a materialist tracking of global mobilities. *Cultural Critique*, *71*, 1–12.

Piazza, J. (2012). The opium trade and patterns of terrorism in the provinces of Afghanistan: An empirical analysis. *Terrorism and Political Violence*, *24*(2), 213–234.

Pomeranz, K., & Topik, S. (1999). *The world that trade created: Society, culture, and the world economy, 1400 to the present*. Armonk, NY: M. E. Sharpe.

Power, M. (2013) *Drugs 2.0: The web revolution that's changing how the world gets high*. London: Portobello Books.

Rengert, G. (1996). *The geography of illegal drugs*. Boulder, CO: West View Press.

Rengert, G., Ratcliffe, J., & Chakravorty, S. (2005). *Policing illegal drug markets: Geographic approaches to crime reduction*. Monsey, NY: Criminal Justice Press.

Reuter, P. (2009). Systemic violence in drug markets. *Crime, Law and Social Change*, *52*(3), 275–284.

Schaefer, S.B., & Furst, P.T. (1997). *People of the peyote: Huichol Indian history, religion, and survival*. Albuquerque, NM: University of New Mexico Press.

Steinberg, M., Hobbs, J., & Mathewson, K. (Eds.). (2004). *Dangerous harvest: Drug plants and the transformation of indigenous landscapes*. Oxford: Oxford University Press.

Taylor, J. (2015). The stimulants of prohibition: Illegality and new synthetic drugs. *Territory, Politics, Governance*, *3*, 407–427.

Taylor, J. S., Jasparro, C., & Mattson, K. (2013). Geographers and drugs: A survey of the literature. *Geographical Review*, *103*, 415–430.

Tempalski, B., & Cooper, H. J. (2014). Place matters: Drug users' health and drug policy. *International Journal of Drug Policy*, *25*(3), 503–507.

Thomas, Y., Richardson, D., & Cheung, I. (Eds.). (2008). *Geography and drug addiction*. Dordrecht: Springer.

Warf, B. (2014). High points: An historical geography of cannabis. *Geographical Review*, *104*, 414–438.

Williams, S. (2010). On islands, insularity and opium poppies: Australia's secret pharmacy. *Environment and Planning D: Society and Space*, *28*, 290–310.

Williams, S. (2013). Licit narcotics production in Australia: Geographies nomospheric and topological. *Geographical Research*, *51*, 364–374

Williams, S. (2014). *Geography of drugs. Oxford annotated bibliographies*. New York, NY: Oxford University Press (online publication).

Wilton, R., & Moreno, C. (2012). Critical geographies of drugs and alcohol. *Social & Cultural Geography*, *13*, 99–108.

World Health Organization. (2014). *Global status report on alcohol and health 2014*. Geneva: Author.

Drug laws, bioprospecting and the agricultural heritage of *Cannabis* in Africa

Chris S. Duvall

Department of Geography and Environmental Studies, University of New Mexico, Albuquerque, USA

For centuries across most of Africa, farmers have valued Cannabis for multiple reasons. Historic crop selection produced genetic diversity that commercial bioprospectors value for marijuana production. African colonial and post-colonial administrations devalued the crop, enacted *Cannabis* controls earlier than most locations worldwide, and excluded *Cannabis* from agricultural development initiatives. Public agricultural institutions exclude *Cannabis* as an extension of drug-control policies. Only private companies conserve crop genetic diversity for psychoactive *Cannabis*, without recognizing intellectual property rights embedded in landraces. *Cannabis* decriminalization initiatives should stimulate evaluation of its roles in African agriculture, and of worldwide control and management of its genetic diversity.

Agricultural development initiatives reflect political opinions about particular crops, and the control of agricultural inputs and knowledge. Seed systems particularly reveal political differences about farming, because seeds represent the fundamental knowledge and inputs of agriculture (Kloppenburg, 2005). Improved seed, including hybrid and genetically modified crops, is an especially contentious topic. Debates about improved seed are far-reaching, ranging from the political-economic structure of agricultural systems, to the nature and control of intellectual property rights (IPRs) (Dutfield, 2004; Institute of Development Studies, 2011; Yapa, 1996).

Efforts to improve African agriculture commonly propose that farmers lack high-quality seed (Pingali, 2012). In particular, the Alliance for a Green Revolution in Africa (AGRA), a major initiative working in 17 countries and funded by the Gates and Rockefeller Foundations, posits that African farmers must replace indigenous landraces with improved, hybrid seedstock distributed through private seed suppliers (Toenniessen, Adesina, & DeVries, 2008). AGRA's seed programme was the first of its six initiatives to be funded, in 2006, and has had more funding than any other (AGRA, 2015).

Critics argue that AGRA and similar initiatives devalue indigenous knowledge by seeking to replace landraces and to transform seed systems from open exchange networks amongst farmers to commercial networks controlled by agribusinesses (Jarosz, 2012; Mbilinyi, 2012; Scoones & Thompson, 2011; Thompson, 2012). AGRA's success would reduce the capacities of existing seed systems to respond to site-specific needs, and hinder farmers from selecting crop attributes through seed saving (African Center for Biodiversity, 2013). Further, AGRA inconspicuously depends upon unimproved seedstock, because this is a vital source of genetic diversity in crop improvement efforts (Smith, Bubeck, Nelson, Stanek, & Gerke, 2015). By failing to acknowledge IPR embedded in indigenous seedstock and to share improved seed openly with the farmers who contributed seeds to research efforts, AGRA facilitates biopiracy – taking of genetic wealth without benefit sharing – by multinational seed companies (Thompson, 2012).

Scholars of agricultural development have not considered the commercial marijuana seed industry, which occupies a unique position: its discourse echoes critics of seed-improvement initiatives, while its practice exemplifies the private, high-tech seed system these initiatives champion.

The commercial marijuana seed industry is large and growing. In 2002, there were 29 "seed banks" doing business over the Internet (Cervantes, 2002). By August 2015, there were 354 (Seedfinder.eu, n.d.). Commercial growers – at least those in Europe and North America – see Africa's *Cannabis* seedstock as a valuable, underexploited resource. "Africa" is an important label on commercial seeds, second only to "Dutch" and "Amsterdam". Company names include African Seeds, Afropips and Seeds of Africa, which seeks to preserve "the legendary [*Cannabis*] strains of Ancient Africa" so that "humanity [...] will not lose them forever in a world dominated by hybridised [...] varieties" (Seeds of Africa, 2013). The most public advocate of Africa's seedstock is Green House Seed Company, whose Strain Hunters bioprospecting documentaries had nearly 10 million views on YouTube by December 2015 (Strain Hunters/YouTube, n.d.). The Strain Hunters have sought *Cannabis* landraces in Malawi, Swaziland, Morocco, Jamaica, Trinidad, St. Vincent, India and Colombia. Importantly, the seed industry is just the visible component of commercial bioprospecting. *Cannabis*-focused pharmaceutical companies – principally Amsterdam-based HortaPharm – have large germplasm collections (Breen, 2004), but do not publicize their bioprospection.

In practice, the marijuana seed industry exemplifies the problems AGRA's critics identify. The industry appears to be heavily concentrated in two Amsterdam-based businesses, Sensi Seeds and Green House Seed Company. These companies (and HortaPharm) use African germplasm in sophisticated breeding programmes, yet acknowledge no IPRs for African farmers and offer no obvious benefits to them. Marijuana seed catalogues almost exclusively offer high yielding, hybrid cultivars (see https://sensiseeds.com/en and http://www.greenhouseseeds.nl/shop).

The parallel between the marijuana seed industry and the seed system AGRA envisions suggests that the fundamental difference between legal agriculture and drug farming is crop choice. However, *Cannabis* is generally not analysed in agricultural terms. Globally, marijuana is primarily a tropical export crop, although production is increasing rapidly in the Global North (Bouchard, Potter, & Decorte, 2011). Agricultural development initiatives in the Global South entirely exclude illegal crops and underemphasize non-food crops generally, even though farmers sometimes choose these crops where food-crop markets are unprofitable. Drug *Cannabis* production responds to prices for legal crops worldwide (Bouchard et al., 2011; United Nations Office on Drugs and Crime [UNODC], 2015), including in African countries where it has been illegal for decades though farmed for centuries. African *Cannabis* landraces persist despite the constraints drug-control laws place on crop selection.

In this paper, I examine the origins and implications of the current situation, wherein African *Cannabis* is simultaneously illegal and a valuable stock of crop genetic diversity. My central argument has two components: (1) African *Cannabis* landraces are diverse because they represent centuries of agricultural selection and (2) African farmers cannot legally produce

Cannabis because drug-control laws devalue the agriculture expertise embedded in the crop. This argument is based on political ecological analysis (Offen, 2004) of historic accounts of farming, and of initial drug laws across the continent. Drug-policy reform is transforming the global political economy of *Cannabis*, yet there has been scant consideration of the implications this transformation might have for agriculture in Africa. I contribute to the relatively thin literatures on *Cannabis* geography (Warf, 2014), and *Cannabis* history in Africa (Akyeampong, 2005; du Toit 1980; Klantschnig, 2014; Kozma, 2011; Paterson, 2009). I generalize about Africa and African farmers to emphasize political ecological conditions that have existed broadly across the continent; nonetheless, I recognize that there are and have been important variations in these conditions.

This remainder of this paper has four sections. First, I define key terms. Next, in two sections I sketch the agricultural past of *Cannabis* in Africa, and outline how drug laws denied the crop's value. Finally, I discuss implications of global drug-policy reform with regard to *Cannabis* in Africa.

Terminology

In this paper, I write "*Cannabis*" to discuss a botanical genus. All *Cannabis* plants produce cannabinoids, a class of over 80 phytochemicals. The most important taxonomically are cannabidiol (CBD) and tetrahydrocannabinol (THC), the primary psychoactive compound. Regarding species, I follow Hillig's concept (2005a) that there are two major groups within *Cannabis*. Simplistically, plants that produce a high THC:CBD ratio are the genetic species *indica* (sensu Hillig), while plants with a high CBD:THC ratio are *sativa* (sensu Hillig). This concept differs from the current, formal taxonomy that considers all plants to represent one species, *Cannabis sativa* L. (Small & Cronquist, 1976). However, genetic analyses support recognition of two species (van Bakel et al., 2011; Datwyler & Weiblen, 2006; Hillig & Mahlberg, 2004; Sawler et al., 2015).

Cannabis indica grows outdoors primarily at low latitudes (approximately < 35°); it is found throughout Africa, except in the driest areas. *C. sativa* grows at higher latitudes (approximately 35–65°). Initially, *sativa* grew only in western Eurasia prior to its introduction to European colonies worldwide. It succeeded in mid-latitude colonies; low-latitude introductions failed. By "African *Cannabis*" I mean the diverse landraces indigenous to the continent. By "landrace" I mean a locally adapted and distinctive population of a cultivated plant that lacks formal improvement. The term "strain" refers to a lineage of plants shaped through agricultural selection. "Variety" is a formal taxonomic rank below the sub-species.

Finally, species names are not synonymous with human uses of *Cannabis*. "Hemp" means *Cannabis* used for fibre or oilseed. By "drug *Cannabis*" I mean plants used as psychoactive or non-psychoactive substances that affect bodily function; I am concerned primarily with psychoactive drugs. The genetic species *indica* and *sativa* have both been used as hemp and drug. Hemp produced in East Asia comes from *indica*; drugs produced from *sativa* are not psychoactive because only *indica* produces a high THC:CBD ratio. By "pharmaceutical *Cannabis*" I mean drugs prepared according to Western pharmacological science.

My terminological definitions are simplified in this paper. For further discussion of *Cannabis* terminology, see Duvall (2015, pp. 9–26). For more on *Cannabis* botany, biogeography and history, see Clarke and Merlin (2013), Small (2015) and Duvall (2015).

Origins and diversity of African *Cannabis*

C. indica originated in South Asia, but arrived in Africa long ago. The earliest evidence is pollen from 650 Before the Current Era (BCE) from central Kenya (Rucina, Muiruri, Downton, &

Marchant, 2010) and 200 BCE from Madagascar (Burney, 1987). The plant experienced some degree of human selection wherever it was used, even before formal agriculture. Farming existed in Egypt by the 1200s CE (Rosenthal, 1971), and in Morocco and Kenya by the 1500s (Muller et al., 2015; Rucina et al., 2010). Smoking pipes in archaeological contexts suggest *Cannabis* use if not agriculture widely across East Africa, especially after 1000 CE (Philips, 1983; Van der Merwe, 2005). European documents, the earliest from the 1580s, suggest the plant's expansion during recent centuries (Figure 1).

In global terms, Africa is a centre of secondary diversification for *C. indica*. Its world history parallels other crops domesticated in South Asia and transferred anciently to Africa. Banana is the most notable crop with this history; African bananas are highly diverse (Carney & Rosomoff, 2009, pp. 35–36). There is scant research on the genetic diversity of African *Cannabis*. Botanists recognize three varieties characteristic respectively of North, Central and Southern Africa (Clarke & Merlin, 2013, p. 330). The only information on landraces are anecdotes from commercial bioprospectors (Strain Hunters, 2013), and participants in online discussion boards (International Cannagraphic, 2015). This information is qualitative and generally unverifiable. Nonetheless, purported landraces are physically distinctive, and from ecologically distinct areas, primarily in North, East and Southern Africa, regions where the crop was earliest present.

Generalizations about the agricultural history of African *Cannabis* are necessary because relevant literature is topically and geographically patchy. Historic descriptions of farming are brief European observations, mostly published after 1850. Although *Cannabis* widely supplied fibre

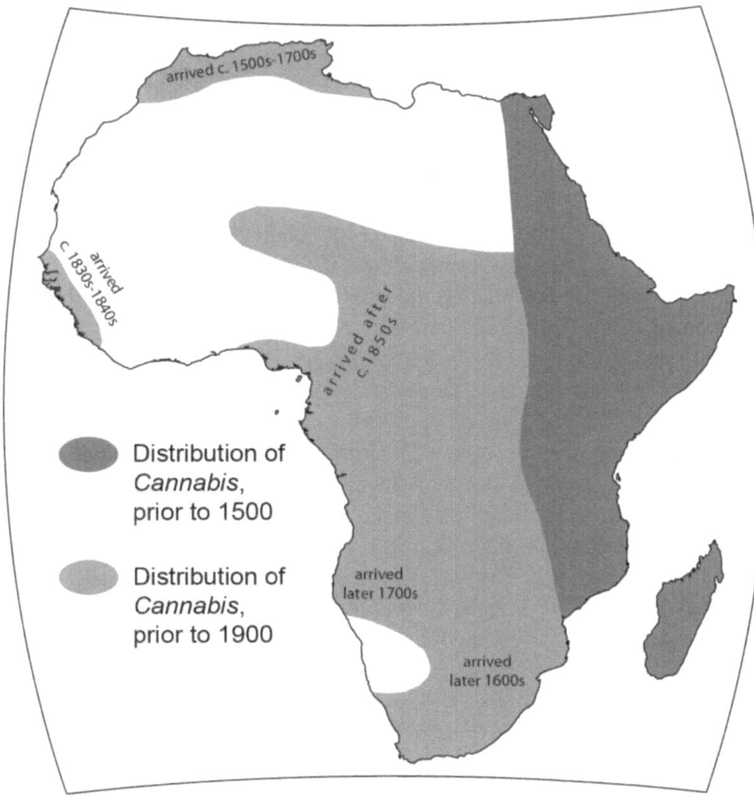

Figure 1. Historic distribution of *Cannabis* in Africa. Map data in Duvall (2015).

and non-psychoactive drugs, it was used principally for psychoactive drugs. *Cannabis* was commonly grown with minimal management on waste heaps and agroecologically marginal locations, such as rocky hillsides and field margins (e.g. Chevalier, 1944; de Ficalho, 1884/1947), but also cultivated more intensively in fertilized, irrigated patches or house gardens (e.g. Baum, 1903, p. 7; Burton, 1860, p. 81; Clarke, 1851; Daniell, 1850; Dias de Carvalho, 1892, p. 50; Du Chaillu, 1861, p. 420; Dukerley, 1866; Foureau, 1903, pp. 467, 519). In Morocco's northern lowlands, *C. sativa* was grown for hemp (du Gast, 1908, pp. 79–80; René-Leclerc, 1905, pp. 245, 347); cross-pollination between *indica* and *sativa* has distinguished the North African variety from the Central and Southern African varieties (Clarke & Merlin, 2013, p. 330).

Little is known of historic plant selection practices, which were embedded in indigenous knowledge systems. Where people did not actively manage *Cannabis* as a crop, it experienced weak selection. For instance, slaves saved seeds in western Central Africa (Du Chaillu, 1861, p. 420), but likely had no choice in plant selection. Where farmers responded to local demand for plant products, selection was stronger. For instance, in 1790s Mozambique, people harvested inflorescences for psychoactive drugs, leaves for non-psychoactive poultices, and stems for fibre, but saved seeds from inflorescences (Barroso da Silva, 1799/1864). Elsewhere, people similarly seem to have selected seeds from inflorescences used as drugs (Bourhill, 1913; Clarke, 1851; Daniell, 1850; Doke, 1931, p. 110; Godard, 1860, p. 178; Kingsley, 1897, pp. 667–668).

Past agricultural selection produced current landraces. Since the 1500s at least, African farmers have widely favoured crops that tolerate uncertainty generated by climate variability and political-economic instability (Carney & Rosomoff, 2009). *Cannabis* likely experienced similar human selection. Cultivation in marginal sites posed natural selection pressures favouring hardy, adaptable plants. Like all crops, *C. indica* benefits from fertilizers, irrigation and other inputs, but it does not require intensive management for high-potency products. Current farmers value the crop because it can succeed in marginal sites (Bloomer, 2008; Chouvy, 2008; Kepe, 2003; Laudati, 2014; Perez & Laniel, 2004).

Selection also affected plant chemistry, which determines the physiological effects of *Cannabis* drug use. There is scant evidence linking the cannabinoid profiles of specific *Cannabis* strains with specific geographic locations, beyond the broadest groups within the genus. However, landraces from Southern Africa have both distinctive phytochemistry and a documentary record of drug effects that parallels the known pharmacology of this phytochemistry. In Southern Africa, the plant drug has long been used as an appetite suppressant. In the 1580s, a Portuguese resident in Mozambique recorded that *Cannabis* "comforted [users'] stomachs [... and] sustained them several days, without eating another thing" (dos Santos, 1609, p. 20B). In 1883, a French traveller found that people in southern Tanzania valued *Cannabis* because it "calms the sufferings of hunger" (Giraud, 1890, p. 73). In Malawi in 2008, a bioprospector reported being "energized by the local weed, sometimes to the point of needing less food than normal" (Strain Hunters, 2010a). For at least the past century, South African labourers have used *Cannabis* to suppress hunger (Bourhill, 1913; Peltzer, Ramlagan, Johnson, & Phaswana-Mafuya, 2010). Marijuana aficionados in the Global North value this effect in the Southern African strains that have entered commercial production, particularly Durban Poison and Malawi Gold.

Southern African plants have elevated levels of the cannabinoid tetrahydrocannabivarin (THCV) (Backes, 2014, pp. 146–147; de Meijer, 2014, p. 101), which is an appetite suppressant (Williams, Whalley, & McCabe, 2015, p. 322). Elevated THCV production is rare globally in *Cannabis*. Hillig and Mahlberg (2004, p. 973), for instance, report only one other sample, from Afghanistan, with high-THCV levels. Although these authors interpret the rarity of high-THCV *Cannabis* as suggesting that humans globally selected *against* THCV production, the pattern as readily suggests that Southern African farmers selected *for* THCV by favouring appetite-suppressing physiological effects.

Of course, drug *Cannabis*' subjective effects depend upon historically and geographically contingent contexts of use, not just biochemistry (Zinberg, 1986). Physiological and subjective effects cannot be disentangled in documentary sources. Historically, *Cannabis* was embedded in numerous geographically specific contexts of use (du Toit, 1980; Duvall, 2015). Contexts sometimes enforced social norms that limited drug consumption: across Central and Southern Africa, people smoked in groups using a shared pipe, thereby controlling the quantity an individual smoked (Bourhill, 1913; Daniell, 1850; Reeve, 1921, p. 51). Other aspects of context seemingly affected drug biochemistry. For instance, *Cannabis* was transported in leaf-wrapped packets in nineteenth-century Central African commerce (Daniell, 1850). Perhaps this was the origin of products like "black Malawi", or herbal material fermented in cornhusk packets, which has subjective effects different from unfermented material (Seshata, 2013; Strain Hunters, 2010a). The cultural and botanical aspects of African *Cannabis* developed conjointly in local production and consumption systems.

Valorizing and devaluing African *Cannabis*

Beyond its sociocultural value, *Cannabis* has had economic value in Africa for centuries. However, beginning in the late 1800s, drug-control laws denied African *Cannabis* had any value; twentieth-century laws solidified its devaluation.

The earliest evidence of *Cannabis* drug markets in Africa is from thirteenth-century Egypt (Rosenthal, 1971). In Southern Africa, by the 1680s *Cannabis* was important in an expansive exchange economy (Gordon, 1996; Paterson, 2009, pp. 23–26). Commercial and exchange markets existed across the continent during the 1800s and early 1900s (Burton, 1876, p. 295; Clarke, 1851; Daniell, 1850; Decazes, 1888; Dukerley, 1866; Giraud, 1890; Söllner, 1897, p. 77; Welwitsch, 1862). North African markets were highly formalized by the late 1800s. In Morocco, before 1860 the royal government began selling an annual monopoly to the *Cannabis* trade (Godard, 1860, p. 179); Ottoman Tunisia followed in 1870 (Say & Chailley, 1892, p. 972). These monopolies, which represented a market-based approach to controlling consumption (Bewley-Taylor, Blickman, & Jelsma, 2014, p. 8), continued under French rule until 1954 (Chouvy, 2008).

European-controlled trades developed within colonial efforts to exploit valuable resources. These trades mostly depended upon demand from hard labourers. In South Africa in the 1700s, Dutch merchants paid Khoisan labourers with the plant drug (Gordon, 1996; Kolben, 1713/1748, p. 513); into the early 1900s white South Africans grew *Cannabis* to supply miners (Paterson, 2009, p. 50). In Angola, slavers valued the crop in their attempts to manage slave health (Daniell, 1850); slaves carried *Cannabis* seeds, including to Sierra Leone and Liberia before 1850 (Büttikofer, 1890, p. 276; Clarke, 1851). In Central Africa, the plant drug was directly commercialized after abolition. Its trade followed the same pathways as the slave trade, with shipments from interior farmlands supplying coastal markets (Silva Porto, 1885/1942, p. 231), and export markets in São Tome and Gabon during the 1870s–1900s (Ivens, 1898; Trivier, 1887). By 1910, European traders in Gabon stocked locally grown *Cannabis* (Seguin, 1910). Elsewhere, Portuguese Mozambique exported the plant drug to British Traansvaal between 1908 and 1913 (Foreign Office and Board of Trade, 1912, 1916). Except in Morocco and Tunisia, legal commerce ended in the 1910s, by which time most African colonies had prohibited drug *Cannabis*.

Even after *Cannabis* was outlawed, it retained value. Black markets grew throughout the 1900s. In Southern and Central Africa, miners were prominent consumers (Higginson, 1990; Laudati, 2014; Paterson, 2009, p. 50). In West Africa, Sierra Leonean merchant sailors trafficked *Cannabis* from Gambia to Nigeria, and transported at least small quantities to New York City by

1938 (Akyeampong, 2005). Colonial troops also carried *Cannabis* widely (du Toit, 1980). Domestic and international trading grew in the 1960s, as middle and upper social classes worldwide adopted the drug (Ellis, 2009; Klantschnig, 2014). In the 1960s, Morocco began producing hashish for export (Chouvy, 2008); farmers have increasingly planted high-yielding strains from Afghanistan and Pakistan, and Moroccan landraces are declining (Strain Hunters 2010b). Since the 1980s, continental production has increased continually (Perez & Laniel, 2004). Domestic markets are important (Kepe, 2003; Laudati, 2014), but trafficking widely links supply and demand across borders (Bloomer, 2008; Bøäs, 2014; Ellis, 2009; Perez & Laniel, 2004). Currently, only Algeria, Egypt and Morocco export significant quantities beyond the continent – hashish bound for Europe (UNODC, 2015).

As European-controlled *Cannabis* trades developed, colonial regimes simultaneously began suppressing non-pharmaceutical *Cannabis* drug use, which was increasingly perceived as a health risk. *Cannabis*-control laws were enacted across the colonial world beginning in the late 1800s (Bewley-Taylor et al., 2014; Duvall, 2015, p. 163; Kozma, 2011). African colonial laws were generally earlier than elsewhere. Before *Cannabis* was first listed in a global drug-control agreement – the League of Nations' 1925 International Opium Convention – its farming, possession, and use were prohibited across most of Central, East and Southern Africa (Table 1). Only Turkey and Greece seem to have enacted similarly stringent prohibitions by 1925 (Bewley-Taylor et al., 2014).

Africa's initial laws mostly mentioned public health as justification (Table 1). Some laws sought to control pharmaceutical practices, though most aimed only generally to protect "native" health. Angola's 1913 law, for instance, stated that *Cannabis* "contribut[ed] to degeneration of the race, [and] debilitation of the native". Its control was based on the "great advisability of [...] restricting the native customs that are absolutely harmful to them" (Ministério das Colónias, 1918, p. 262). Indeed, most *Cannabis*-control laws served ulterior concerns, particularly labour control (Higginson, 1990, p. 251; Paterson, 2009; Payeur-Didelot, 1898; Redinha, 1946, p. 27) and religious proselytizing (Hunt, 1999, p. 56; Reeve, 1921, p. 180). Several laws identified specific labour groups, including Angola's law that sought to end drug-taking amongst colonial troops, and make farmers shift to tobacco production (Ministério das Colónias, 1918, p. 262).

Colonial laws effectively excluded *Cannabis* from legal agriculture, even if its consumption continued. Most laws not only prohibited *Cannabis* farming, but ordered the destruction of fields and produce, thereby legally redefining agriculture by excluding a crop based on European prerogatives. Colonial regimes broadly devalued African farming expertise *Cannabis*-control laws specifically devalued the crop in several ways.

First, *Cannabis* was portrayed as a one-dimensional drug crop, only a poor, "native" substitute for tobacco. No laws recognized non-psychoactive, indigenous uses, which were widespread even if secondary. Many Europeans were ignorant of these because they focused on the exotic psychoactive use, which seemed wasteful because they presumed the plant was most valuable for fibre, as in Europe (Chapaux, 1894, pp. 482, 492; Dewèvre, 1894, p. 31). However, African preference for *Cannabis* drug uses made economic botanical sense: a small patch could supply abundant smokeable material but scant fibre; many other wild and farmed plants supplied fibre; and high-quality hemp was labour intensive.

Second, control laws considered *Cannabis*' indigenous psychoactive uses valueless, despite legal markets. Mozambique's initial law ended without mention a formal export trade to Transvaal; all colonies outlawed active internal markets. In most locations, *Cannabis* remained legal if grown with government authorization to supply pharmaceutical *Cannabis*, a Western drug. Indeed, colonial authorities accepted drug crops, but only those specified through their absence in drug-control laws and presence in agricultural policies – particularly tobacco, tea and

Table 1. *Cannabis*-control laws in Africa enacted prior to implementation of the 1925 International Opium Convention.

Colony	Year	Law	Stated purposes	Prohibited behaviours
British Natal	1870	Law No. 2, 1870, to Amend and Consolidate the Laws relating to the Introduction of Coolie Immigrants into this Colony […]	Control behaviour and health of Indian labourers	Farming, possession and use of *Cannabis* by Indian labourers; sale/gift of *Cannabis* to Indian labourers
Khedivate of Egypt	1879	[unknown law, cited in Indian Hemp Drugs Commission, 1894, p. 270]	Control public health and behaviour; strengthen earlier law (1868)	Farming, import and use of *Cannabis*
German East Africa	1891	Verordaung des kaiserlichen Gouverneurs vom 2 September 1891	Control native health, and behaviour of colonial troops	Farming, sale and use of *Cannabis*
French Madagascar	1901	Arrêté du gouverneur général du 3 décembre 1901	Control native behaviours	Sale and use of *Cannabis*
Congo Free State	1903	Décret du 1er mars 1903	Control native health; preserve labour quality; prevent crime	Farming, sale and use of *Cannabis*
Orange Free State	1903	Ordinance 48	Control native health; prevent crime	Farming, sale, and use of *Cannabis*
Anglo-Egyptian Sudan	1907	Hashish Ordinance 1907	Prevent use of *Cannabis* drugs; control access to pharmaceuticals; clarify and strengthen earlier law (1901)	Farming, manufacture, sale, possession, import, export and transport of *Cannabis*, without authorization; use of *Cannabis* pharmaceutical preparations without authorization
French Congo	1909	Circulaire au sujet des mesures à prendre contre l'usage et la diffusion du chanvre	Control native health; preserve labour quality; prevent crime	Farming, sale and use of *Cannabis*
Portuguese São Tome e Principe	1911	Decreto […] proibe a cultura, venda e importação de cânhamo indiano	Control health of labourers	Farming, import, sale and use of *Cannabis*
German South-west Africa	1912	Verordaung des kaiserlichen Gouverneurs vom 25 Mai 1912	Control native health; control behaviour of colonial troops	Farming, sale and use of *Cannabis*
British Nyassaland	1912	Sale of Drugs and Poisons Ordinance, 1912	Control native health	Sale of *Cannabis* without authorization
Portuguese Angola	1913	Portaria provincial proibindo […] o fornecimento a indigenas da *riamba*, ou *liamba*, por ter efeitos perniciosos semelhantes aos do ópio	Control native health; control behaviour of colonial troops; encourage tobacco farming	Farming *Cannabis* without authorization; sale/giving drug *Cannabis* to 'natives'

(*Continued*)

Table 1. Continued.

Colony	Year	Law	Stated purposes	Prohibited behaviours
British East Africa	1913	Abuse of Opiates Prevention Ordinance, 1913	Control access to pharmaceuticals; control native health	Use of *Cannabis* except pharmaceutical preparations; pharmaceutical use without authorization
British East Africa	1914	Government Notice 100	Control native health	Farming and sale of *Cannabis* without authorization
Portuguese Moçambique	1914	Portaria provincial proibindo […] a importação, cultura, venda e consumo da planta conhecida cafrealmente por bangue ou suruma	Control native health	Farming, import, sale and use of *Cannabis*
French West Africa, French Equatorial Africa	1916	Decrèt du 30 décembre 1916	Prevent use of harmful drugs; control access to pharmaceuticals; apply metropolitan law to colonies	Import, sale, possession and use of *Cannabis*
Union of South Africa	1922	No. 35: Customs and Excise Duties Amendment Act [cited in Chanock, 2001, p. 94]	Control native health; prevent crime; preserve labour quality	Farming, sale, possession and use of *Cannabis*
British Mauritius	1923	Ordinance No. 8	Control native health; control access to pharmaceuticals	Farming, import, sale and possession of *Cannabis*; pharmaceutical use without authorization
French Equatorial Africa	1926	Interdiction de la culture du chanvre et répression de son emploi comme stupéfiant en Afrique équatoriale française	Control native health; preserve labour quality; prevent crime; clarify earlier laws (1916 [above] and 1918)	Farming, sale, possession and use of *Cannabis*

Note: Two errors exist in recent accounts of African colonial *Cannabis* laws: (1) several colonies enacted laws prohibiting opium, cocaine, "and similar drugs" in 1913, to comply with the 1912 Opium Convention (see *Journal of the Society of Comparative Legislation*, vol. 15 [1915]). *Cannabis* was not listed in these laws. (2) British Cape Colony's Medical and Pharmacy Act of 1891 does not list *Cannabis*.

coffee. Colonial agricultural institutions actively supported these crops; *Cannabis* has been completely excluded from African agricultural research and development.

Third, African *Cannabis* was devalued as merely an introduced plant that Africans had passively accepted without any agricultural agency. By the 1850s, biogeographers recognized that *Cannabis* had been anciently introduced to Africa, and not from Europe (de Candolle, 1855, p. 833). Three centuries of botanical literature had established psychoactive *C. indica* as an Oriental object, "Indian hemp" rather than non-psychoactive, European hemp (*C. sativa*). African *Cannabis* signified Oriental influence, a counterpoint to the civilizing influence of European colonialism. "The tobacco introduced by the Portuguese has contended successfully against the stupefying or maddening hemp [...] from the far Muhammadan north-east", celebrated a British administrator in Belgian Congo (Johnston, 1908, p. 78). Africans were simply recipients, having no role in facilitating crop dispersal through farming, or in resisting *Cannabis*' "gradual but sure advances" into new lands (Du Chaillu, 1861, p. 420).

By extension, African agriculture was devalued through the belief that the introduced crop had only degenerated under African farmers. Europeans considered African *Cannabis* a second-rate version of the global drug crop. For instance, in East Africa about 1860, the local *Cannabis* was "a fine large species [...] grow[n] before every cottage door" according to a British traveller with experience in India. Nonetheless, he compared the East African crop to South Asian "jungle bhang", or feral *Cannabis* (Burton, 1860, p. 81). Similarly, French colonial law described "Indian hemp" – drug *Cannabis* grown in India – as "particularly rich in [psychoactive] resin". In contrast, "Congo hemp" had a "lesser quantity of [psycho]active principles", even though, paradoxically, it was used "to make preparations quite like [those of Indian hemp], with similar effects" (Ministère des Colonies, 1926).

Colonial *Cannabis* controls in Africa were strict in global terms. Indeed, *Cannabis*' listing in the 1925 Opium Convention began with the request of South Africa's white minority government supported by newly independent Egypt (Mills, 2003), whose authorities had since the 1860s legally suppressed *Cannabis* in order to control labourers (Kozma, 2011). The 1925 agreement established a regulatory approach to drug control; the United Nations' 1961 Single Convention on Narcotic Drugs (SCND) shifted international policy to strict legal prohibition, modelled on U.S. policies (Bewley-Taylor et al., 2014). In much of Africa, however, strict controls had been in place for decades and were unchanged after independence, to maintain compliance with international agreements. Of the African states party to the United Nations, only Somalia and Ethiopia opposed the SCND during its negotiation (Sinha, 2001, pp. 19–20). Other colonial and independent states remained neutral, thereby disclaiming indigenous traditions of *Cannabis* use, in contrast to South Asian countries that sought to protect longstanding practices. In the 1960s and 1970s, *Cannabis* became concerning to authorities in Africa and worldwide as it increasingly symbolized resistance to authority (Ellis, 2009; Klantschnig, 2014; Paterson, 2009). Ultimately, all African states except Equatorial Guinea, Somalia and South Sudan have signed key United Nations conventions from 1971 and 1988 that firmly marked *Cannabis* as an illegal crop.

Re-thinking African *Cannabis*

Drug-policy reform is unfolding worldwide because some civil societies and governments have concluded that criminalizing drug use creates more harms than benefits. *Cannabis* policy reform has been pursued primarily in North America and Europe, where several jurisdictions have decriminalized certain instances of cultivation, sales, possession and use. In the Global South, only Uruguay has formally stepped in the same direction, enacting decriminalization in 2013. Court decisions in Brazil and Mexico in late 2015, and ongoing legislative debates in Morocco,

Rwanda and South Africa suggest these countries may follow. There are seemingly no other significant, open movements towards decriminalization in Africa.

Possible effects of drug-policy reform on agricultural development in the Global South have received little attention. Participation in illegal *Cannabis* farming entails numerous and complex causes and consequences (Blackwell, 2014; Chouvy & Laniel, 2007; Zurayk, 2013). Implications of *Cannabis* policy reform on agriculture are similarly multifaceted, but three are noteworthy with regard to *Cannabis*' African agricultural past.

First, colonial *Cannabis* prohibitions were exogenous, even if indigenous societies had varying opinions about the drug, and norms that limited its use. Central Africans resisted *Cannabis* prohibitions when they were first enacted (Berriedale Keith, 1919, p. 195; Hunt, 1999, p. 56; Likaka, 2009, p. 46; Reeve, 1921, p. 180). Continued farming and use there and elsewhere arguably constitutes continued resistance (Zurayk, 2013). Despite longstanding prohibitions, African *Cannabis* cultures and agricultures persist. Farmers adopted *Cannabis* long ago because it provided products distinct from those of existing crops and wild plants; these products were valued for household consumption and/or income generation. *Cannabis* widely maintains this role in African agricultural systems, even though farmers cannot legally grow, use or sell it. Drug-policy reform could allow African societies to re-examine the definitions of agriculture implicit in drug-control laws.

Second, African *Cannabis* is undervalued in terms of global agricultural heritage. *Cannabis* experienced secondary diversification in Africa because farmers selected the crop to meet their agricultural needs and local demand for plant products. Although there is scant research-based evidence about *Cannabis* landrace diversity in Africa (Clarke & Merlin, 2013, p. 330), the world's *de facto* experts on *indica* diversity – commercial bioprospectors – consider the continental crop highly significant.

Commercial bioprospectors are the world's experts because mainstream agricultural institutions ignore African *Cannabis* specifically and *indica* more generally. For instance, Biodiversity International, part of the Consultative Group for International Agricultural Research, works to "deliver scientific evidence, management practices and policy options" to conserve underutilized crops, under the vision that "agricultural biodiversity matters" (Biodiversity International, 2014). The organization, however, has considered only European *C. sativa* used for hemp (Pavelek & Lipman, 2010). Yet, *C. sativa* is reasonably represented in *ex situ* seed banks (see Hillig, 2004, 2005b), while African drug strains are essentially absent except in private, commercial collections held by seed sellers or pharmaceutical companies. Scholarly research on *indica* genetic diversity relies heavily on these collections (e.g. Hillig, 2005a Sawler et al., 2015). Private control of germplasm is exactly what critics of seed-improvement initiatives like AGRA oppose with regard to food crops (Thompson, 2012).

The germplasm collections of commercial marijuana seed companies and pharmaceutical firms are important for conserving crop genetic diversity. However, these companies make no clear efforts to preserve IPRs potentially embedded in landraces, and seemingly make their products available only through sales; only the seed companies sell germplasm. Jamaica is the sole country to claim a *Cannabis* strain as intellectual property (Cadogan, 2015). If *Cannabis* IPRs exist in Jamaica, they exist elsewhere: the plant arrived in Jamaica not before the 1840s, carried by Central African and South Asian labourers whose forebears had cultivated the crop for centuries (Duvall, 2015, pp. 102–104). Debates over private versus public control of germplasm are unresolved, centring on whether property rights can or should be embedded in life forms. Regardless the outcome of these debates, private, commercial control is the default for *C. indica* because public institutions, whether governments or organizations like Biodiversity International, exclude the crop as an extension of drug policy. Societies should assess how *Cannabis* genetic diversity is managed as an aspect of drug-policy reform.

Finally, the African *Cannabis* crop earns less than its potential value in terms of monetary worth. The decriminalization of *Cannabis* in North American and European jurisdictions has opened lucrative markets. However, non-tariff trade barriers (that is, drug trafficking laws) hinder Global Southern producers from participating in these markets, despite the comparative advantages Southern producers have through low-input outdoor production and lower labour costs. Import substitution in the Global North (via indoor horticulture) is simultaneously foreclosing potential export markets for Southerners and generating wealth for Northerners (Bouchard et al., 2011; Zurayk, 2013). Further, countries in the Global South continue to expend resources on *Cannabis* control even as Northern countries have loosened controls in apparent violation of multilateral drug-control agreements (International Narcotics Control Board, 2015).

For *Cannabis*, drug policy implies agricultural policy. This relationship is recognized in the drug-control strategy of alternative development, which centres on providing incentives for farmers to switch to legal crops (UNODC, 2015). Alternative development has been hardly pursued in Africa. The only alternative development intervention, in Morocco, failed because European demand for hashish remained strong and provided a reliable market for farmers with few other options (Chouvy, 2008). Proponents of alternative development have not enunciated any relationship between alternative development and the globally shifting legality of *Cannabis* (e.g. UNODC, 2015). Agricultural development efforts similarly neglect to enunciate how drug policy might impact farming.

A truly alternative development strategy would be to decriminalize *Cannabis* production in a way that allows Global Southern farmers to access lucrative markets, whether domestic or international (Buxton, 2015; Laudati, 2014). Of course, open *Cannabis* markets would favour well-capitalized farmers, probably not those who currently grow (Kepe, 2003; Zurayk, 2013). Still, decriminalizing production would increase the legal crop choices farmers have for generating income.

In any case, past African farmers produced globally significant *Cannabis* crop diversity, and current farmers capture little of the crop's global value.

Disclosure statement

No potential conflict of interest was reported by the author.

References

African Center for Biodiversity. (2013). *Giving with one hand and taking with two: A critique of AGRA's African Agriculture Status Report 2013*. Melville: ACB.

Akyeampong, E. (2005). Diaspora and drug trafficking in West Africa: A case study of Ghana. *African Affairs*, *104*(416), 429–447.

Alliance for a Green Revolution in Africa. (2015). *Progress report 2007–2014*. Nairobi: AGRA.

Backes, M. (2014). *Cannabis pharmacy: The practical guide to medical Marijuana*. New York, NY: Black Dog & Leventhal.

van Bakel, H., Stout, J. M., Cote, A. G., Tallon, C. M., Sharpe, A. G., Hughes, T. R., & Page, J. E. (2011). The draft genome and transcriptome of *Cannabis sativa*. *Genome Biology*, *12*(10), article R102.

Barroso da Silva, F. M. (1799/1864). Descripção de algumas drogas e medicamentos da India [Description of some Indian spices and medicines]. *Archivo de Pharmacia e Sciencias Accessorias da India Portugueza, 1*(12), 185–191.

Baum, H. (1903). *Kunene-Sambesi-expedition*. Berlin: Kolonial-Wirtschaftlichen Komitees.

Berriedale Keith, A. (1919). *The Belgian Congo and the Berlin act*. Oxford: Clarendon.

Bewley-Taylor, D., Blickman, T., & Jelsma, M. (2014). *The rise and decline of Cannabis prohibition*. Amsterdam: Transnational Institute.

Biodiversity International. (2014). Who we are [website]. *Biodiversity International*. Retrieved December 29, 2015, from http://www.bioversityinternational.org/about-us/who-we-are/

Blackwell, J. M. (2014). The costs and consequences of U.S. drug prohibition for the peoples of developing nations. *Indiana International and Comparative Law Review, 24*(3), 665–692.

Bloomer, J. (2008). Using a political ecology framework to examine extra-legal livelihood strategies: A Lesotho-based case study of cultivation of and trade in cannabis. *Journal of Political Ecology, 16*, 49–69.

Bøäs, M. (2014). North Kivu, Eastern Congo: Buffer, battleground, sanctuary. In B. Vassort-Rousset (Ed.), *Building sustainable couples in international relations: A strategy towards peaceful cooperation* (pp. 146–164). New York, NY: Palgrave Macmillan.

Bouchard, M., Potter, G., & Decorte, T. (Eds.). (2011). *World wide weed: Global trends in Cannabis cultivation and its control*. Farnham: Ashgate.

Bourhill, C. J. G. (1913). The smoking of dagga (Indian hemp) among the native races of South Africa and the resultant evils (*Unpublished doctoral dissertation*). University of Edinburgh, Edinburgh.

Breen, B. (2004). Dr. Dope's connection [website]. *Fast Company.* Retrieved December 29, 2015, from http://www.fastcompany.com/48172/dr-dopes-connection

Burney, D. A. (1987). Pre-settlement vegetation changes at Lake Tritrivakely, Madagascar. *Paleoecology of Africa, 18*, 357–381.

Burton, R. F. (1860). *The lake regions of central Africa*. New York, NY: Harper & Brothers.

Burton, R. F. (1876). *Two trips to Gorilla land and the Cataracts of the Congo* (Vol. 2). London: Sampson Low.

Büttikofer, J. (1890). *Reisebilder aus Liberia* [Travel Pictures from Liberia] (Vol. 2). Leiden: Brill.

Buxton, J. (2015). *Drugs and development: The great disconnect*. Singleton Park: Global Drug Policy Observatory.

Cadogan, M. (2015). The legal implications of medical marijuana as a geographical imdication for Jamaica [website]. *Intellectual Property Watch*. Retrieved December 29, 2015, from http://www.ip-watch.org/2015/03/02/the-legal-implications-of-medicinal-marijuana-as-a-geographical-indication-for-jamaica/

de Candolle, A. (1855). *Géographie botanique raisonnée* (Vol. 2). Paris: Masson.

Carney, J. A., & Rosomoff, R. N. (2009). *In the shadow of slavery: Africa's botanical legacy in the Atlantic world*. Berkeley: University of California Press.

Cervantes, J. (2002). World's greatest seed banks [website]. *High Times*. Retrieved December 29, 2015, from http://hightimes.com/read/worlds-greatest-seed-banks

Chanock, M. (2001). *Making of South African legal culture, 1902-1936: Fear, favour, and prejudice*. Cambridge: Cambridge University Press.

Chapaux, A. (1894). *Le Congo* [The Congo]. Brussels: Charles Rozez.

Chevalier, A. (1944). Histoire de deux plantes cultivées d'importance primordiale: Le Lin et le Chanvre [History of two cultivated plants of primordial importance: Flax and hemp]. *Revue de Botanique Appliquée et d'Agriculture Coloniale, 24*, 51–71.

Chouvy, P.-A. (2008). Production de cannabis et de haschich au Maroc [Production of cannabis and hashish in Morocco]. *L'Espace Politique, 4*(1), Article 59.

Chouvy, P.-A., & Laniel, L. (2007). Agricultural drug economies: Cause or alternative to intra-state conflicts? *Crime, Law and Social Change, 48*, 133–150.

Clarke, R. C., & Merlin, M. D. (2013). *Cannabis: Evolution and ethnobotany.* Berkeley: University of California Press.

Clarke, R. O. (1851). Short notice of the African plant Diamba, commonly called Congo Tobacco. *Hooker's Journal of Botany, 3*, 9–11.

Daniell, W. F. (1850). On the D'amba, or dakka, of southern Africa. *Pharmaceutical Journal and Transactions, 9*(8), 363–365.

Datwyler, S. L., & Weiblen, G. D. (2006). Genetic variation in hemp and marijuana according to amplified fragment length polymorphisms. *Journal of Forensic Sciences, 51*(2), 371–375.

de Ficalho, C. (1884/1947). *Plantas úteis da África portuguesa* [Useful plants of Portuguese Africa]. Lisbon: Agência Geral das Colónias.

Decazes, M. (1888). L'ouest africain. Relation de voyage [West Africa. Travel narrative]. *Société Normande de Géographie, Bulletin de l'Année, 10*, 37–63.
Dewèvre, A. (1894). *Les plants utiles du Congo* [Useful plants of the Congo]. Brussels: Jules Vanderauwera.
Dias de Carvalho, H. A. (1892). *Expedição Portugueza ao Muatiânvua: Descripção da Viagem á Mussumba do Muatiânvua* [Portuguese expedition to the Muatiânvua: Description of the Voyage to Mussumba from the Muatiânvua] (Vol. 2). Lisbon: Imprensa Nacional.
Doke, C. M. (1931). *The Lambas of Northen Rhodesia*. London: George Harrap.
dos Santos, J. (1609). *Ethiopia oriental e varia historia de covsas* [Eastern Ethiopia and Ranging History of Things]. Evora: Conuento de S. Domingos.
Du Chaillu, P. B. (1861). *Explorations and adventures in equatorial Africa* (1st ed.). New York, NY: Harper Brothers.
du Gast, C. (1908). *Le Maroc agricole* [Agricultural Morocco]. Paris: Imprimerie Nationale.
du Toit, B. M. (1980). *Cannabis in Africa*. Rotterdam: Balkema.
Dukerley, I. (1866). Note sur les différences que présente avec le chanvre ordinaire et la variété de cette espèce connue en Algérie sous les noms de *kif* et de *tekrouri* [Note on the differences between ordinary hemp and the variety of this species known in Algeria under the names kif and *tekrouri*]. *Bulletin de la Société Botanique de France, 3*, 401–406.
Dutfield, G. (2004). *Intellectual property, biogenetic resources, and traditional knowledge*. London: Earthscan.
Duvall, C. S. (2015). *Cannabis*. London: Reaktion Books.
Ellis, S. (2009). West Africa's international drug trade. *African Affairs, 108*(431), 171–196.
Foreign Office and Board of Trade (Ed.). (1912). *Report for the year 1911 on the trade and commerce of the Portuguese Possessions in East Africa* (No. 4881 Annual Series). London: His Majesty's Stationery Office.
Foreign Office and Board of Trade (Ed.). (1916). *Report for the year 1914 on the trade and commerce of Lourenço Marques and other Portuguese Possessions in East Africa* (No. 5558 Annual Series). London: His Majesty's Stationery Office.
Foureau, F. (1903). *Documents scientifiques de la Mission Saharienne* [Scientific documents from the Saharan mission] (Vol. 1). Paris: Masson.
Giraud, V. (1890). *Les lacs d'Afrique équatoriale* [The lakes of equatorial Africa]. Paris: Hachette.
Godard, L. (1860). *Description et histoire du Maroc* [Description and history of Morocco]. Paris: Tanera.
Gordon, D. (1996). From rituals of rapture to dependence: The political economy of Khoikhoi narcotic consumption. *South African Historical Journal, 35*, 62–88.
Higginson, J. (1990). *A working class in the making: Belgian colonial labor policy, private enterprise, and the African mineworker*. Madison: University of Wisconsin Press.
Hillig, K. W. (2004). A multivariate analysis of allozyme variation in 93 *Cannabis* accessions from the VIR germplasm collection. *Journal of Industrial Hemp, 9*(2), 5–22.
Hillig, K. W. (2005a). Genetic evidence for speciation in *Cannabis* (Cannabaceae). *Genetic Resources and Crop Evolution, 52*, 161–180.
Hillig, K. W. (2005b). A combined analysis of agronomic traits and allozyme allele frequencies for 69 *Cannabis* accessions. *Journal of Industrial Hemp, 10*(1), 17–30.
Hillig, K. W., & Mahlberg, P. G. (2004). A chemotaxonomic analysis of cannabinoid variation in *Cannabis* (Cannabaceae). *American Journal of Botany, 91*(6), 966–975.
Hunt, N. R. (1999). *A colonial Lexicon: Of birth ritual, medicalization, and mobility in the Congo*. Durham: Duke University Press.
Indian Hemp Drugs Commission. (1894). *Report of the Indian Hemp Drugs Commission*. Simla: Government Printing Office.
Institute of Development Studies. (2011). Special issue: The politics of seed in Africa's Green Revolution. *IDS Bulletin, 42*(4), 1–120.
International Cannagraphic. (2015). Forum: Landraces [website]. *International Cannagraphic*. Retrieved December 29, 2015, from https://www.icmag.com/ic/forumdisplay.php?f=65686.
International Narcotics Control Board. (2015). *Report of the International Narcotics Control Board for 2014*. New York, NY: United Nations.
Ivens, C. (1898). L'Angola méridional [Southern Angola]. *Société d'Études Coloniales, 5*(5), 233–269.
Jarosz, L. (2012). Growing inequality: Agricultural revolutions and the political ecology of rural development. *International Journal of Agricultural Sustainability, 10*(2), 192–199.
Johnston, H. (1908). *George Grenfell and the Congo: A history and description of the Congo independent state* (Vol. 1). London: Hutchinson.

Kepe, T. (2003). *Cannabis sativa* and rural livelihoods in South Africa: Politics of cultivation, trade and value in Pondoland. *Development Southern Africa, 20*(5), 605–615.

Kingsley, M. H. (1897). *Travels in West Africa*. London: Macmillan.

Klantschnig, G. (2014). Histories of cannabis use and control in Nigeria, 1927–1967. In G. Klantschnig, N. Carrier, & C. Ambler (Eds.), *Drugs in Africa: Histories and ethnographies of use* (pp. 69–88). Gordonsville: Palgrave Macmillan.

Kloppenburg, J. (2005). *First the seed: The political economy of plant biotechnology* (2nd ed.). Madison: University of Wisconsin Press.

Kolben, P. (1713/1748). Histoire naturelle du Cap de Bonne-Esperance & des Pays voisins [Natural history of the Cape of Good Hope and the neighboring countries]. In L. A. Prevost (Ed.), *Histoire générale des voyages*, Vol. 6 (pp. 505–533). The Hague: Pierre de Hondt.

Kozma, L. (2011). Cannabis prohibition in Egypt, 1880–1939: From local ban to league of nations diplomacy. *Middle Eastern Studies, 47*(3), 443–460.

Laudati, A. A. (2014). Out of the shadows: Negotiations and networks in the cannabis trade in eastern democratic republic of Congo. In G. Klantschnig, N. Carrier, & C. Ambler (Eds.), *Drugs in Africa: Histories and ethnographies of use* (pp. 161–181). Gordonsville: Palgrave Macmillan.

Likaka, O. (2009). *Naming colonialism: History and collective memory in the Congo*. Madison: University of Wisconsin Press.

Mbilinyi, M. (2012). Struggles over land and livelihoods in African agriculture. *Development, 55*, 390–392.

de Meijer, E. P. M. (2014). The chemical phenotypes (chemotypes) of *Cannabis*. In R. Pertwee (Ed.), *Handbook of Cannabis* (pp. 89–110). Oxford: Oxford University Press.

Mills, J. H. (2003). *Cannabis Britannica: Empire, trade, and prohibition*. Oxford: Oxford University Press.

Ministério das Colónias. (1918). *Colecção da Legislação Colonial da República Portuguesa* [Collection of colonial legislation of the Portuguese republic]. *1913* (Vol. 4). Lisbon: Imprensa Nacional.

Ministère des Colonies. (1926). Interdiction de la culture du chanvre et répression de son emploi comme stupéfiant en Afrique équatoriale française [Prohibition of hemp cultivation and repression of its employment as a narcotic in French Equatorial Africa]. *Journal Officiel de la République Française, 58*(207), 10017.

Muller, S. D., Rhazi, L., Andrieux, B., Bottollier-Curtet, M., Fauquette, S., Saber, E.-R., … Daoud-Bouattour, A. (2015). Vegetation history of the western Rif mountains (NW Morocco): Origin, late-Holocene dynamics and human impact. *Vegetation History and Archaeobotany, 24*(4), 487–501.

Offen, K. (2004). Historical political ecology: An introduction. *Historical Geography, 32*, 19–42.

Paterson, C. (2009). *Prohibition and resistance: A socio-political exploration of the changing dynamics of the Southern African Cannabis trade* (*Unpublished thesis*). Rhodes University, Johannesburg.

Pavelek, M., & Lipman, E. (2010). *Report of a working group on Fibre Crops (Flax and Hemp)*. Velké Losiny: Biodiversity International.

Payeur-Didelot, J. F. (1898). Colonisation, commerce, industrie et agriculture au Congo [Colonization, commerce, industry and agriculture in the Congo]. *Bulletin de la Société de Géographie de l'Est, 20*, 17–43.

Peltzer, K., Ramlagan, S., Johnson, B. D., & Phaswana-Mafuya, N. (2010). Illicit drug use and treatment in South Africa. *Substance Use & Misuse, 45*(13), 2221–2243.

Perez, P., & Laniel, L. (2004). Croissance et … croissance de l'économie du cannabis en Afrique subsaharienne [Growth and … growth of the cannabis economy in sub-Saharan Africa]. *Hérodote, 112*(1), 122–138.

Philips, J. E. (1983). African smoking and pipes. *The Journal of African History, 24*(3), 303–319.

Pingali, P. L. (2012). Green revolution: Impacts, limits, and the path ahead. *Proceedings of the National Academy of Sciences, 109*(31), 12302–12308.

Redinha, J. (1946). *Relatorio Annual 1945* [Annual report 1945]. Dundo: Companhia de Diamantes de Angola.

Reeve, T. E. (1921). *In Wembo Nyama's Land*. Nashville: Methodist Episcopal Church.

René-Leclerc, C. (1905). Le commerce et l'industrie à Fez [Commerce and industry at Fez]. *Bulletin du Comité de l'Afrique Française, 4* (Supplement), 229–350.

Rosenthal, F. (1971). *The herb: Hashish versus medieval Muslim society*. Leiden: Brill.

Rucina, S. M., Muiruri, V. M., Downton, L., & Marchant, R. (2010). Late-Holocene savanna dynamics in the Amboseli Basin, Kenya. *The Holocene, 20*(5), 667–677.

Sawler, J., Stout, J. M., Gardner, K. M., Hudson, D., Vidmar, J., Butler, L., … Myles, S. (2015). The genetic structure of marijuana and hemp. *PLoS ONE, 10*(8), e0133292.

Say, L., & Chailley, J. (1892). *Nouveau dictionnaire d'économie politique* (Vol. 2). Paris: Guillaumin.

Scoones, I., & Thompson, J. (2011). The politics of seed in Africa's green revolution: Alternative narratives and competing pathways. *IDS Bulletin*, *42*(4), 1–23.

Seedfinder.eu. (n.d.). Breeder & seedbanks [website]. *Seedfinder.eu*. Retrieved December 29, 2015, from http://en.seedfinder.eu/database/breeder/

Seeds of Africa. (2013). About SOA seedbank [website]. *Seeds of Africa*. Retrieved December 29, 2015, from http://www.seeds-of-africa.com/about-soa-seedbank/

Seguin, C. (1910). Les hallucinations d'un fumeur de chanvre au Gabon [The hallucinations of a hemp smoker in Gabon]. *Journal des Voyages*, *704*, 427.

Seshata. (2013). Cannabis in Malawi. *Sensi Seeds*. Retrieved December 29, 2015, from http://sensiseeds.com/en/blog/cannabis-in-malawi/

Silva Porto, A. (1885/1942). *Viagens e Apontamentos de um Portuense em África* [Travel and notes of an Oporto Native in Africa]. Lisbon: Agência Geral das Colónias.

Sinha, J. (2001). *The history and development of the leading international drug control conventions*. Ottawa: Library of Parliament.

Small, E. (2015). Evolution and classification of *Cannabis sativa* in relation to human utilization. *The Botanical Review*, *81*, 189–294.

Small, E., & Cronquist, A. (1976). A practical and natural taxonomy for *Cannabis*. *Taxon*, *25*(4), 405–435.

Smith, S., Bubeck, D., Nelson, B., Stanek, J., & Gerke, J. (2015). Genetic diversity and modern plant breeding. In M. R. Ahuja & S. M. Jain (Eds.), *Genetic diversity and erosion in plants* (pp. 55–88). Geneva: Springer International.

Söllner, C. (1897). *Un voyage au Congo* [A voyage to the Congo] (2nd ed.). Namur: Auguste Godenne.

Strain Hunters. (2010a). Morocco expedition. *Strain Hunters*. Retrieved December 29, 2015, from http://forums.strainhunters.com/site/index.php/index.html/_/expeditions/africa-expedition-malawi-r5

Strain Hunters. (2010b). Africa expedition – Malawi. *Strain Hunters*. Retrieved from http://forums.strainhunters.com/site/index.php/index.html/_/expeditions/morocco-expedition-r2

Strain Hunters. (2013). Landraces. *Strain Hunters*. Retrieved December 29, 2015, from http://forums.strainhunters.com/site/index.php/index.html/_/articles/landraces/

Strain Hunters/YouTube. (n.d.). Strain Hunters channel. *YouTube*. Retrieved December 29, 2015, from https://www.youtube.com/user/strainhunters

Thompson, C. B. (2012). Alliance for a green revolution in Africa (AGRA): Advancing the theft of African genetic wealth. *Review of African Political Economy*, *39*(132), 345–350.

Toenniessen, G., Adesina, A., & DeVries, J. (2008). Building an alliance for a green revolution in Africa. *Annals of the New York Academy of Sciences*, *1136*, 233–242.

Trivier, M. (1887). D'Ambriz au Gabon [From Ambriz to Gabon]. *Bulletin de la Société de Géographie de Rochefort*, *8*, 203–211.

United Nations Office on Drugs and Crime. (2015). *World drug report 2015*. New York, NY: United Nations.

Van der Merwe, N. J. (2005). Antiquity of the smoking habit in Africa. *Transactions of the Royal Society of South Africa*, *60*(2), 147–150.

Warf, B. (2014). High points: An historical geography of cannabis. *Geographical Review*, *104*(4), 414–438.

Welwitsch, F. (1862). *Synopse explicativa das amostras de madeiras e drogas medicinaes e de otros objectivos mormente ethnographicos colligidos na provincia de Angola* [Explanatory synopsis of wood and medicinal drug samples and other especially ethnographic objects collected in the province of Angola]. Lisbon: Imprensa Nacional.

Williams, C. M., Whalley, B. J., & McCabe, C. (2015). Cannabinoids and appetite (dys)regulation. In L. Fattore (Ed.), *Cannabinoids in neurologic and mental disease* (pp. 315–339). London: Academic Press.

Yapa, L. (1996). Improved seeds and constructed scarcity. In R. Peet & M. J. Watts (Eds.), *Liberation ecologies: Environment, development, and social movements* (pp. 69–85). New York, NY: Routledge.

Zinberg, N. E. (1986). *Drug, set, and setting: The basis for controlled intoxicant use*. New Haven: Yale University Press.

Zurayk, R. (2013). Should farmers just say no? *Journal of Agriculture, Food Systems, and Community Development*, *4*(1), 11–14.

The myth of the narco-state

Pierre-Arnaud Chouvy

Centre national de la recherche scientifique (CNRS), Paris, France

Despite being used repeatedly in different contexts, the term "narco-state" has never been satisfactorily defined or explained. In fact, the existence of the narco-state is almost always taken for granted. This article will argue, on the basis of a review of existing definitions and of selected case studies, that there is no such thing as a narco-state and that using the term tends to oversimplify if not mask the complex socio-political and economic realities of drug-producing countries. The narco-state notion will be debated and opposed in terms of politics, territory, and economics.

Introduction

Virtually every single illegal drug-producing and/or drug-trafficking country in the world has one day or another been referred to as a narco-state or has been issued warnings against becoming a narco-state, whether by the United Nations Office on Drugs and Crime (UNODC), by senior counternarcotics officials, by heads of states and other politicians or, of course, by journalists and academics. The term has become extremely common despite a pervasive lack of definition. It seems that what a narco-state is, or is supposed to be, provided that it exists, is mostly assumed. As a consequence, the menace or threat that the simple reference to the narco-state implies is also assumed, maybe in part because something that is undefined is pretty much unknown and makes for the ideal menace or threat. While this is not the subject of this article, it must be stressed from the onset that the elusiveness of the term explains much of its discursive power and success as its undefined nature makes it an amorphous category that can be used to refer to very diverse states: this makes labelling a country a narco-state all the easier and can serve the interests of foreign powers by delegitimizing particular regimes or states and by calling for various forms of interventions and political interference.

In this article, we first briefly review the range of definitions that exist in the literature and address their limitations, especially how their vagueness tends to trivialize the notion of the narco-state by qualifying most countries as narco-states on the sole basis of their drug-tainted economies. We then determine what criteria we deem the most pertinent to describe so-called narco-states: the economic importance of the drug industry relative to a country's economy; the surface areas dedicated to illegal drug crops compared to the arable or cultivated land of a given country; the active involvement of the state in the illegal drug economy. It is on the basis of such criteria that we show that neither Afghanistan nor North Korea, arguably the world's two most drug-tainted economies, qualify as narco-states. We consequently argue that narco-states are nowhere to be found.

The ubiquitous but elusive narco-state

Guinea-Bissau's narco-state story is typical of how the news media very often refer to so-called – and alleged – narco-states: either by being content with quoting official reports or statements, sometimes inaccurately, or by sensationalizing their titles. This happened when the British newspaper The Observer reported in 2008 on "How a tiny West African country became the world's first narco state", stating, without defining what a narco-state was, that the UNODC called Guinea-Bissau the continent's – not the world's – "first narco-state" (How a tiny West African country became the world's first narco state, 2008). In fact, the UNODC has repeatedly warned against Afghanistan and other countries "being on the brink of becoming narco-states", or "moving from narcoeconomy to narco-state" (2006, p. iii), yet without defining what a narco-state is, or what a narcoeconomy is, or how it differs in degree or nature from a narco-state. Lack of definition is actually often made worse by the frequent association of highly debated and confusing notions. Such is the case of the "narcokleptocracy" first mentioned in 1989 to describe how the Panamanian government ended being funded with drug money (US Congress, 1989, p. 84). There are also mentions, without definitions of any sort, of "failed narco-states" (Marcy, 2010, p. 71) or of "narco-mafia states" (Tadjbakhsh, 2008, p. 6).

While the lack of definition can explain the prevalence of the narco-state phrase amongst politicians who want to delegitimize a given country or who wish to pressure a given government into action, the use of such an undefined notion by academics is less understandable. In fact, many if not most academics resort to the "narco-state" notion without defining it, as is the case with Jonathan Marshall who explains, in an otherwise significant book, that "Lebanon arguably declined from a narco-state to a failed state" (Marshall, 2012, p. 3): as if a narco-state was a superior state category. Still, some academics have provided various levels of definition of what a narco-state is or is supposed to be. In his 1972 seminal work *The Politics of Heroin* Alfred W. McCoy did not refer to the narco-state. Nor can any such mention be found in a 1991 revised edition. However, in a largely updated 2003 edition, McCoy referred to what had then become a widely used notion, as if it had become so pervasive that it could no longer be avoided. He explained how in Pakistan and Mexico "drugs had achieved the multifaceted mix of economic and institutional influence that defines a narco-state" (McCoy, 2003, p. 23). Yet, while such a description gives a sense of a narco-state's nature, it does not explain at which point a given state becomes a narco-state. In fact, so-called narco-states do not seem to be defined by most authors by much more than by reference to government corruption in drug-producing and/or -trafficking countries, despite the fact that corruption is usually described according to its nature, or to its scale and/or to the sector it affects, not according to the economic resource at stake. Why, then, is drug-related corruption singled out as it is when referring to a narco-state?

Most attempts at defining alleged narco-states basically describe forms and levels of drug-related corruption, not why or how a given state can legitimately be called a narco-state rather than a corrupt state. This is the case with Jordan who does not define the narco-state *per se* but rather what he calls narcostatization: "the corruption of the political regime as a result of narcotics trafficking" (1999, p. 9). He distinguishes between "narcodemocracies", "narcoauthoritarian regimes" and "narcoanocracies", and proposes five levels of narcostatization (from incipient to advanced) according to which a narco-state would be characterized by the "compliance of ministries, in addition to judiciary and police, with organized crime"; with "a president surrounded by compromised officials"; with a "possible complicity of the presidency itself" (Jordan, 1999, table 2). This typology – rather than a proper definition – eventually focuses more on the corruption of the state than on any supposed "narco" nature of the state, and it also proves too vague and limited in scope to determine which countries are or are not narco-states.

In a Ph.D. thesis questioning the narco-state and failed state statuses of Guinea-Bissau, Ashley Neese Bybee stresses that "as often as the term is used, consensus on a single definition of 'Narco-State' has not emerged". Despite warning against the use of the term "narco-state", Neese Bybee eventually refrains from a critical approach and simply defines the narco-state as "a state whose political, economic, security, or social institutions have been impacted to some extent by the drug trade" (2011, p. 97), yet without usable metrics and/or thresholds. As for Julia Buxton, she explains that "the term 'narco-state' refers to those countries where criminal organizations connected to the drug trade acquire an institutionalized presence in the state". Although institutionalization is obviously a very important phenomenon when the state is concerned, she does not explain what she means by an "institutionalized presence", nor does she detail the process behind it. In fact it seems that Buxton refers to the penetration of the state's institutions by the criminal organizations through what she calls "narco-corruption" (2006, p. 129). Here again the definition of the narco-state is rather incomplete and unconvincing for its criteria cannot be used to determine precisely which countries are narco-states or not.

Only Weiner critically addressed the issue of the narco-state's definition, stressing how the "use of the prefix 'narco', mainly by politicians and journalists, has ballooned to become almost ludicrous" (2004, p. 4). Yet Weiner bases most of his efforts at definition on a short description by the International Monetary Fund that explains that a narco-state is "where all legitimate institutions become penetrated by the power and wealth of traffickers" (IMF, 2003, p. 45). Weiner, after rightly dismissing various definition efforts by other authors for being often "vague and distracted by irrelevant terms" (p. 6), eventually defines the narco-state as "a state where drug networks are able to control and regulate the coercive instruments of the state, financial apparatus and government executive and policy to facilitate narcotics production, refining and trafficking" (p. 18). The problem with his definition is that it refers to a state that became controlled by drug-trafficking organizations rather than to a state that actively controls, if not encourages, drug productions and networks. In the end, rather oddly, Weiner cannot find any state to match his definition but refrains, nevertheless, from dismissing the narco-state notion. Still, he explains that a narco-state "may exist only in a Weberian 'ideal-type' manifestation" (p. 11), as if a narco-state could exist only as an idea and not in reality (ideal-types are pure types of existing phenomenon, which means that, to exist, the narco-state's ideal-type needs to be extrapolated on the basis of real-world narco-states).

It is on the basis of Weiner's definition that Letizia Paoli, Victoria A. Greenfield and Peter Reuter have asked to what extent Afghanistan and Burma are "narco-states". In the cases of both countries, the authors eventually dismiss the narco-state notion, mainly, and rightly in my opinion (see *infra*), because of the lack of control exerted by both the Afghan and Burmese states over their territories. In their chapter on Afghanistan and Burma the authors do not define what a narco-state is but they explain that there are two main conditions for a narco-state to exist: "a country that is economically dependent on the illicit drug economy" and "in which the government elites are complicit in the illicit drug trade" (Paoli, Greenfield, & Reuter, 2009, pp. 142–143). The authors stop short of explaining what degree and form of dependence they refer to or what they mean by complicity. However, later on, the same authors posit the rise of a narco-state in Tajikistan on the basis of different criteria, that is, where "leaders of the most powerful trafficking groups occupy high-ranking government positions and misuse state structures for their own illicit businesses" (p. 181). This is based on such an equivocal definition that the authors then declare that "Tajikistan has become, in less than 10 years, a veritable narco-state" (p. 197) (suggesting, it seems, that there are false narco-states).

The last definition to be mentioned here is that of the French Geopolitical Drug Watch that described a narco-state as "a state that, or in which state institutions, benefit directly and in a significant or even a major way, from illegal drug proceeds" (Observatoire géopolitique des drogues, 1994, pp. 12–14). Here again the definition proves too vague to be used to determine accurately which countries are narco-states. Moreover, the narco-state is oddly described as a state that benefits rather passively from – instead of actively developing – the illegal drug trade.

All the above attempts to define the narco-state are lacking in various ways. As Weiner rightfully put it, too many attempts of this sort are "vague and distracted by irrelevant terms". Also, most of them refer to the corruption of state and/or government officials by illegal drug funds but do not explain why speaking of narco-states rather than of corrupt states is justified (as if naming a state after the resource used for corruption is only justified when illegal drug production or trafficking is the resource). In any case, the extent of the drug-related corruption, or of the economic dependence of a given state or country on an illegal drug industry, is never defined precisely enough, whether in terms of metrics or threshold. Nor is the level of penetration of state institutions. The lack of territorial control experienced by the state in many drug-producing countries and its consequence on the pertinence of calling such states narco-states are also barely addressed. Pertinent criteria are therefore needed in order to decide if narco-states exist or not and, if they do, which countries qualify as narco-states.

Is a narco-state a rentier state?

The first thing about a narco-state, obviously, is that it is a state, that is, according to Migdal, an

> organization, composed of numerous agencies led and coordinated by the state's leadership (executive authority) that has the ability or authority to make and implement the binding rules for all the people as well as the parameters of rule making for other social organizations in a given territory, using force if necessary to have its way. (Migdal, 1988, p. 19)

States that are referred to as narco-states, rightly or not, all happen to be those late and less developed states that Douglass C. North et al. call "natural states" or "limited access orders" whose patterns are characterized, notably, by "polities without generalized consent of the governed" and by a "predominance of social relationships organized along personal lines, including privileges, social hierarchies, laws that are enforced unequally, insecure property rights, and a pervasive sense that not all individuals were created or are equal" (North, Walls, & Weingats, 2009, p. 12). In such natural states, "the positions, privileges, and rents of the individual elites in the dominant coalition depend on the limited entry enforced by the continued existence of the regime" and rent-seeking can easily amount to corruption or other unequal competitive processes (North et al., 2009, p. 20). This is in part why Migdal warns that there is a danger in making the state anthropomorphic, and that "where state coherence is low, reference to the state leadership or executive authority as if it *were* the state or, worse yet, reference to *the* state without regard to differences within it could be downright misleading" (Migdal, 1988, p. 19).

This is one reason why calling Afghanistan a narco-state is somehow problematic since the country has been under no or very little state authority for years. In this case and in that of many other weak or even failed states, the state clearly lacks the "ability or authority to make and implement the binding rules for all the people as well as the parameters of rule making for other social organizations" in its territory, even by force. The same is true of Burma, where some of the world's longest armed insurgencies persist and where the state, far from being a monolithic and homogenous organization, has never had the political and material means to enforce official anti-drug laws (whether through repression or economic incentives) over its territory (whether or not state actors and successive governments have ever been willing to do so). Reducing or suppressing illegal drug production and/or trafficking in weak or failed states is most often beyond governmental and institutional capabilities, because of power rivalries and armed contestations, or (geo)political realism and pragmatism (such as in Morocco). Even basic economic laws and legal procedures can be difficult if not impossible to enforce, as exemplified by the fact that, very often, "natural states cannot issue something as seemingly simple as a driver's license on impersonal basis" (North et al., 2009, p. 11).

The absolute and relative importance of illegal crop superficies would then seem to be an important criterion to include in a definition of the narco-state, provided that the illegal crops are grown in areas under the effective control of the state. Following the same logic, the absolute and relative economic importance of an illegal drug industry in a given country can be related to the penetration of the state institutions by drug-trafficking organizations and to the corruption of the government. All things considered, it seems that a so-called narco-state must be a country in which the resort to illegal drug production and/or trafficking is part of the official state policy with the government organizing drug production and/or trafficking through the involvement of state and/or non-state actors. Without going as far as Aureano (2001, p. 3) when he writes that the narco-state "implies the existence of a state who would devote its most important resources and those of the civil society to the benefit of the drug industry", we can say that for a narco-state to exist illegal drug production and/or trafficking must be sponsored and planned by the state, whether the state's most important resources are devoted to drug production and/or trafficking, or not.

Obviously, no state resorts to illegal drug production or trafficking as part of an official policy as no such ideal narco-state can exist within the international system without becoming a pariah. In fact, the only country that could well be a narco-state, on the sole basis of resorting to drug production and trafficking as part of a state's (unofficial) policy, the Democratic People's Republic of Korea, can be said to be a pariah. Since defaulting on its international debt in 1975 the North Korean state allegedly resorts to illegal activities such as counterfeiting money and producing and trafficking opium, heroin and methamphetamine, in part so that its embassies can be financially autonomous (Chestnut, 2007, pp. 85, 89). Yet very little is known about illegal drug production and trafficking by the North Korean state, whether about the areas cultivated with opium poppies or the revenues obtained from heroin and methamphetamine production and trafficking. What is known is that opium production and exportation (trafficking) was reportedly developed after a countrywide public order to produce opium was issued by the Korean state in the early 1990s (until then opiates were reportedly only purchased by North Korean diplomats for resale). It is also known from defectors that "drug processing and counterfeit currency manufacturing took place at state-run factories", and that "opiates, and later methamphetamines, were processed and plastic-wrapped at refinement plants established in consultation with Southeast Asian experts and run by state security" (Chestnut, 2007, p. 89). How much North Korea earns from illegal activities is not known in detail but US officials estimated in 2005 the country's "total income from criminal activities at $500 million, an amount roughly equal to income from arms sales and 35–40 percent of the income provided by legitimate exports" (p. 92).

If these figures are accurate North Korea is most likely the closest to what a narco-state (i.e. a rentier state comparable to a petro-state) would be if the economic criterion were to be considered the most pertinent. Yet for a state to be called a narco-state purely on an economic basis, the revenues procured to the state through illegal drug production and/or trafficking have to be vital to state stability: as we will see, both resource abundance and dependence are needed to qualify a state as a rentier state. While North Korea clearly relies on illegal drug revenues and other illegal activities, it is not clear to US officials and various observers if the "contribution of criminal activity to regime stability" is vital or not (Chestnut, 2007, p. 93). In any case, calling North

Korea a narco-state remains problematic since illegal drug proceeds are most likely matched, if not surpassed (according to most observers), by illegal arms sales (Hurst, 2005; Perl, 2003): North Korea would therefore qualify more as an "arm-state" than as a similarly awkwardly named "narco-state". Interestingly, while the US Department of State mentions estimates of 4200–7000 hectares of poppy cultivation and of 30–44 metric tons of opium being produced annually (with an expected yield of 3–4.5 metric tons of heroin) in the early 2000s, it also makes clear that such "estimates have not been confirmed", that "reports of extensive opium cultivation in North Korea are dated" and that "agricultural problems in North Korea, including flooding and shortages of fertilizer and insecticides, suggest that current opium production might well be below these estimates" (US Department of State, 2002, pp. VIII-46–47). What brings North Korea closer to an ideal narco-state is the fact that it is most probably the only country in which state-sponsored illegal drug production and trafficking takes place.

Only Afghanistan could match or rival North Korea when, in the 2000s, its drug economy was estimated to be *equivalent to* 61% of Afghanistan's GDP, that is, when it amounted to 37% of the entire (legal and illegal) Afghan economy (UNODC, 2006, p. 9). But that was until Afghanistan's legal economy grew enough to significantly reduce the relative importance of its drug economy (despite an increase in cultivation) with the Afghan opium industry *equivalent to* only 15% of the country's GDP in 2013, that is, when it amounted to about 13% of the entire Afghan economy (UNODC, 2013, p. 70). In Morocco, the hashish industry was estimated by the UNODC to be *equivalent to* only 0.57% of the GDP in 2003, when production was likely to be at its highest (UNODC, 2003, p. 5). Yet, in the mid-1990s, the hashish industry was said to be the country's main foreign exchange earner and to *be equivalent to* 55% of the country's official export earnings (OGD, 1994, pp. 31–55). It would be difficult, in the end, to call Afghanistan and Morocco narco-states based on such "low" incomes derived from their respective drug industries; or, for that matter, as we will see later, on the basis of their surface areas cultivated with poppies and/or cannabis.

According to the above-mentioned economic data, can so-called narco-states qualify as rentier states? According to their drug production outputs and their absolute and relative economic importance, neither Afghanistan's nor North Korea's states are characterized by both the resource abundance and resource dependence that define rentier states (Brunnschweiler, 2008, p. 401). They clearly cannot be compared to those petro-states that Terry Lynn Karl described as the rentier states "par excellence" (Karl, 1999, p. 36) or to other "mineral economies" that Gobind Nankani qualified as "developing countries in which the share of mineral production in GDP and of mineral exports in total exports render the keystone of the economy", with "guiding thresholds" of 10% or more of GDP and 40% of total merchandise exports (in the mid-1970s) (Nankani, 1979: p. i, note 1). While Afghanistan and North Korea may be compared to petro-states on the basis of such metrics and thresholds, they clearly do not qualify as rentier states because their drug economies do not provide them with the "substantial *external rent*" that characterizes a rentier economy according to Hazem Beblawi. Rather, their drug economies result from a "domestic productive sector", that is, "a situation of domestic payment transfer in a productive economy" that should not be confused with a rent (Beblawi, 1990, p. 51). Also, in a rentier state, the state (or the government) must be "the principal recipient of the external rent in the economy", a rent that is redistributed to the population and makes the rentier state, to use Giacomo Luciani's distinction, an allocative state rather than a productive state (Beblawi, 1990, p. 53; Luciani, 1987).

North Korea is most likely the principal recipient of what is an internal rent rather than an external rent but it remains, like Afghanistan, Burma, Colombia, Morocco, etc., a production state. While states that derive a large source of revenues solely from drug trafficking (an external rent) could be considered rentier states and therefore narco-states, none of the alleged narco-states are allocative states and therefore none of them are rentier states. Indeed, according to Luciani, a rentier state differs from a "production state" ("a state that relies on taxation of the domestic economy for its income") in that it is an "allocation state" that "does not depend on domestic sources of revenue but rather *is* the primary source of revenue itself in the domestic economy" (Luciani, 1987, p. 63; Yates, 1996, p. 15). Luciani refers to the "allocation state" that depends on a "rentier economy" to perform its allocative function: according to him, a rentier or allocation state is a state "whose revenue derives predominantly (more than 40%) from oil or other foreign sources" and "whose expenditure is a substantial share of GDP", so that allocation (without taxation) is "the only relationship that they need to have with their domestic economy" (Luciani, 1987, pp. 70–71). This is clearly not the case in the alleged narco-states of Afghanistan, Guinea-Bissau or North Korea. Moreover, the relative importance of their drug economies to their global economy (GDP) derives in part from the usually limited size of their economy (legal and illegal, for there are non-drug-related illegal activities in every single country). Indeed, as stressed by Gavin Wright and Jesse Czelusta in their critical review of the resource curse hypothesis and literature, "the relative size of resource exports is at best an indicator of *comparative* advantage in resource products", which means that "comparative advantage in natural resources may simply reflect an absence of other internationally competitive sectors in the economy – in a word, underdevelopment" (Wright & Czelusta, 2004, p. 4). This is exemplified in Afghanistan where the growth of the legal economy lessened the relative importance of the country's drug industry in a matter of a few years (Chouvy, 2009).

This is not to say, though, that when (as in Afghanistan or in Guinea-Bissau) the size of the legal economy is small, or even smaller than that of the illegal economy, the revenue generated through illegal drug production and/or trafficking is not "central to sustaining competition within the elite", or that there are no "sufficient powerful actors […] who have a vested interest in its continuation" (Transparency International, 2014, p. 27). Indeed, as "the non-drug economy provides very few rents which could sustain patronage networks, the drugs trade is of central political importance" (Transparency International, 2014, p. 27). In fact, the existence of highly valuable resources and rents is likely to increase rent-seeking and corruption, along with political bargaining between state and private actors. According to the traditional rent-seeking theory, corruption can be seen as a particular type of rent-seeking activity (as opposed to the legitimate lobbying's open competition): "rent-seeking is called corruption when competition for preferential treatment is restricted to a few insiders and when rent-seeking expenses are valuable to the recipient" (Lambsdorff, 2002, p. 120). But, according to Lambsdorff (2002, p. 121), "corruption motivates the creation of inefficient rules that generate rents", something that does not truly fit the idea of the narco-state where corruption does not motivate the creation of rules but merely manages to avoid or bend the rules: the illegality of drug production and trafficking is not the result of rent-seeking processes in any alleged narco-state or, for that matter, in any state at all.

The narco-state vs. the lack of political and territorial control of resources

The literature about rentier states is vastly dominated by references to extraction economies, that is, mineral economies among which so-called petro-states form a large majority. In this literature as well as in the resource curse literature, references to production economies and especially to agriculturally based resource rents are almost nonexistent. In fact, some studies stress that "oil and minerals give rise to massive rents in a way that food or agricultural resources do not" (Sala-i-Martin & Subramanian, 2003, p. 9). Despite their relatively high value (at least compared to most other agricultural products), even agriculturally based illegal drug economies are absent from the literature on resource rents and rentier states. Conversely, and rather oddly, the literature on narco-states does not resort to the notions of rentier state or of rentier economies. While the latter is difficult to understand, the fact that narco-states are not mentioned in the rentier state literature is more understandable since the value of illegal drugs at the farm gate compares unfavourably with the value of mineral resources such as oil, diamond, ore minerals, etc., but also because the geographical dimensions or spatial characteristics of agricultural drug production (closer to small-scale subsistence agriculture than to large-scale plantation agriculture) define the drug resource as distant (as opposed to proximate) and diffuse (as opposed to point). This is actually another reason why states faced with illegal drug production cannot qualify as rentier states, and even less as narco-states: because the resource that could provide a rent (even an internal one) is most often beyond the direct and complete reach and control of the state.

Distant resources are resources that are far from the centre of power, "whether through a physical relationship or a socially constructed one", or both (such as poppy, coca or cannabis cultivation in Afghanistan, in Burma, in Colombia, in Morocco) (Le Billon, 2001, pp. 569–570). Diffuse resources "are spatially spread over vast areas and access to their revenue is socio-economically dispersed", which makes them less accessible, and therefore less taxable and/or "lootable", than extracted resources: illegal drug cultivation (often small and remote fields in poorly accessible – and often peripheral – areas) is clearly a perfect example of a diffuse resource (Auty, 2001; Le Billon, 2012, pp. 28–29). Indeed, as stressed by Goodhand and Mansfield, the "diffuse, high value (and price elasticity) and fugitive qualities of drugs makes them inherently difficult for state actors to monopolise" and, one could add, to control (2010, p. 29). Also, agricultural drug production (being a lootable resource not in the sense of extracted resource but in the sense that it can be easily produced by independent individuals outside of the government's knowledge/taxation and/or opposition) is a diffuse and most often distant resource that is difficult for state actors to monopolize because, as explained by Snyder, "the *low economic barriers to entry* that characterize lootable resources make it hard for rulers to gain monopoly control of them" and also because "a further impediment to public extraction concerns the *illegality*" of such a lootable resource: state actors risk international sanctions and "illegality poses a barrier to entry for the public sector" (Snyder, 2006, p. 950). Joint extraction (meaning shared income generated by exploiting resources, whether through taxation or government-run protection rackets) is also often impossible because of international pressure and, most often, because of the state actors' incapacity to "make a credible threat of enforcing no extraction if private actors refuse to share their income" (Snyder, 2006, p. 953).

The same is true of the conditionality of so-called state-sponsored protection rackets, that is, "informal institutions through which public officials refrain from enforcing the law or, alternatively, enforce it selectively against the rivals of a criminal organization, in exchange for a share of the profits generated by the organization" (Snyder & Duran-Martinez, 2009, p. 253). Such rackets are possible provided that the state is in a position to threaten private actors with law enforcement (so that the promise not to enforce the law can be sold to those private actors who agree to share their income with state actors), which is rarely the case in Afghanistan or in Burma for example. Whether in Afghanistan, in Burma, in Pakistan or even in Morocco, forced eradication has always been difficult (politically, strategically and even materially) to implement by the state or by foreign paramilitary outfits (such as DynCorp in Afghanistan: see Chouvy, 2009, p. 115) as violent encounters between opium or cannabis farmers (or anti-government militants such as the Taliban in southern Afghanistan) and eradication teams often prevent crop destruction from occurring (Chouvy, 2009, pp. 157–170). Also, the threat of eradication is rarely a deterrent if only because, in Afghanistan for example, "the opportunity cost of planting opium poppy and having it destroyed is equal to the wheat crop that might have been cultivated in the place of poppy" (Mansfield & Pain, 2006, p. 7).

Another key criterion of the inadequacy of the narco-state notion, at least when agricultural drug production (and not drug trafficking) is concerned, is the surface area over which cultivation takes place, territorial control being paramount for a state. Agricultural drug production would then be one significant criterion defining a narco-state. Here absolute and relative data need to be considered carefully in order to determine if a given cultivated surface area is important enough for a state to deserve being called a narco-state. For instance, Afghanistan and Morocco could hardly qualify as narco-states when they respectively cultivated 131,000 hectares of opium poppy in 2004 and 134,000 hectares of cannabis in 2003 (UNODC, 2003, 2004). Yet what matters the most here is not absolute data, even though it points to the degree of state territorial control or toleration, the Afghan state having obviously much less control over its territory than Morocco. What matters the most are relative data, both Afghanistan and Morocco devoting very limited parts of their arable lands (respectively 1.67% and 1.57%) to illegal drug crop cultivation (UNODC, 2003, 2004). Neither Afghanistan nor Morocco, then reportedly and respectively the world's foremost opium- and hashish-producing countries, devoted enough arable land to illegal poppy and cannabis cultivation to deserve being called narco-states on this basis alone: in both countries the vast majority of the arable land was then and still is cultivated with cereals, and not poppies or cannabis.

The only real difference here is that in 2003 the Afghan state was then being (re)built and was clearly not in control of the entire country, even though the insurgency had not yet reached the levels known in the mid-2010s. In terms of absolute territorial control, the Afghan state was at the time lacking the means to enforce the monopoly of the legitimate use of force over its territory. Law enforcement was then – and still is – extremely difficult if not impossible to achieve. As Goodhand wrote in, 2008: "Large swathes of the south have now become 'non-state spaces' where the government has neither the capacity nor the legitimacy to mobilize capital or coercion in order to enforce institutions of joint control (or no extraction)" (2008, p. 414).

To the contrary, the Moroccan state was and still is in full control of its territory, where its writ is unchallenged by armed insurgencies. Yet the tense socio-economic situation of the impoverished Rif region, where cannabis is grown, most likely prevents the authorities from acting decisively against the hashish economy. The Moroccan state formally controls its territory but has no other choice, economically, socially and even politically, than to tacitly tolerate hashish production and trafficking in the centre of the Rif: a region where cannabis cultivation has been inherited from a long, complex and violent history of rivalries, tolerance and contestation (Chouvy, 2005, 2008). Cannabis cultivation in Morocco can be said to benefit from the socio-political and economic context of the Rif, as well as from large-scale corruption, but it clearly does not entitle Morocco to be considered a narco-state.

It is obviously difficult to label a weak state – that is, a state that lacks the means of effective territorial control (a vulnerable state) – or even worse, a failed state – that is, a state that cannot perform any of "the core state functions in the fields of security, representation and welfare" (a state in overt crisis) – as a narco-state (Boege, Brown, Clements, & Nolan, 2009, p. 3). Although this is not to say that a large-scale illegal opium economy, such as the one in Afghanistan, has not had "several direct and indirect impacts upon both the degree of the state and the kind of state", or that the drug economy has not "become a vehicle for accumulating power" (Goodhand, 2008, pp. 411, 412). Goodhand is correct when he writes that the "drugs economy provides a mode of accumulation that enables military and political entrepreneurs to 'capture' parts of the state"; and also when he stresses that "although drugs are a factor in political decision-making, the "narco-state" discourse exaggerates their role by raising them to a position of primacy" (2008, pp. 412, 413).

In Afghanistan as well as in all illegal drug-producing countries, North Korea apart, the drug industry is developed through private extraction regimes or through joint extraction regimes that involve rulers and private actors (Goodhand, 2008; Snyder, 2006). Only in North Korea, where the state is the closest to what a narco-state could supposedly consist of, has the illegal drug industry been developed through a public extraction regime, the state (and not only some state actors of government officials) reportedly coercing some farmers to produce opium rather than grain on parts of the state farms land they till. That very specific case apart, most illegal drug-producing countries are weak or failing states where non-state actors are too strong to be suppressed or ignored by the state. As Migdal explains, "there can be no understanding of state capabilities in the Third World without first comprehending the social structure of which states are only one part" (1988, p. 34). He explains how "in circumstances of fragmented social control, the state has become an arena of accommodations", something that is echoed by the limited access order of North's natural state (Migdal, 1988, p. 264; North et al., 2009). It therefore appears that weak, failed or natural states that cannot reign in their strongmen-turned-drug lords, and other powerful potentially anti-government non-state actors, cannot reasonably be called narco-states. Weak and failed states are characterized by a lack of state control over certain parts of a population and/or territory while the alleged existence of a narco-state necessarily implies control and governing over drug-trafficking organizations and/or drug-producing areas. In any case – and to acknowledge that no state, whether natural or modern, weak or strong, can fully control its territory to totally prevent drug cultivation (including the USA where illegal cannabis cultivation occurs on large areas in state-owned forests) – what so-called narco-state would devote less than 2% of its arable land to drug crops, mostly, at that, outside of its direct territorial control?

Conclusion

The three most pertinent criteria by which to judge whether a given country qualifies as a narco-state are: the surface area covered by illegal drug crops; the size of the illegal drug economy relative to the overall economy and, most importantly, the state-sponsorship of illegal drug production and/or trafficking.

Contrary to what most definition attempts have described, the ideal narco-state is the opposite of a state whose institutions have been penetrated by drug-trafficking organizations or of a state whose officials have been corrupted by drug money. A state cannot qualify as a narco-state unless illegal drug production and/or trafficking are/is the result of top-down economics where the state developed, if not initiated, an illegal drug industry. For a state to be rightly categorized as a narco-state, the illegal drug industry must be state sponsored and must contribute to the majority of a country's overall economy (GDP + illegal economy or, as is now the case within the European Union, GDP that includes the illegal economy).

According to such a restrictive definition, neither North Korea nor Afghanistan, arguably the world's two most drug-tainted economies, are narco-states. This leads to the conclusion that there is no existing narco-state, and that mentions of alleged narco-states can be explained by what Alfred North Whitehead described as the "Fallacy of Misplaced Concreteness", that is, the "error of mistaking the abstract for the concrete" (Whitehead, 1925). In fact, and as James Stuart Mill wrote:

> The tendency has always been strong to believe that whatever received a name must be an entity or being, having an independent existence of its own. And if no real entity answering to the name could be found, men did not for that reason suppose that none existed, but imagined that it was something peculiarly abstruse and mysterious.[1]

The future existence of narco-states remains of course a possibility. They are part of what John Leslie terms Plato's "necessarily existing realm of possibilities" but that does not mean that any such state presently exists (Holt, 2012, p. 198). Qualifying existing states as narco-states is only possible because of a lack of proper definitions, which makes it a perfect example of reification.

Acknowledgements

The author wishes to acknowledge the comments of Kenza Afsahi, Guillermo Aureano, Stewart Williams and two anonymous reviewers on earlier drafts of this text.

Disclosure statement

No potential conflict of interest was reported by the author.

Note

1. A note (no. 2) by John Stuart Mill in a book by Mill (1869, p. 5).

References

Aureano, G. R. (2001). L'Etat et la prohibition de (certaines) drogues [The state and the prohibition of (certain) drugs]. *Cemoti*, *32*, Dossier « Drogue et politique », 15–38.
Auty, R. (2001). *Resource abundance and economic development*. Oxford: Oxford University Press.
Beblawi, H. (1990). The rentier state in the Arab world. In G. Luciani (Ed.), *The Arab state* (pp. 49–62). Berkeley: University of California Press.
Boege, V., Brown, A., Clements, K., & Nolan, A. (2009). *On hybrid political orders and emerging states: State formation in the context of "fragility"*. Berghof Handbook Dialogue n° 8, Berghof Research Center for Constructive Conflict Management, Berlin.
Brunnschweiler, C. N. (2008). Cursing the blessings? Natural resource abundance, institutions, and economic growth. *World Development*, *36*(3), 399–419.
Buxton, J. (2006). *The political economy of narcotics. Production, consumption, and global markets*. London: Zed Books.
Chestnut, S. (2007). Illicit activity and proliferation. North Korean smuggling networks. *International Security*, *32*(1), 80–111.
Chouvy, P.-A. (2005). Morocco said to produce nearly half of the world's hashish supply. *Jane's Intelligence Review*, *17*(11), 32–35.
Chouvy, P.-A. (2008). Production de cannabis et de haschich au Maroc: contexte et enjeux. *L'espace politique*, *4*, 5–19.
Chouvy, P.-A. (2009). *Opium. Uncovering the politics of the poppy*. London: I.B. Tauris.
Goodhand, J. (2008). Corrupting or consolidating the peace? The drugs economy and post-conflict peacebuilding in Afghanistan. *International Peacekeeping*, *15*, 405–423.
Goodhand, J., & Mansfield, D. (2010). *Drugs and (dis)order: A study of the opium trade, political settlements and state-making in Afghanistan*. Crisis states working papers series n° 2, working paper n° 83, London: Crisis States Research Centre.
Holt, J. (2012). *Why does the world exist*? New York: Liveright Publishing Corporation.
How a tiny West African country became the world's first narco state. (2008, March 9). *The Observer*.
Hurst, C. (2005). North Korea. A government-sponsored drug trafficking network. *Military Review*, September–October 2005.
International Monetary Fund. (2003). *Islamic state of Afghanistan: Rebuilding a macroeconomic framework for reconstruction and growth* (IMF country report n° 03/299). Washington, DC: Author.
Jordan, J. (1999). *Drug politics: Dirty money and democracies*. Norman: University of Oklahoma Press.

Karl, T. L. (1999). The perils of the petro-state: Reflections on the paradox of plenty. *Journal of International Affairs*, *53*(1), 31–48.
Lambsdorff, J. G. (2002). Corruption and rent-seeking. *Public Choice*, *113*, 97–125.
Le Billon, P. (2001). The political ecology of war: Natural resources and armed conflicts. *Political Geography*, *20*, 561–584.
Le Billon, P. (2012). *Wars of plunder. Conflicts, profits and the politics of resources*. London: Hurst & Company.
Luciani, G. (1987). Allocation vs. production states: A theoretical framework. In G. Luciani & H. Beblawi (Eds.), *The rentier state* (pp. 63–82). London: Croom Helm.
Mansfield, D., & Pain, A. (2006). *Opium poppy eradication: How to raise risk when there is nothing to lose?* AREU Briefing Paper, August 2006, Kabul: Afghanistan Research and Evaluation Unit.
Marcy, W. L. (2010). *The politics of cocaine: How US. Policy has created a thriving drug industry in central and South America*. Chicago, IL: Lawrence Hill Books.
Marshall, J. V. (2012). *The Lebanese connection. Corruption, civil war, and the international drug traffic*. Stanford, CA: Stanford University Press.
McCoy, A. W. (2003). *The politics of heroin. CIA complicity in the global drug trade (Afghanistan, Southeast Asia, Central America, Colombia)*. New York: Lawrence Hill Books.
Migdal, J. S. (1988). *Strong societies and weak states. State-society relations and state capabilities in the third world*. Princeton, NJ: Princeton University Press.
Mill, J. (1869). *Analysis of the phenomena of the human mind*. Volume 2. London: Longmans, Green, Reader, and Dyer.
Nankani, G. T. (1979). *Development problems of mineral exporting countries*. World Bank staff working paper 354, Washington: World Bank.
Neese Bybee, A. (2011). *Narco-state or failed state? Narcotics and politics in guinea-bissau*. PhD in Public Policy. George Mason University.
North, D. C., Walls, J. J., & Weingats, B. R. (2009). *Violence and social orders. A conceptual framework for interpreting recorded human history*. Cambridge: Cambridge University Press.
Observatoire géopolitique des drogues [Geopolitical Drug Watch]. (1994). *Etat des drogues, drogues des Etats* [State of the drugs, drugs of the states]. Paris: Hachette.
Paoli, L., Greenfield, V. A., Reuter, P. (2009). *The world heroin market. Can supply be Cut?* Oxford: Oxford University Press.
Perl, R. F. (2003). *Drug trafficking and North Korea: Issues for US policy*. CRS Report for Congress, Congressional Research Service. Washington, DC: United States Congress.
Sala-i-Martin, X., & Subramanian, A. (2003). *Addressing the natural resource curse: An illustration from Nigeria*. Working paper 9804, NBER working paper series. Cambridge: National Bureau of Economic Research.
Snyder, R. (2006). Does lootable wealth breed disorder? A political economy of extraction framework. *Comparative Political Studies*, *39*, 943–968.
Snyder, R., & Duran-Martinez, A. (2009). Does illegality breed violence? Drug trafficking and state-sponsored protection rackets. *Crime, Law and Social Change*, *52*(3), 253–273.
Tadjbakhsh, S. (2008). Failed narco-state or a human security failure? Ethical and methodological ruptures with a traditional read of the Afghan Quagmire. In H. G. Brauch, Ú. O. Spring, J. Grin, C. Mesjasz, P. Kameri-Mbote, N. Behera, … H. Krummenacher (Eds.), *Facing global environmental change: Environmental, human, energy, food, health and water security concepts* (pp. 1127–1244). Berlin: Springer.
Transparency International. (2014). *Corruption as a threat to stability and peace*. Berlin: Author.
United Nations Office on Drugs and Crime (UNODC). (2003). *Maroc. EEnquête sur le cannabis 2003*. Vienna: United Nations.
UNODC. (2004). *Afghanistan opium survey 2004*. Vienna: United Nations.
UNODC. (2006). *Afghanistan opium survey 2006*. Vienna: United Nations.
UNODC. (2013). *Afghanistan opium survey 2013*. Vienna: United Nations.
US Congress. (1989). *Drugs, law enforcement and foreign policy*. House of representatives. Committee on foreign relations. Subcommittee on terrorism, narcotics and international operations. Report in the matter of representative John F. Kerry.100th Cong., 2d sess., S. Prt. 100–165.
US Department of State (2002). *International narcotics control strategy report 2001*. Bureau of international narcotics and law enforcement affairs, US state department, March 2002.
Weiner, M. (2004). *An Afghan "narco-state"? Dynamics, assessment and security implications if the Afghan opium industry*. Canberra Papers on Strategy and Defence n° 58. Strategic Defence Studies Centre. Canberra: Australian National University.

Whitehead, A. N. (1925). *Science and the modern world*. Cambridge: Cambridge University Press.
Wright, G., & Czelusta, J. (2004). *Mineral resources and economic development* (Working Paper n° 209). Stanford Center for International Development, Stanford: Stanford University.
Yates, D. A. (1996). *The rentier state in Africa: Oil rent dependency and neocolonialism in the republic of Gabon*. Trenton: Africa World Press.

From *rakı* to *ayran*: regulating the place and practice of drinking in Turkey

Emine Ö. Evered[a] and Kyle T. Evered[a,b]

[a]*Department of History, Michigan State University, East Lansing, USA;* [b]*Department of Geography, Michigan State University, East Lansing, USA*

Despite religious proscriptions and practices, currents of alcohol never wholly ceased in Ottoman or Republican Turkey. Rather, Anatolian history overflows with examples of regulated consumption – and futile schemes for prohibition. Recently, prohibitionist discourse returned amid regulatory initiatives and in ways reifying secular-Islamist divides. Integral to permutations in policy implementation, even schemes of socio-spatial control arose that entail regimes of zoning and separation for trade and consumption. Accounting for narratives of regulationism and prohibitionism from a vantage acknowledging the republic's past, we map today's dynamic and ongoing shifts in Turkey's regulatory and discursive engagements with the place and practice of drinking.

> Every major industrialized nation has **A BEER** (you can't be a **Real Country** unless you have **A BEER** and an **airline** – it helps if you have some kind of a *football team*, or some *nuclear weapons*, but *at the very least* you need **A BEER**).
>
> (Zappa & Occhiogrosso, 1989, p. 231)

1. National drinks and the laws of nation-states

In spring and summer 2013, Turkey attracted international scrutiny owing both to protests over plans for demolishing/redeveloping green space (and adjacent neighbourhoods) in central Istanbul and to the state's reactions to these demonstrations. Most protesters and scholars of Turkey interpreted this struggle over Gezi Park as signifying far more than the fate of a single site of greenery adjacent to Istanbul's Taksim Square. For many involved directly and for those familiar with ongoing trends within the country, this confrontation appeared rooted in and emblematic of wider anxieties over a multitude of ongoing shifts in Turkey's socio-political landscapes that permeate people's very existence. Indeed, the demonstrations themselves drew activists and other participants concerned with issues transcending those of the urban environment and acutely top-down schemes for its modification. In the ensuing protests – and in numerous other cities, citizens thus voiced a plurality of political agendas that focused upon, among other causes, the country's Islamist-secularist divisions, neoliberal policies of austerity, privatization, deregulation, and restructuring, the state's posture vis-à-vis the crisis in Syria, a history of state abuses of civil liberties and human rights (extending from restrictions on social media and the press, on the one hand, to allegations of police brutality, on the other hand), accusations of anti-democratic, autocratic and corrupt dealings by senior state officials, and the precarious status of frequently marginalized populations (ranging from ethno-religious minorities, such as Turkey's Kurdish and Alevi populations, to the lesbian, gay, bisexual, and transgender community). Integral to most concerns echoed in these rallies and in related expressions of opposition at that time (and since) were claims that the state, as led by Prime Minister (PM) Recep Tayyip Erdoğan (b. 1954), was neglecting increasingly – if not thoroughly running roughshod over – the interests, rights and necessities of citizens and parties not aligned unconditionally with either the *Adalet ve Kalkınma Partisi* (the AKP or Justice and Development Party; the pro-neoliberal Islamist party that has maintained majority control of the Turkish state ever since a November 2002 general election) or those economic interests associated with the party that bolster its electoral prominence. In particular, critics in Turkey (and beyond) voiced grievances over a perceptible set of regulatory–deregulatory trends towards asserting state authority over people's freedoms of expression and morality, on the one hand, and abdicating of state responsibilities pertaining to other aspects of people's lives (i.e. one that is in-step with commercial deregulation and privatization – concerns that resurfaced tragically following the May 2014 Soma mine disaster; see Turkish mine disaster: Unions hold protest strike, 2014), on the other hand. Amid such shifts, many protesters in Istanbul were motivated by commercial development schemes for cosmopolitan public spaces like the Gezi Park, Taksim Square and İstikal Caddesi location – a project celebrating in its design the Ottoman past (i.e. an "Islamic" and/or "imperial" past, in the view of secularist and nationalist critics), but they were also agitated by coinciding local impositions of moral authority and national legislative trends to restrict public displays of artistic expression and of affection (e.g. kissing) and any public consumption or advertising of alcoholic beverages. Coming shortly after the AKP-led state's and its officials' ongoing vocal advocacy for larger families and their recent drive to legislatively constrain (if not abolish) abortion rights, the enhanced governmental (and even societal) policing of kissing on public transportation, of artwork, and of drinking and its endorsements in public places inflamed concerns over a presumed legislative overreach of neoliberal-fuelled Islamism in Turkey's political and public spheres. In the particular case of alcohol, though proposed (and subsequently enacted) regulations restricted the times and places of consumption, commerce, and advertising (and did not entirely outlaw the production, sale or consumption of alcohol), critics charged that this was merely the beginning of a regulatory slide towards a state of universal prohibition. For such detractors, the prior emergence of "alcohol zones" and impositions of increasingly costly excise taxes provided ample evidence of such intentions. Slogans, images and acts of drinking thus were (and continue to be) commonplace in contexts of demonstrations and other confrontations of the state, of the PM, and of the AKP stemming from the Spring–Summer 2013 events at Gezi Park (Figure 1). As one *New York Times* correspondent even noted in the title of his June 2013 article, the Turks in Taksim Square and elsewhere were "Resisting by Raising a Glass" (Arango, 2013).

Conversely, elected leaders of the Turkish state and supporters of its initiatives to curtail public consumption and marketing of alcohol declared adamantly that their motivations had no basis in their religiosity or politics. Rather, they steadfastly proclaimed that their actions were ones of moderate "regulation" – and *not* "prohibition" (e.g. see Milliyet, 2013b; Sabah, 2013). Moreover, they announced that this agenda was consistent with limits established by other "Western" and "modern" states, and they asserted that their motivations were grounded in concerns over population, public health, and the nation's youth; policies construed as guided both

Figure 1. Sold along İstikal Caddesi, near Gezi Park, in June 2013, this t-shirt proclaims "Şerefine Tayyip!" (essentially "Cheers Tayyip!" – referencing quite informally PM Erdoğan; or, literally "To your honor, Tayyip!") with an image of toasting mugs of beer.
Source: Photo by authors, June 2013.

by the constitution and by medical and social science (see HaberTurk, 2013). Furthermore, as a precedent for the declared limits to their policy-making ambitions and associated results, advocates of further regulating alcohol marketing and consumption pointed to Turkey's recent adoption and enforcement of legislation advocating "smoke-free" public and work environments; a programme lauded by the World Health Organization (WHO) at the time of its promulgation for its initiative and since its enactment for its efficacy (Adams, 2012; Chan, 2013b; WHO, 2014). Anticipating (and later responding to) criticisms of further regulating the consumption and marketing of alcohol, proponents of greater restrictions also charged that their political opponents were guilty both of making exaggerated claims of an illusory "prohibition" agenda and of inciting people's fears of political Islam (see HaberTurk, 2013).

In our introduction to this article about Turkey's present day regulationist discourse and legislation involving alcohol, we first provide an overview of the socio-historical and geopolitical contexts of drink and drinking as observable within the nation-state since the years of its establishment. In doing so, we trace how producing, marketing and consuming alcohol were depicted by particular interests in both state and society as fundamental aspects of Turkish national culture and identity. While we connect a drinking with the nation-state through its history, our survey also reveals that there has been a consistent regulatory presence throughout, as well. In particular, we address briefly how (until recently) the wider economies of alcohol functioned largely (and sometimes exclusively) as ventures integral to the state itself.

Second – and based upon our socio-historical grounding that underlay the republic's cultural and legal landscapes of alcohol consumption and marketing, we turn to examine the actual legislative shifts that the AKP-led state enacted, on the one hand, and the discourse of present debates over escalating regulation both from the perspective of the state and key political leaders, on the other hand. Along the way, we also engage with public criticisms and statist responses. Ordering this section somewhat chronologically into several sub-sections, we confront how, since the

AKP's emergence as a majority power in Turkey, the state reversed course and instituted an agenda not only geared towards commercial privatization but also established step-by-step a regulatory regime controlling all aspects of alcohol production, marketing and consumption. Basing its actions on a partial re-reading of the constitution, leaders vowed to "protect" the youth, launching their initial efforts to restrict advertising accordingly. In addition to limiting commercial media, there were profound efforts to limit spatially (i.e. segregate) the places for acceptable commerce in and consumption of alcohol; a programme that *The Guardian*'s European editor Ian Traynor characterized as a conspicuous plan by PM Erdoğan to "to limit and 'ghettoise' the supply and consumption of alcohol" (Traynor, 2005). Regulation via taxation also continued steadily, appearing to many as another means to further restrict the trade in and practice of drinking – especially for the country's lower income majority. By spring 2013, Erdoğan and the AKP-led republic issued a number of statements forewarning of enhanced regulation and thereafter proceeded legislatively to further eliminate alcohol from much of Turkey's public sphere; actions that coalesced with the many other grievances voiced throughout and since the Gezi Park experience. Examining this legislative achievement and public relations debacle, we also analyse criticisms voiced within Turkey and abroad in order to critically interrogate how the continuities and inconsistencies in all of these narratives reveal both the realities of regulationist (and/or prohibitionist) policies, on the one hand, and the ways in which they are connected inextricably to broader tensions and conflicts over ongoing socio-spatial and political trends within Turkey, on the other hand.

Third, we conclude by connecting this debate not only with broader matters positioned along a so-called secularist-Islamist divide; we reveal how many aspects of this controversy are linked more so with matters of governance in terms of the appropriate roles of states in overseeing public health, youth and behaviour; the tensions between democratic and authoritarian tendencies within the Turkish political arena and, the ways in which the alcohol question informs prevailing views as to Turkey's widespread endorsement of privatization and free trade/neoliberalism. In these ways, our engagement illuminates how this debate has been depicted both by its participants and by the media, it establishes a foundation for subsequent analysis of this matter, and it taps into how the geopolitics of alcohol provide perspectives on the (un)acceptability of particular "drugs" in particular contexts and how such inquiries enable more rigorous research into the socio-political, cultural and economic fault lines that potentially divide all societies over matters of citizens' rights and the exercise of states' powers.

1.1. *A nation of rakı – and of regulation*

To situate historically our analysis of alcohol and its regulation in Turkey, it is significant to note that it was present in Anatolia long before the arrival either of the Turkic peoples from Eurasia or of Islam from Arabia. Among Eurasian pastoral societies, fermented mares' milk (or *kumys*) had been produced for centuries, and even with the regional spread of Islam, provisions for the acceptance of non-Muslims and their customs ensured that alcohol (especially wine; religiously significant for both Christians and Jews) maintained a place in Anatolian ecologies, trade and traditions – if only as limited to non-Muslim communities. In the quarters of the Ottoman Empire's larger, cosmopolitan, port cities, alcohol was thus available readily throughout most the empire's duration, particularly in the taverns, markets and households of its many non-Muslim minorities (Evered & Evered, in press; Georgeon, 2002). Moreover, most troops serving in the empire's legendary janissary corps were members of the *Bektaşi tarikat*; a Sufi (i.e. Islamic) order that ritualized drinking (and drunkenness, especially involving wine) to such an extent that *Bektaşism* has ever since been synonymous (to varying degrees, for many) not only with imbibing but with inebriation – and frequently with disorder and defiance, as well (Evered

& Evered, in press). By the nineteenth and early-twentieth centuries, the consumption of alcohol (to include imported varieties) emerged ever more as not just a signifier of minority (or foreign) status but increasingly of socio-economic differentiation, Europeanization and modernization for specific strata within Ottoman society (Georgeon, 2002; Matthee, 2014). Amid shifts in prevailing perceptions of consumption during the late-Ottoman and early-republican eras, arguments advocating the regulation and/or prohibition of alcohol also underwent changes; based previously almost entirely upon overlying moral, religious and legal (e.g. *Sharia*) considerations, regulationist and prohibitionist narratives increasingly invoked arguments steeped in the rationale of public health and science (Evered & Evered, in press; Georgeon, 2002). Indeed, noting trends observable within modernizing states of this period concerning their modes of governing, shifts towards regulatory controls of a wide range of behaviours by states' populations as justified by medicine and science constituted a universal theme (Howell, 2009, pp. 2–11).

Though the late-Ottoman state committed itself – albeit exasperatingly – to a modernist agenda, given this global trend towards states' medicalized regulation of their citizenries, it is perhaps not surprising that some of the more progressive figures within the new republic to emerge amid the empire's dissolution (culminating in 1922), the Allied occupation of Istanbul (1918–1923) and the War of Independence (1919–1923) (especially those from within its medical community and those appointed to the newly formed *Sıhhat ve İçtimai Muavenet Vekaleti*, or Ministry of Health and Social Assistance) also pursued a progressive and "scientific" prohibitionist agenda. As the revolutionary body for what became the Turkish republic's parliament emerged with a 19 March 1920 proclamation by Mustafa Kemal (1881–1938; the surname Atatürk was not added until 1934), within just days following its initial 23 April meeting, the Grand National Assembly of Turkey (the Türkiye Büyük Millet Meclisi, 1982, or TBMM; abbreviated simply in this article as the GNA) took up the debate over mandating universal prohibition to cover production, marketing and consumption of alcohol, with only a few exceptions (as justified for scientific applications and for the purposes of research). Politically, the early GNA consisted of those supporting the Western and modernist agenda of Mustafa Kemal, on the one hand, and an assemblage that constituted a disparate opposition labelled broadly as the *İkinci Grup* (or "Second Group"), on the other hand. What emerged as an unanticipated union of traditional populists (and Islamists) from the *İkinci Grup* (who advocated prohibition on religious and moral grounds) and medical and public health officials (equipped with medical and social science) from the Kemalist modernists became the basis for the embryonic republic's push towards prohibition. Despite a prolonged debate and opposition from interests arguing for an appreciation of the cultural (especially for non-Muslim citizens), political and economic significance of alcohol in Anatolia (i.e. it was one of the state's more reliable generators of revenue) (see Evered & Evered, in press; Karahanoğulları, 2008; Üçüncü, 2012; Zat, 2008), the prohibitionist agenda emerged as law by the narrowest of margins within the GNA in September 1920, going into effect in February 1921 (Men-i Müskirat Kanunu 1920–1921).

Not long after the February 1921 enactment of the ban by the Ankara-based budding republic, there were pressures to revisit the severity of the law. GNA MPs from wine-producing provinces conveyed economic hardships endured by their constituents; others later noted that alternative uses for wine grapes (e.g. raisins or preservatives) ultimately proved fruitless (Evered & Evered, in press). Once the competing empire and sultanate fell (in late 1922) and the GNA's first session concluded (in early 1923), Mustafa Kemal exercised greater influence over those admitted to candidacy for the parliament's second session. In addition to other dramatic steps, like abolishing the Caliphate in March 1923 (see Evered & Evered, 2010), the second session debated and quickly approved a revision to the existing ban in April 1924. Though phrased as a "modification" of the state's prohibition, the new law effectively reversed the state's posture from prohibitionism to regulationism, with provisions for improved inventories, tax collection and controls over establishments serving alcohol. Though other legislative changes followed, since that time, Turkey could be characterized aptly as a decidedly "wet" but regulated polity (to employ vocabulary of the era from the USA; a case followed – and interpreted very differently – by all parties to the Turkish debate), albeit one with a very large number of citizens abstaining entirely (Evered & Evered, in press). Only in particular places and under certain circumstances [e. g. as in Turkey's licensed brothels – another republican context wherein a distinct sort of regulationism was manifest (see Evered & Evered, 2012, 2013a, 2013b)] would we witness outright bans on the presence and/or consumption of alcohol. In the new Kemalist socio-cultural and political climate, drinking emerged as an even more prominent marker of Turkey's status as a Western and modern nation-state (acts that anthropologist Jenny White likened to women's decisions to display their hair; 2010, pp. 221, 225). Indeed, the image of drinking – especially the consumption of *rakı* (an anise-flavoured alcoholic drink of Turkey, similar to *arak*, *ouzo* and *sambuca*) – was regarded by many as a mainstay both of Anatolia and of the Turkish nation (especially for men electing to drink). Though present in Ottoman contexts (Georgeon, 2002; Mrgić, 2011), its particularity to Anatolia and the empire made *rakı* a symbol of consequence for the emergent nation seeking to distinguish itself. Additionally, Mustafa Kemal reportedly consumed prodigious volumes of it and thus forged an enduring bond between *rakı*, the nation and the leader (who, according to most accounts, was diagnosed with and presumably died at age 57 from cirrhosis of the liver; e.g. Blacker, 1970; Howe, 2000, p. 14; Mango, 2000, p. 36). Under these circumstances, *rakı* came to be viewed as the nation's preeminent drink; though other alcoholic (e.g. beer – especially Efes Pilsen) and non-alcoholic beverages (e.g. *ayran* and tea; on the latter, see Hann, 1990) may also be seen competing for such notoriety.

Within the Kemalist republic, *rakı* was not the only alcoholic drink available – or even the only one associated with Anatolia or with the Turkish nation. Indeed, *rakı* has a strong gendered association that often precludes wider consumption (i.e. it is regarded as a "man's drink"); wine, beer and other beverages thus are viewed as more common staples for drinking women and youth. In addition to centuries-long customs of vineyards in Anatolia, by the late-nineteenth and early-twentieth centuries, breweries also opened. When demands for beer (among other drinks) arose in the late-Ottoman era, Bomonti emerged as Anatolia's most prominent brewer. Thereafter, breweries and "beer parks" (or "gardens") appeared not only as private enterprises but as key sites within the eventual republic's state-designed landscape; entities that participated in international competitions and that hosted social and state functions. Given this history, the Turkish republic clearly encouraged its population to undergo a "culturally grounded habituation" to social drinking (i.e. the concept that tastes are learned/taught, as advanced by anthropologist Sidney Mintz, 1986, p. 109 and applied to research on drugs and alcohol by historian Courtwright, 2001, p. 28; also note Figure 2). In this context, citizens adhering to the Kemalist vision of a modern Turkey may have learned to drink as an act of not only recreation but also as an expression of nationalism, secularism and/or their abandonment of traditional moral and societal conformity.

In the late 1920s and the 1930s, as with other commodities and products (notably tobacco and cigarettes), the republic nationalized alcohol production; it was thereafter consolidated – along with tobacco – under the state monopoly TEKEL (associated with Turkish words *tek* and *el*; or, "single" and "hand", and taken in combined form to mean "monopoly"). By the late 1960s, in a context of diminishing regulatory control over private businesses, the Efes brewing company formed in Izmir, and the beer Efes Pilsen emerged thereafter as its leading product. Efes' production and marketing continue today, under the management of the privately held concern Anadolu Efes. Leading with sales of Efes Pilsen beer, Anadolu Efes today records a dominant place as Turkey's largest brewer, posting a 76% market share for 2013. The company oversees its growing European operations through the Holland-based Efes Breweries International N.V., boasts over 40 beer brands and is Europe's fifth (and the world's 10th)

Figure 2. 1930s poster promoting the beer brewed at *Gazi Orman Çiftliği* (later renamed as *Atatürk Orman Çiftliği*). Located in what would become the centre of Ankara, this "forest farm" was established to not only promote modern (and scientific) agriculture but also lifestyles enlightened by secular modernity – conveyed by both subjects, their obvious class and their attire.
Source: Featured on the Istanbul Research Institute's "poster of the month" blog from July 2012; retrieved from http://blog.iae.org.tr/index.php/diger/ayin-afisi-ankara-birasi/?lang=en – last accessed June 25, 2014.

largest brewer (Anadolu Efes, 2014, pp. 3–9). Fielding sports teams, having its own iconic bottle (though not yet as recognizable in the USA as, for example, the bottles of now French-owned but still Swedish-produced Absolut Vodka), and maintaining its national (and expanding its overseas) market share, should we limit our identification of Turkey's national drink to just beers (per our epigraph from Frank Zappa) – or to that percentage of Turkish drinkers born during or since the 1970s, Efes Pilsen might also be viewed as Turkey's premier drink.

Under the state's TEKEL-regulated market, activities associated with alcohol production and sales endured as state operations until the recent decades' neoliberal push towards privatization, as encouraged by the International Monetary Fund (or IMF) and as carried out by the AKP-led state in the 2000s. Additionally, as the republic prepared to privatize alcohol, tobacco and other industries – with many holdings eventually passing to various transnational corporations, it also established TAPDK, the Tütün ve Alkol Piyasası Düzenleme Kurumu (or Tobacco and Alcohol Market Regulatory Authority) (under Law no. 4733; see 4733 Sayılı: Tütün ve Alkol Piyasası Düzenleme Kurumu Teşkilat ve Görevleri Hakkında Kanun, 2002). Symbolically, this was a dramatic governmental shift that entailed a significant move both away from production and marketing (as undertaken by TEKEL), on the one hand, and closer to TAPDK's self-declared "mission and vision" statement's promise to achieve "social regulation" designed "to protect the rights of society and increase its well-being" – introducing considerations of "public health and well-being" to an industry that, according to TAPDK, focused previously too heavily upon just profit, on the other hand (see TAPDK, 2002; authors' translation). Just as regulated production and consumption of alcohol in Turkey were integral to the republic's own processes of national self-definition throughout the twentieth century, so too were its twenty-first century shifts towards economic liberalization (e.g. privatization) and stricter moral regulation (or prohibition, as some charge) fundamental to the rise of the AKP and its policies both to foster a neoliberal reform of the economy and to redefine the (once-)Kemalist nation in ways that proposed to cultivate a more caring – or, perhaps, a more religiously conscious/observant – state.

2. Regulating a republic from *rakı* to *ayran*

In addition to legislation introduced in the spring 2013, frequent pronouncements and several events greatly inflamed ongoing contestations over the place of alcohol and its regulation within Turkey. Most visible internationally – and symbolic of the cultural politics of these changes, we identify PM Erdoğan's afternoon address to the Global Alcohol Policy Symposium, hosted in Istanbul on 26–27 April 2013. Organized by the anti-addiction NGO *Türkiye Yeşilay Cemiyeti* (known in English as the Turkish Green Crescent Society) and co-sponsored by WHO, the event brought together over 1200 attendees from 53 countries (see GAPS). In his speech, which we engage with in greater detail below, Erdoğan resolutely criticized the republic's past alcohol-related policies and its promotion of drinking, the founder of modern Turkey – on account of both Atatürk's position on alcohol and his personal example, and the impacts that he claimed alcohol had upon society. Amid his denunciation – and the remark that most in the media and from opposing perspectives took note of, Erdoğan decried what he viewed as a false tradition of viewing *rakı* (or even beer) as the nation's drink (despite national declarations to the contrary; see Acar, 2013); rather, he avowed that *ayran* (an alcohol-free, yogurt-based beverage – one that is truly ubiquitous in many homes and public eateries) is Turkey's true "national drink" (HaberTurk, 2013). For critics, this proclamation rejecting *rakı* (a drink with profound symbolic connections to the secularists' venerated founder of the republic) and promoting *ayran* were not merely indicative either of a public health agenda (one consistent with the sponsors of the symposium) or of an overbearing paternalism; these comments were signs of a deep and religiously rooted prohibitionist programme, and they were evidence of a presumably broader AKP/Erdoğan agenda to restrict civil liberties while re-writing the republic's history.

In this section, we thus examine both the evolving laws of regulation and the state's and its leadership's discourse on alcohol and regulationist trends. Ultimately, while the laws themselves are incredibly important, public perceptions of legitimacy are vital, as well. We contend that, while the laws unto themselves provide some basis for popular resistance, the paternalistic, moralistic and ultimately dogmatic narrative emanating from the state and from some of its highest elected and appointed officials contributed overwhelmingly to the politicization of the question of further regulating alcohol – both independently and in association with the many issues coalescing around the Gezi Park experience. This rhetorical confrontation escalated into what many Turkish citizens and foreign critics ultimately framed (inappropriately or otherwise) as a conflict over *prohibition*. In these regards, legislative implementation and enforceability are only part of the story; popular views, acceptance/legitimacy and/or instances of contesting such laws are also significant, and thus so is the state's strategy – and its record of gaffes – for engaging with the public regarding initiatives both to regulate drinking and to govern effectively.

2.1. *"Protecting the youth"*

Given the recency of Turkey's 2013 regulations and controversies concerning alcohol and associated restrictions on marketing, most secondary sources available thus far are journalistic articles or opinion-editorial pieces. Due to their news media orientation, many works about the regulationist debate have not examined the 2013 legislation in terms of the regulatory chronology that preceded its passage. As a result, there is a critical absence in many popular accounts regarding how this legislation may be viewed as a culmination of prior acts that enabled its passage; just as it is crucial for any analysis to acknowledge the limits of actual laws enacted, it is also vital to engage the societal and legislative processes preceding their adoption. Examining Turkey's recent history of regulationism, one of the earliest sources cited repeatedly by lawmakers derives directly from the republic's 1982 constitution. In Article 58 of this foundational document, which mandates the "Protection of the Youth", it is declared that,

> The State shall take measures to ensure the education and development of the youth into whose keeping our independence and our Republic are entrusted, in the light of positive science, in line with the principles and reforms of Atatürk, and in opposition to ideas aiming at the destruction of the indivisible integrity of the State with its territory and nation.
>
> The State shall take necessary measures to protect youth from addiction to alcohol and drugs, crime, gambling, and similar vices, and ignorance. (Türkiye Cumhuriyeti Anayasası, 1982; the Turkish government's English-language translation of Article 58 cited from TBMM, pp. 26–27)

Although this two-sentence article initially stipulates emulating of "the principles and reforms of Atatürk", proponents of today's regulationist efforts generally refrain from citing this first provision. Rather, the article's second-line specification for the state to "protect [its] youth" from alcohol and drug addiction, criminality and vices, and "ignorance" is emphasized continually as justification for subsequent regulations restricting the consumption and marketing of alcohol throughout the country. In addition to this constitutional basis, the afore-mentioned establishment of TAPDK by Law no. 4733 in 2002 as a regulatory body devoted to controlling tobacco and alcohol commerce created an additional mechanism for subsequent state interventions involving alcohol and drinking. In particular, TAPDK's mandate to "regulate and prevent any kind of public, social, and medical kinds of harm caused by tobacco and alcohol consumption" (4733 Sayılı: Tütün ve Alkol Piyasası Düzenleme Kurumu Teşkilat ve Görevleri Hakkında Kanun, 2002; authors' translation) enabled it to exercise considerable authority at national, provincial and local scales over the subsequent years.

The combined significance of the selective reading of the 1982 constitution's Article 58 and the mission established for TAPDK was underscored three years later. On 18 January 2005, the state promulgated a regulation curtailing promotions of alcoholic beverages (titled *Alkollü İçki Reklamlarında Uyulacak İlkeler Hakkında Tebliğ*; see Alkollü İçki Reklamlarında Uyulacak İlkeler Hakkında Tebliğ, 2005). Through this directive, the state greatly restricted advertising of alcohol in Turkey. Mandating that commercials and advertisements for alcohol should not be oriented towards minors (i.e. those under 18 years) and that that they should not employ minors (or those appearing to be minors), the rule also banned any commercial claims as to the effectiveness or capacities of alcoholic products to render: curative, stimulating or relaxing benefits; resolution for individuals' personal problems; social distinction (e.g. as a marker of maturity, social status, bravery or courage); improved athleticism; or, satisfaction for one's thirst. Conversely, it was also illegal to imply that non-consumption, lesser levels of consumption or termination of consumption may be equated with weakness, poor decision-making skills, or suffering from mental or social deficiencies. Finally, this act prohibited advertising from employing any endorsements by individuals who are noteworthy or distinguished in their field, who are in positions of public trust, who work with welfare organizations or on behalf of children, or who have a public persona – especially any individuals, characters or groups who are (or have potential to be – either directly or indirectly) role models for minors (Alkollü İçki Reklamlarında Uyulacak İlkeler Hakkında Tebliğ, 2005). For many casual observers who otherwise paid no attention to the content of alcohol advertisements, this TAPDK regulation and subsequent restrictions and interpretations eventually compelled the Efes-sponsored basketball team to change its very name (and its especially visible logo; see Figure 3) from "Efes Pilsen Spor Kulübü" *to* "Anadolu Efes Spor Kulübü" on 7 January 2011 (as articulated by the organization in its own online history of the team and its logo; see Anadolu Efes, n.d.). Caring for their long-time fans, however, the club continues to offer in their online "Fan Store" a t-shirt bearing the pre-TAPDK-imposed name and logo; advertized as *Nostalji Forma* (Figure 4).

2.2. *Regulation via segregation and taxation*

Beyond the January 2005 regulatory restrictions on advertising (Alkollü İçki Reklamlarında Uyulacak İlkeler Hakkında Tebliğ, 2005), in August of that year, the state enacted a new 48-article regulation that applied broadly to the opening of businesses and to the acquisition of permits (titled *İşyeri Açma ve Çalışma Ruhsatlarına İlişkin Yönetmelik*, it appeared in İşyeri Açma ve Çalışma Ruhsatlarına İlişkin Yönetmelik, 2005). Though mandating sundry matters in its numerous provisions, Articles 29 and 30 of this regulation generated considerable debate as they dealt with those businesses serving alcohol. Promoting the spatial definition of special "alcohol zones" – to be determined with the guidance of local governing authorities and in coordination with municipal and/or provincial bodies, the article stipulated that establishments serving alcohol were prohibited from operating outside of a designated "alcohol zone". In the regulation's subsequent Article 30, such zones were defined further by distinguishing the types of buildings, populations and activities that were prohibited from consideration for enclosure. Excluded sites and activities included: state buildings, prisons and other correctional facilities; sites of religious institutions and places of prayer; art institutions; mining and construction sites; places associated with the production, storage, or commerce of explosive or other dangerous materials; service stations (i.e. selling gas or fuel); 200 meters of highways or roads, except the establishments allowing for overnight accommodations; bus stations; and, anywhere within 100 meters of public and private school buildings, elementary and middle-school dormitories, and kindergartens (İşyeri Açma ve Çalışma Ruhsatlarına İlişkin Yönetmelik, 2005). Although Article 29 of the August 2005 regulation designated simply those parties with authority to determine an "alcohol zone" (İşyeri Açma ve Çalışma Ruhsatlarına İlişkin Yönetmelik, 2005), within a short period of time, Minister of Interior Abdülkadir Aksu sent an official circular to all provincial governors of Turkey. Within this circular, Minister Aksu requested that all governors initiate

Figure 3. In imparting its history as an athletic organization, the Efes-/Anadolu-sponsored basketball team *Anadolu Efes Spor Kulübü* relates the details of not only its 2011 name change but also the most dramatic change in the history of the team's logo – noting that these modifications were imposed by TAPDK (referencing the shift to the last – and latest – of the above images).
Source: Anadolu Efes (n.d.)

Figure 4. Anadolu Efes Spor Kulübü's *Nostalji Forma* t-shirt; for those commemorating the team's (and perhaps Turkey's) pre-TAPDK era.
Source: The Anadolu Efes S.K. "Fan Store" website as of June 25, 2014; retrieved from https://www.anadoluefessporkulubu.org/magaza/detay/nostaljik-forma-beyaz.

implementation of the portions of the August 2005 regulation relevant to sites of public recreation and entertainment venues, and he highlighted sections from the initial regulation that focused on the imperative for area security forces to grant authorization in order to establish/operate businesses involved with alcohol (implying that they have means and authority to access such sites to enforce state regulations dealing with public safety and security) and the requirement of such businesses to obtain permits for lawful operation (TC İçişleri Bakanlığı Basın ve Halkla İlişkiler Müşavirliği Basın Açıklaması, 2005).

Once officials commenced defining "alcohol zones" (and thus delineating consequent spaces excluding any establishments with alcohol), references to these sites as so-called *kırmızı sokaklar* or *kırmızı bölgeler* ("red streets" or "red zones") began to enter commonly into vernacular Turkish to refer to these places of regulated consumption. The popularization of such colloquialisms – which conveyed simultaneously officials' views of disdain and other citizens' notions of defiance and/or resistance – were aided by advocates of the regulations, too. This was particularly noteworthy in November 2005 when the enthusiastic AKP vice-mayor of Osmangazi (a town in Bursa province) Abdullah Karadağ made a statement that attracted national media attention. Proclaiming that the municipality would gather all alcohol-serving businesses and site them in one location, he continued, "as in Europe, we plan to create 'red streets' where only alcohol-serving establishments exist" (Milliyet, 2005a; authors' translation). In the eyes of many, it seemed apparent that the "red streets" of Turkey were framed by AKP officials as the country's equivalent to the "red-light districts" of some European cities. Reacting against such associations – and conveying what he perceived to be the AKP politicians' true motives, opposition politician Kemal Anadol asserted, "What they want is Tehran not Luxembourg" (Traynor, 2005).

Likewise, other officials not only remarked upon these areas of regulated access to alcohol in terms conveying perceptions of derision (and even depravity); they also associated strongly – and sought to situate – such "alcohol zones" alongside or within spaces of urban and industrial disamenity. In Denizli, another city wherein officials embraced the new regulations, Nihat Zeybekci sought to relocate the city's alcohol-serving establishments to an outside district where tanneries were located and operated. When criticized, the AKP mayor responded by questioning if drinking alcohol was so much better than cigarette smoking; if not, how could it be acceptable to ban smoking in public places, on the one hand, and to not do the same with alcohol, on the other hand – especially with objections from the media? Though he referenced a nation-wide uproar in the media, he continued by affirming that this matter was a non-issue within Denizli; adding, "We are determined … [this] is not an alcohol ban. We are [simply] implementing a new regulation" (Milliyet, 2005b; authors' translation).

Following the publication of the initial regulation and the subsequent dissemination of Minister Aksu's circular that emphasized implementation and enforcement of particular sections of the regulation, there appeared to be a wave of businesses that were compelled to shut down. This seeming campaign of forced closures resulted in accusations that overzealous and conservative governors and municipal officials were abusing their positions of authority in their consequent enforcements of this regulation. In essence, such allegations charged that these officials utilized this law to compel businesses involved with alcohol to relocate to places outside of their cities and their jurisdictions. Within two years, the Ankara Bar Association filed a suit against the Ministry of Interior regarding this circular. Though the courts determined that such provisions (i.e. determined to be absent from the actual regulation) violated the law itself and contributed to unauthorized instances of segregation, administrative processes associated with these regulations and their implementation continue in many localities throughout the country and are associated strongly with a trend for many places serving alcohol to ultimately close down (Armutçu, 2012). Moreover – and in line with these policies, state-owned restaurants, cafes, guesthouses, and other venues for teachers, police and other state workers for the secular state also stopped serving alcohol.

Another strategy to diminish the sales and/or consumption of alcohol in Turkey has been the imposition of dramatically increasing excise taxes on alcohol purchases. These special consumption taxes that target immediately the consumer at the point of sale have been a matter of contention well before the events of spring and summer 2013 (concerns over which even appeared in the English-language media disseminated from Turkish sources since the mid- to late-2000s; e.g. see Hürriyet Daily News, 2010). Writing in October 2012, columnist Şükrü Kızılot observed that taxes on alcohol increased 114% over the preceding three years; calculating (at the time) since the AKP were elected to majority rule in Turkey, the tax increased 655% (Kızılot, 2012). Noting the same percentage increase (i.e. 655%) since the beginning of the AKP's rule (a figure that apparently did not increase in the intervening months), Koray Çalışkan (an Associate Professor of Political Science at Boğaziçi University) noted in his weekly column for the newspaper *Radikal* that a bottle of *rakı* that cost 13 US dollars in 2004 would cost 30 US dollars by 2013 (Çalışkan, 2013).

2.3. *Spring 2013, and since: regulatory progress, political regress*

Recalling PM Erdoğan's remarks from the April 2013 Global Alcohol Policy Symposium in Istanbul, we are able to witness the beginning of when the alcohol issue returned with prominence to public discourse in the divisive way that facilitated its coalescence in coming months with the array of other grievances voiced during the Gezi Park experience. Beyond simply hosting this venue, however, this forum was also one wherein Turkey's leadership received unambiguous cues from the international community that its approach with tobacco was a global success story – and that continued regulationism with alcohol was *highly* desirable (Chan, 2013a). Delivering the opening remarks in a presentation titled "Support for strong alcohol policies", Dr Margaret Chan, Director-General of the WHO, declared in the later third of her address,

> In short, national alcohol policies are needed, desired, entirely feasible, and highly effective.
>
> ... The most important requirement for success, the item that heads that list of ten recommended target areas, is leadership, awareness, and commitment. Turkey has this leadership at the highest political level.
>
> Prime Minister Erdogan [*sic.*] is leading the initiative to reduce the harmful use of alcohol within Turkey. He is also the driving force behind this symposium.
>
> The leadership he has shown in forging tough policies for tobacco control and road safety goes beyond safeguarding the health of the Turkish people. It is a model for other countries to follow, and it is a source of great encouragement. (2013a)

Despite this explicit endorsement by the WHO's leading executive for further alcohol regulation and for Erdoğan's leadership with public health, headlines following the symposium focused solely upon the PM's mis-steps (especially his remarks on *rakı*, beer and *ayran*). In addition to his most publicized comments regarding Turkey's "national drink", founder and history of promoting alcohol, he spoke of alcohol as a cause of traffic deaths and violent crime and of his view that alcohol-related vehicular homicides merited increased penalties. Referencing draft legislation that was under preparation, he pledged further advertising restrictions, place-based restrictions (e.g. schools), warning labels and additional excise taxes on alcohol purchases, among other measures. Though he acknowledged that he and his supporters would be accused of "Islamization", he declared that he was committed to this public health agenda (see full video of his remarks at: HaberTurk, 2013).

Noting inconsistencies between Erdoğan's claims and his policy declarations, some criticized the PM for conveying that Turkey had a "real" alcohol problem (one that might be statistically or otherwise appreciable, for example, as compared with other Western states). Pursuing this line of inquiry, one editorial that appeared in *Cumhuriyet* concluded that this was not a valid state concern and cited Turkey's annual rate of consumption at just 1.4 litres per person; a figure that would rank the country 143 out of 193 (Sirmen, 2013). Also demonstrating an alternative narrative in late April 2013 – in so far as declarations of Turkey's "national drink" were concerned, representatives from GİSDER (the *Türkiye Geleneksel Alkollü İçki Üreticileri Derneği*; Turkey's association of traditional alcoholic beverage producers) were applying to the European Union Commission for *rakı*'s designation as Turkey's "national drink". Pledging to introduce Turkish *rakı* to parts of Europe where it was not yet consumed (Cumhuriyet, 2013), GİSDER's leader Egemen Demirtaş thus was pursuing internationally the claim that Turkey's *rakı* resulted from his country's unique agricultural characteristics and distillation processes. According to Turkish law, this claim had a precedent; the *Türk Patent Enstitüsü* (the Turkish Patent Institute) ruled in 2009 that *rakı* was Turkey's "national drink" – at least to the extent of asserting its both unique and national derivation (Acar, 2013).

In addition to criticisms, in the days and weeks that followed the symposium, there were also many who voiced support for Erdoğan and his efforts – both from within and beyond the state. In a televised appearance on the station *Radyo Televizyon Üst Kurulu'nun* in early May, Vice-PM Bülent Arınç noted that both cigarettes and alcohol pose dangers, and he questioned the quality of values conveyed in entertainment media and in advertising that portray depictions of so-called hospitality that involves alcohol. Though he speculated that the state may or may not pursue further regulations, he declared his support for any measures and added, "I like our youth and families" (Milliyet, 2013a). Later in May, Minister of Health Mehmet Müezzinoğlu also echoed his support, and he provided his own figures and the observation that, though Turkey did not seem to be drinking more, it did appear that the percentage of alcohol consumers rose from 10.9% in 2008 to 12.6% in 2010, and again to 14.3% in 2011; figures that seem to validate concerns over whether or not Turkey had a "real" alcohol problem (i.e. if the 1.5 litre per capita is constant for the nation's population, one might construe that these increasing percentages convey that more people are drinking – but more are drinking less (i.e. they are drinking with more restraint and responsibility)). Aside from the numbers, Müezzinoğlu stated that per capita consumption in some countries was as high as 15 litres, and that the state thus needed healthy regulations, and he criticized how such regulations were being misinterpreted in the media as reflective of a "prohibitionist mentality" that does not exist in Turkey (Milliyet, 2013b).

Maintaining his position throughout May, Erdoğan continued to declare in public venues that his state "is not banning alcohol" and instead sought to convey the draft legislation's merits; focusing on spatial segregation from mosques and schools, further limits to advertising and conveying how enhanced regulation coincides with his interpretation of the mandate inherent to Article 58 of the 1982 constitution. Despite what may have been his best efforts, however, Erdoğan created additional public relations problems for himself, the AKP, and his proposition to further regulate alcohol. He declared, *Kafası kıyak nesil istemiyoruz* (or, "we don't want a drunken generation"; see Başbakan Erdoğan, 2013; also note Sabah, 2013). Though many foreign news organizations interpreted this statement more politely (e.g. many utilized the English term "tipsy"; we utilized the term "drunken", though the vernacular really implies something more akin to a chronic state of being "wasted"), his words were demonstrative of the sometimes coarse language that the PM has been known to invoke when defensive; reaction in the Turkish media (and in ensuing protests) was colourful and profuse. Though Erdoğan would be known internationally more so for later referring in early June to the demonstrators at Gezi Park as traitors and as *çapulcu* (translated loosely oftentimes as "looters", or even as "brigands") – largely because of the ways in which activists immediately seized upon and laid claim to the latter term, appropriated it thoroughly, and began to use it self-referentially (with absolutely no lack of pride), his remarks about Turkey's "drunken generation" continue to resonate within the country, as well, and they reflect ways in which the ostensibly regulationist agenda simultaneously acquired an intractably divisive presence and became integrally connected to the political upheavals that transpired thereafter.

At the same time – during this month following PM Erdoğan's April 2013 speech at the Global Alcohol Policy Symposium, the GNA debated and eventually approved further regulations (first proposed on 10 May, and then circulated through various committees) on 23 May as contained in Law no. 6487. In the sometimes heated exchanges that transpired from one day into the following morning, an array of criticisms were levelled on the basis of procedural irregularities, content and presumed intent. Procedurally, this initiative was presented to the GNA as part of a collection of regulations that also included amendments to assorted laws; it was not presented as a distinct law unto itself. In this regard, it was not unlike Articles 29 and 30 of the broader regulations that were decreed in August 2005 to govern the opening of businesses and to the acquisition of permits (i.e. the sections that resulted in the creation of segregated "red streets"; İşyeri Açma ve Çalışma Ruhsatlarına İlişkin Yönetmelik, 2005). Indeed, as some critical observers speculate, it is an ongoing pattern to regulate alcohol in Turkey without specific pieces of universal legislation that bear corresponding titles; presuming an intent to create a complex network of laws (ones that lack individually the symbolic weight of, for example, the Eighteenth Amendment to the Constitution in American history) and/or to avoid attracting undo public scrutiny – at least until after the acts are ratified and applied. Additionally, other GNA representatives commented in session that the proposal was actually more a finalized "draft law" rather than merely a motion for review (see TBMM Tutanak Dergisi, Dönem 24, Cilt 51, 2013).

In GNA deliberations that pertained more to the content of (and presumed intentions underlying) the proposed legislation, Erhan Akçay of the *Milliyetçi Hareket Partisi* (Turkey's MHP or "Nationalist Action Party") stated that, though he wholeheartedly supports Article 58 of the country's 1982 constitution, the proposed legislation focused mostly on matters of proscription and penalties – especially with an almost exclusive focus on advertising, promotion and public visibility. In short, he decried the measure's lack of resolve to truthfully assist the nation's youth through fostering education, awareness, individual rights and any sense of responsible freedoms. Such an approach by the AKP, he continued, represented a failure to understand the real causes behind consumption of alcohol by the nation's youth; pointing to the roles played by friends, family and social and psychological problems. Further, he argued that an advertising focus was ill-informed and avoided dealing meaningfully with educational and societal challenges (TBMM Tutanak Dergisi, Dönem 24, Cilt 51, 2013, pp. 989–990). Speaking on behalf of the *Cumhuriyet Halk Partisi* (Republican People's Party), Mehmet Akif Hamzaçebi questioned directly the intentions behind the proposal. Arguing that the state's real effort should focus on the problem of addiction, he charged that the AKP-sponsored initiative instead reveals an ideological bias against alcohol itself; continuing, he declared,

> This is wrong. No country that cares about its people promotes alcohol consumption but they also do not prevent an individual's choice to consume alcohol. The duty of the state is to inform people and society about the harm that alcohol poses to individual health. Going beyond that and envisioning itself as an individual, the state cannot interfere in the freedoms [of others] … or ban alcohol production and consumption. … [Though] Islam regards alcohol to be *haram* (a sin), a state cannot impose a legal regulation based [simply] on the notion of sin. (TBMM Tutanak Dergisi, Dönem 24, Cilt 51, 2013, p. 996; authors' translation)

From this critique of the approach and nature of the law, MP Hamzaçebi launched into a more severe condemnation of the AKP and how he interpreted their wider agenda, as discernible through the move to regulate alcohol. Accusing the AKP of seeking to redesign Turkish society – despite a hypocritical condemnation of Kemalist social engineering, he charged that they now move as "boorishly as an elephant in a glass shop" as they re-engineer society according to "Sunni conservatism". Claiming that a transparent and universal ban on alcohol would be too bold for the AKP, he charged that they began a campaign of imposing laws and regulations to restrict alcohol – even on Turkish airlines – in order to frame alcohol consumption as a shameful act that people must only do in secret and out of public scrutiny. In the AKP's depictions of alcohol consumers as fallen souls given to bad habits, he continued, they target them as outcasts in their own society, on the one hand, while continuing to facilitate consumption in particular places (especially in luxury hotels, restaurants and touristic establishments) and collecting the increasingly extraordinary taxes that they levy – effectively creating and privileging an upper-class and foreign minority of consumers, on the other hand. Accusing AKP MPs of imposing their own conservatism on the lifestyles of others and of ignoring the social and cultural contexts of food and drink, he declared, had nothing to do with a struggle to protect the youth or promote public health; adding that, "if the goal was [really] to protect [the] health [of our youth], there would be a priority to instead ban soda products containing artificial flavors that are far more harmful" (TBMM Tutanak Dergisi, Dönem 24, Cilt 51, 2013, pp. 996–1000; authors' translation). Despite the prolonged debate, the measures were adopted as Law no. 6487.

Upon Law no. 6487's 11 June publication, the law imposed a dramatic and stark distinction between alcohol as sold and consumed within Turkey, as opposed to sales and consumption that might occur beyond the republic's borders. It required that beverages produced within the country – and those permitted for importation – must include a warning label written in Turkish that communicates the harms of alcohol; sales of products lacking this warning label were prohibited. According to the law, the size and content of this warning message were to be determined by both the Ministry of Health and TAPDK. Alcohol produced for export, however, was exempted from carrying the required warning label. The law also banned most remaining means for advertising or otherwise promoting alcoholic beverages within the physical (and virtual) territories of the Turkish republic. Under its provisions, only events that promoted the purchase of alcohol for scientific research or for international markets were allowed to continue. All other advertising campaigns and associated special events promoting alcohol were banned, including: (a) any sponsorship of events and associated uses of logos, emblems or distinguishing images; (b) any free distribution of alcoholic beverages or promotional gifts by companies producing or marketing alcohol and, (c) the use of signs, advertising, or other publicly disseminated information by those establishments permitted to serve alcoholic beverages. Further, television shows, movies and music videos were prohibited from featuring scenes involving alcoholic beverages in ways that might make them tempting or induce consumption. Finally, any sales or serving of alcohol to minors was prohibited, as were any sales within: educational institutions; student dormitories; places providing health services; stadiums or other sports venues; coffeehouses, bakeries, salons for playing bridge (i.e. cards); stores and restaurants that also function as gas stations; roadside or highway rest locations – where consumption was also prohibited; and, retail markets or stores between the hours of 10:00 pm and 6:00 am (6487 Bazı Kanunlar ile 375 Sayılı Kanun Hükmünde Kararnamede Değişiklik Yapılması Hakkında Kanun, 2013).

In reactions to the debate and eventual legislation, one dimension that Turkish commentators noted (that many foreign correspondents did not comment on) entailed the ways in which these regulations were further dividing Turkish society, on the one hand, and extending particular privileges to foreign tourists, on the other hand. Confident that the flexibility in applying some of these regulations as they pertained to particular establishments that serve alcohol would result in exemptions for those businesses catering to Turkey's upper-class and foreign drinkers, critics discerned obvious class and citizen/non-citizen dimensions. For many working-class Turkish citizens, the economic (and increasingly the social) costs of drinking would make it an activity that would be legally inaccessible. Viewing this in more than nationalistic terms that distinguished between resident and touristic establishments, "a tourist can have it but you cannot" sensibility reflected not only a differentiation between foreigners and nationals; it also reflected the state's claim to decision-making freedoms previously held by the citizens themselves (Alçı, 2013). In other ways, the perspectives of critics within Turkey were also very consistent with those from abroad; concerns focused on matters of moral authority and political Islam, intrusions into a cosmopolitan public sphere, and a less-than-democratic authoritarianism – sentiments that seemed well-suited for the symbols of alienation that Erdoğan was providing them with (e.g. his *rakı*-ayran distinction, his references to youth who drink – and to Atatürk – as drunkards, his belittling of critics and protestors as traitors or *çapulcu*, and his regulationist and political efforts to restrict not only advertising but also social media).

Leading up to and during the Gezi Park experience of spring and summer 2013, international news organizations focused on Turkey and sought to cover not only the ensuing sensational images of protest and of police responses. Many journalists and foreign media outlets also initiated their own analyses of what was transpiring beyond the imagery of a defiled green space, on the one hand, and the proclamations issued by PM Erdoğan and the state as to protesters' "traitorous" motives, on the other hand. While some covered Erdoğan's polarizing statements at the Global Alcohol Policy Symposium (e.g. Burch, 2013), most sources did not begin to engage with the question of alcohol in Turkey until after the protests commenced. Once lauded as a reformer and agent for democracy, many sources were less sanguine about Erdoğan's achievements since the 2007 end of his first term – and his future as a respected leader. "[N]o longer the gifted politician who turned Turkey upside down 10 years ago", one article in

Spiegel Online observed that the PM "who broke up the fossilized Turkish state, now rules with the methods of those who once persecuted him" (Steinvorth & Zand, 2013). Reading beyond just the questions of alcohol and Gezi Park, the larger questions perceived by many foreign correspondents turn to not only an enduring secularist-Islamist divide but also towards what some view as a more recent pattern of awkward authoritarian conduct; as noted in *The Guardian*, "What infuriated protestors is what they perceive as Erdoğan's clunking attempts to impose values on everyone else" (Harding, 2013).

3. Summary and conclusions

Writing in mid-May 2013 – prior to the ratification and implementation of Law no. 6487, columnist Mehveş Evin warned her readers of the state's looming alcohol regulations and what she viewed as a power grab by AKP officials. Focusing on Manisa MP Recai Berber's endorsement of banning alcohol advertising to the extent that brands of particular drinks would disappear from public view, she identified one vital aspect of this push often obscured by concentrating solely on alcohol itself; in adopting and applying this law, the national government was removing authorities once vested in municipalities and conferring them to the provincial governors and the republic. As Evin observed, all alcohol-related policing and regulatory authority would now be in the hands of the central government (2013). In other words, should her misgivings about Erdoğan's and his supporters' motives be valid, the public health initiative to further regulate alcohol would not only further religious objectives; it would also facilitate a greater shift towards exclusive AKP control over political decision-making throughout the republic.

Though the actual reach of the legislation that was adopted did mandate a heightened regime of regulation, it is a set of controls that does not come close to an absolute prohibition of alcohol production, marketing or consumption. Nonetheless, in the realms of public perception – both among citizens within Turkey who are critical of the state, of PM Erdoğan, and of the AKP – and among many foreign observers, both interpretations of and representations of this regulatory advance have conveyed unambiguously an ongoing progression towards a prohibitionist outcome. To be sure, a good measure of these concerns derive from general anxieties about the ambitions and manifestations of tendencies towards escalations of political Islam and/or authoritarianism within the republic (the veracity or legitimacy of which we do not engage with directly in the limited scope of this study). Without a doubt, however, such concerns have also been fuelled by state and AKP leaders at both local levels (e.g. as with past attempts to impose restrictions/prohibitions unilaterally) and at national levels (e.g. as when leaders like Erdoğan have promoted their policies with narratives that clearly infringe upon other citizens' notions of what it means to be Turkish, national, secular and free). Indeed, in recalling the Turkish state's now successful efforts to achieve similar regulationist outcomes for tobacco, the political and public relations mis-steps exhibited with initiatives to further regulate alcohol could not stand in starker contrast.

Although the AKP-led state under Erdoğan accomplished its legislative victory by eliminating alcohol-related advertising from within Turkey, this achievement seems particularly hollow when one walks through the still tourist-friendly Taksim and Beyoğlu neighbourhoods adjacent to Gezi Park – where alcohol still flows freely, albeit no longer under establishment signs carrying endorsements for *rakı*, beer or other intoxicants. Likewise, in considering the proclaimed public health goals of the initiative in comparison with contemporary public health trends, the regulationist achievements in Turkey render a less-than-optimistic glimpse of any anticipated outcomes. While geographers Jayne, Valentine and Holloway note from their review of contemporary policy trends in the West and scholarship that statist approaches have been steadily shifting away from merely seeking to push alcohol out of the public sphere to instead engaging more meaningfully with underlying causes of drinking (and of addiction) (2011, pp. 44–46), this trend is not at all evident in the Turkish record – a case imposing and/or reifying society's class-based and spatial divides. Indeed, where is such a push for such progressive interventions in the lives of Turkey's drinking citizens? Rather, as vociferously confronted by MHP MP Akçay amid the May 2013 GNA debates (TBMM Tutanak Dergisi, Dönem 24, Cilt 51, 2013, pp. 989–990), the 2013 – and preceding – regulations in Turkey have achieved very little other than socially marginalizing and spatially segregating alcohol consumption and trade. While this study demonstrates the imperative for states and leaders to devote themselves as much to cultivating a culture for consenting to regulation as they do to drafting and declaring regulatory laws, it also reveals profound limitations when interventions in the public sphere and in individual freedoms are socio-spatially divisive and substitute for progressive social policies.

Acknowledgements

The authors would like to thank Stewart Williams and Barney Warf for their invitation to include our research on this topic in their special issue of *Space and Polity*. We would also like to thank editor Ronan Paddison and the anonymous reviewers who read and critiqued our submission.

Disclosure statement

No potential conflict of interest was reported by the authors.

Funding

Support for the research that enabled this manuscript came from Michigan State University's Asian Studies Program and Muslim Studies Program.

References

4733 Sayılı: Tütün ve Alkol Piyasası Düzenleme Kurumu Teşkilat ve Görevleri Hakkında Kanun. (2002, January 9). *Resmî Gazete*, no. 24635.

6487 Bazı Kanunlar ile 375 Sayılı Kanun Hükmünde Kararnamede Değişiklik Yapılması Hakkında Kanun. (2013, June 11). *Resmî Gazete*, no. 28674.

Acar, Ö. (2013, April 30). İçki ve içecek! *Cumhuriyet*. Retrieved June 25, 2014, from http://www.cumhuriyet.com.tr/koseyazisi/418930/icki_ve_icecek_.html

Adams, P. (2012). Turkey's transformation. *Bulletin of the World Health Organization*, *90*(6), 408–409.

Alçı, N. (2013, May 26). Nafile çaba. *Milliyet*. Retrieved June 25, 2014, from http://www.milliyet.com.tr/nafile-caba/gundem/ydetay/1714118/default.htm

Alkollü İçki Reklamlarında Uyulacak İlkeler Hakkında Tebliğ. (2005, January 18). *Resmî Gazete*, no. 25704.

Anadolu Efes, S. K. (2014). *Anadolu Efes annual report 2013*. Retrieved June 25, 2014, from http://www.anadoluefes.com/dosya/faaliyetraporu_in/20140417-ANADOLUEFES_FR13ENG____.pdf

Anadolu Efes, S. K. n.d. *Tarihçe* [History]. Retrieved June 12, 2015, from https://www.anadoluefessporkulubu.org/kulup/tarihce

Arango, T. (2013, June 9). Resisting by raising a glass. *The New York Times*. Retrieved June 25, 2014, from http://www.nytimes.com/2013/06/10/world/europe/pushing-back-and-raising-a-glass-in-turkey.html

Armutçu, O. (2012, October 16). Alkol yasağı lokal yayılıyor. *Hürriyet*. Retrieved June 25, 2014, from http://www.hurriyet.com.tr/gundem/21700617.asp

Başbakan'dan 'alkol' çıkışı! "Bizim milli içkimiz ayrandır". (2013, April 26). *HaberTurk*. Article (with linked video of PM Erdoğan's symposium address). Retrieved June 25, 2014, from http://www.haberturk.com/gundem/haber/839295-basbakandan-alkol-cikisi

Başbakan Erdoğan. (2013, May 24). Kafası kıyak nesil istemiyoruz. *Türkiye Gazetesi*. Retrieved June 25, 2014, from http://www.turkiyegazetesi.com.tr/politika/41513.aspx.

Blacker, H. (1970). Mustafa Kemal – Ataturk (1881–1938). *Alcohol and Alcoholism*, *5*(2), 64–68.

Burch, J. (2013, April 27). Turkey's leader hits a nerve over country's "national drink." *Reuters*. Retrieved June 25, 2014, from http://in.reuters.com/article/2013/04/27/turkey-alcohol-idINDEE93Q02C20130427

Çalışkan, K. (2013, May 24). Rakı vergisine yüzde 655 zam. *Radikal*. Retrieved June 25, 2014, from http://www.radikal.com.tr/yazarlar/koray_caliskan/raki_vergisine_yuzde_655_zam-1134772

Chan, M. (2013a, April 26). *Support for strong alcohol policies*. Opening address at the Global Alcohol Policy Symposium, Istanbul, Turkey. Retrieved June 25, 2014, from http://www.who.int/dg/speeches/2013/global_alcohol_policy_symposium_20130426/en/

Chan, M. (2013b, May 31). *Speech: Success of tobacco control in Turkey and release of the Global Adult Tobacco Survey 2013*. Remarks on World No Tobacco Day, Istanbul, Turkey. Retrieved June 25, 2014, from http://www.euro.who.int/en/health-topics/disease-prevention/tobacco/world-no-tobacco-day/2013-ban-tobacco-advertising,-promotion-and-sponsorship/speech-success-of-tobacco-control-in-turkey-and-release-of-the-global-adult-tobacco-survey-2013

Courtwright, D. T. (2001). *Forces of habit: Drugs and the making of the modern world*. Cambridge: Harvard University Press.

Cumhuriyet. (2013, April 28). Rakı için "Milli" başvurusu. *Cumhuriyet*. Retrieved from June 25, 2014, http://www.cumhuriyet.com.tr/haber/diger/418680/Raki_icin__Milli__basvurusu.html

Evered, E. Ö., & Evered, K. T. (2010). Decolonization through secularization: A geopolitical reframing of Turkey's 1924 abolition of the Caliphate. *The Arab World Geographer*, *13*(1), 1–19.

Evered, E. Ö., & Evered, K. T. (2013a). Sex and the capital city: The political framing of syphilis and prostitution in early republican Ankara. *Journal of the History of Medicine and Allied Sciences*, *68*(2), 266–299. doi:10.1093/jhmas/jrr054

Evered, E. Ö., & Evered, K. T. (2013b). "Protecting the national body": Regulating the practice and the place of prostitution in early republican Turkey. *Gender, Place, and Culture: A Journal of Feminist Geography*, *20*(7), 839–857.

Evered, E. Ö., & Evered, K. T. (in press). A geopolitics of drinking: Debating the place of alcohol in early republican Turkey. *Political Geography*.

Evered, K. T., & Evered, E. Ö. (2012). Syphilis and prostitution in the socio-medical geographies of Turkey's early republican provinces. *Health and Place*, *18*(3), 528–535. doi:10.1016/j.healthplace.2012.02.001

Evin, M. (2013, May 13). Alkole bitmeyen ayar. *Milliyet*. Retrieved June 25, 2014, from http://www.milliyet.com.tr/alkole-bitmeyen-ayar/gundem/ydetay/1707565/default.htm

Georgeon, F. (2002). Ottomans and drinkers: The consumption of alcohol in Istanbul in the nineteenth century. In E. Rogan (Ed.), *Outside in: On the margins of the modern Middle East* (pp. 7–30). London: I.B. Tauris.

Global Alcohol Policy Symposium. (2013, April 26–27). *Global alcohol policy symposium Istanbul* (event's English-language website). Retrieved from June 25, 2014, http://www.gaps-istanbul.com/eng/news.aspx

Hann, C. M. (1990). *Tea and the domestication of the Turkish state*. Huntingdon: Eothen Press.

Harding, L. (2013, June 8). Turkey's protesters proclaim themselves the true heirs of their nation's founding father. *The Guardian*. Retrieved June 25, 2014, from http://www.theguardian.com/world/2013/jun/08/turkey-protesters-proclaim-heirs-ataturk

Howe, M. (2000). *Turkey today: A nation divided over Islam's revival*. Boulder, CO: Westview Press.

Howell, P. (2009). *Geographies of regulation: Policing prostitution in nineteenth-century Britain and the empire*. Cambridge: Cambridge University Press.

Hürriyet Daily News. (2010, October 29). Turkish consumers dazed by another alcohol tax increase. *Hürriyet Daily News*. Retrieved June 25, 2014, from http://www.hurriyetdailynews.com/default.aspx?pageid=438&n=turkish-consumers-dizzy-of-excessive-alcohol-tax-2010–10–29

İşyeri Açma ve Çalışma Ruhsatlarına İlişkin Yönetmelik. (2005, August 10). *Resmî Gazete*, no. 25902.

Jayne, M., Valentine, G., & Holloway, S. L. (2011). *Alcohol, drinking, drunkenness: (Dis)Orderly spaces*. Aldershot: Ashgate.

Karahanoğulları, O. (2008). *Birinci Meclis'in içki yasağı: Men-i Müskirat Kanunu*. Ankara: Phoenix Yayınevi.

Kızılot, Ş. (2012, October 8). Alkollü içki ÖTV'sinde dünya rekoru Türkiye'de. *Hürriyet*. Retrieved June 25, 2014, from http://www.hurriyet.com.tr/yazarlar/21645925.asp

Mango, A. (2000). *Atatürk: The biography of the founder of modern Turkey*. Woodstock: Overlook Press.

Matthee, R. (2014). Alcohol in the Islamic Middle East: Ambivalence and ambiguity. *Past and Present*, *222* (suppl. 9), 100–125.

Men-i Müskirat Kanunu (1920, September 14–1921, February 28). *Resmî Gazete*, no. 4.

Milliyet. (2005a, November 23). Osmangazi'ye "kırmızı sokak". *Milliyet*. Retrieved June 25, 2014, from http://www.milliyet.com.tr/2005/11/23/guncel/axgun02.html

Milliyet. (2005b, December 11). Üsküdar'da iç içebilirsen! *Milliyet*. Retrieved June 25, 2014, from http://www.milliyet.com.tr/2005/12/11/siyaset/asiy.html

Milliyet. (2013a, May 3). Arınç'tan alkolü 'buzlama' sinyali. *Milliyet*. Retrieved June 25, 2014, from http://www.milliyet.com.tr/arinc-tan-alkolu-buzlama-sinyali/gundem/detay/1702550/default.htm

Milliyet. (2013b, May 24). Sağlık Bakanı Müezzinoğlu: Türkiye'de kişi başına içki tüketimi 1.5 litre. *Milliyet*. Retrieved June 25, 2014, from http://www.milliyet.com.tr/saglik-bakani-muezzinoglu-/gundem/detay/1713240/default.htm

Mintz, S. W. (1986). *Sweetness and power: The place of sugar in modern history*. New York, NY: Penguin Books.

Mrgić, J. (2011). Wine or raki: The interplay of climate and society in early modern Ottoman Bosnia. *Environment and History*, *17*(4), 613–637. doi:10.3197/096734011X13150366551652

Sabah. (2013, May 28). Başbakan alkol düzenlemesini anlattı. *Sabah*. Retrieved June 25, 2014, from http://www.sabah.com.tr/gundem/2013/05/28/basbakan-erdogan-konusuyor

Sirmen, A. (2013, April 30). Milli Duygun Yok ki Milli İçkin Olsun!. *Cumhuriyet*. Retrieved June 25, 2014, from http://www.cumhuriyet.com.tr/koseyazisi/418926/Milli_Duygun_Yok_ki_Milli_ickin_Olsun_... html

Steinvorth, D., & Zand, B. (2013, June 24). A country divided: Where is Turkey headed? *Spiegel Online*. Retrieved June 25, 2014, from http://www.spiegel.de/international/world/protests-reveal-the-deep-divisions-in-turkish-society-a-907498.html

TBMM Tutanak Dergisi. (2013, May 23). Dönem 24, Cilt 51.

TC İçişleri Bakanlığı Basın ve Halkla İlişkiler Müşavirliği Basın Açıklaması. (2005, September 15). *Umuma Açık İstirahat ve Eğlence Yerlerine Ait Genelge*, no. 2005/20. Retrieved from June 25, 2014, http://www.icisleri.gov.tr/default.icisleri_2.aspx?id=3072.

Traynor, I. (2005, December 22). Alcohol the battleground in east-west conflict. *The Guardian*. Retrieved June 25, 2014, from http://www.theguardian.com/world/2005/dec/23/turkey.iantraynor

Turkish mine disaster: Unions hold protest strike. (2014, May 15). *BBC News*. Retrieved June 25, 2014from http://www.bbc.com/news/world-europe-27415822

Türkiye Büyük Millet Meclisi. (1982). *Constitution of the Republic of Turkey*. Retrieved from June 25, 2014, http://global.tbmm.gov.tr/docs/constitution_en.pdf

Türkiye Cumhuriyeti Anayasası. (1982, November 9). *Resmî Gazete*, no. 17863.

Tütün ve Alkol Piyasası Düzenleme Kurumu. (2002). *Misyon & Vizyon*. Retrieved from June 16, 2015, http://www.tapdk.gov.tr/tr/kurumsal/misyon-vizyon.aspx.

Üçüncü, U. (2012). *Milli Mücadele yıllarında bir yasak denemesi: Men-i Müskirat (İçki Yasağı) Kanunu ve toplumsal hayata yansımaları*. Konya: Çizgi Kitabevi.

Valentine, G., Holloway, S. L., Jayne, M., & Knell, C. (2007). *Drinking places: Where people drink and why?* York: Joseph Rowntree Foundation.

White, J. (2010). Fear and loathing in the Turkish national imagination [reprint of a November 2009 public lecture sponsored jointly by The Chair in Contemporary Turkish Studies, London School of Economics and Political Science and the Turkish Studies Programme at the School of Oriental and African Studies (SOAS)]. *New Perspectives on Turkey*, *42*, 215–236.

World Health Organization. (2014). *Raising tax on tobacco: What you need to know*. Geneva: Author.

Zappa, F., & Occhiogrosso, P. (1989). *The real Frank Zappa book*. New York, NY: Poseidon Press.

Zat, V. (2008). *Biz rakı içeriz: Rakının geçmişi ve bugünü*. Istanbul: Overteam Yayınları.

Neoliberalism and the alcohol industry in Ireland

Julien Mercille

School of Geography, University College Dublin, Belfield, Ireland

This paper sheds light on the development of the Irish alcohol industry and its regulation since the 1980s by situating it within the politico-economic context of neoliberalism at the national, European and global scales. First, a conceptualisation of neoliberalism is presented and the alcohol industry is related to it. Second, the connections between neoliberalism, the drinks industry and alcohol legislation are explained and illustrated at the three spatial scales mentioned above, emphasising the following components of neoliberalism: deregulation, liberalisation, commodification, free trade agreements and transnational capital flows. The paper provides a theoretical template for future research.

1. Introduction

Alcohol occupies a significant place in Irish life, culture, politics and economy. In the European Union (EU), Ireland ranks sixth in terms of pure alcohol consumption, at 11.9 l per capita, compared to a European average of 10.7 l. A report by the Royal College of Physicians of Ireland (2013, pp. 6–8) states that as "a nation, the Irish are heavy alcohol consumers" and that the "place of the pub as a centre of Irish social life is indisputable" as "there is scarcely a small village or parish in the country that does not have" one. The drinks industry is an important component of the economy. Diageo, the owner of Guinness, is the dominant drinks company nationally. The industry provides full- or part-time employment for 62,000 persons and generates about €2 billion per year in tax revenues from alcohol manufacturing and retail sales, in addition to approximately €1 billion in drinks exports (Foley, 2013, p. 5).

The health effects, however, have been highly negative. It is estimated that alcohol caused 4.4% (6584) of deaths in Ireland between 2000 and 2004 (Martin et al., 2010). It is also strongly linked to suicide, particularly among young men: one study showed that over half of all people who died by suicide had alcohol in their blood and between 2000 and 2004, alcohol was the major contributing factor in 823 suicides (Royal College of Physicians of Ireland, 2013, p. 10). Lastly, as many as 25% of injury admissions to hospitals' emergency rooms are related to alcohol (Royal College of Physicians of Ireland, 2013, p. 14).

It is often suggested, in particular, by the drinks industry, that Ireland has long had a drinking culture and that such a factor should be taken into account to explain the relatively high consumption of alcohol in the country and the significance of its drinks industry. Indeed, it is clear that Ireland was never a "temperance culture" involving the existence of a large and sustained temperance movement advocating the view that alcohol is inherently evil and calling for prohibition as a policy measure (Butler, 2002, p. 19). However, it would be incorrect to believe that the levels of alcohol consumption of recent years have always characterised drinking habits. Indeed, alcohol consumption per capita almost tripled between 1960 and 2001, rising from 4.9 l (1960) to 7.0 (1970) to 9.6 (1980) to 11.2 (1990) to a peak of 14.5 (2001) and down to 11.6 (2012, most recent data) (OECD, 2015). This points to the influence of factors other than traditions and culture to account for the changing significance of the industry and consumption. In any case, this paper's analysis does not claim that cultural factors play no role in accounting for alcohol consumption patterns. Rather, it seeks to identify and explain the political economic forces of the last few decades that have played an important role in shaping the alcohol industry and its regulation.

2. Neoliberalism and alcohol studies

In geography, studies of substance abuse, including alcohol, have not been numerous, but there is a growing corpus of research on the subject (for reviews, see Jayne, Valentine, & Holloway, 2008a, 2008b; Wilton and Moreno, 2012). Existing investigations have examined issues ranging from the complex relations between place, space and drug addiction and consumption to treatment and recovery problems and their institutional contexts (Draus, Roddy, & Greenwald, 2010; Jayne, Valentine, & Holloway, 2010, 2011; Kneale & French, 2008; Love, Wilton, & DeVerteuil, 2012; Wilton & DeVerteuil, 2006). In particular, it has been pointed out that geographical research has tended to adopt a case study approach, leaving the relations between alcohol and people and places undertheorised (Jayne et al., 2008a). Similarly, although the field of alcohol studies has paid some attention to the political and economic processes within which alcohol production and consumption are embedded, theorisation has often remained underdeveloped or absent. This can be seen, in particular, in studies of the influence of the drinks industry on laws and legislation (Alavaikko & Österberg, 2000; Giesbrecht, 2000; Grieshaber-Otto, Sinclair, & Schacter, 2000; Hawkins, Holden, & McCambridge, 2012).

This paper seeks to shed light on the development of the alcohol industry and its regulation in Ireland since the 1980s by situating it within the politico-economic context of neoliberalism at the national, European and global scales. It is argued that a number of key features of the restructuring of the drinks industry and its regulation flow directly or indirectly from the neoliberalisation of the Irish and world economies since the 1980s. Theoretically, interpreting the political economy of the drinks industry by relating it to neoliberalism is novel, with a few exceptions (Butler, 2009; Haydock, 2014). It is thus hoped that the paper may provide a template for future studies. The remainder of this section outlines the conceptualisation of neoliberalism that is used in this paper and explains in schematic form how the alcohol industry fits within this context. Subsequent sections illustrate in more detail the connections between neoliberalism, the drinks industry and alcohol legislation at the national, European and global scales.

Neoliberalism has become a relatively popular concept in critical scholarship, having been used in a variety of contexts while taking on a range of meanings (Boas & Gans-Morse, 2009; Saad-Filho & Johnston, 2005). In this paper, the word is used to refer to a set of ideas and practices whose objective is to restore, increase and maintain the power of the corporate sector relative to ordinary people since the late 1970s. It is a class project that has developed as a response to the erosion of the corporate sector's economic power during capitalism's "golden age" that lasted from the end of World War II until the late 1960s (Duménil & Lévy, 2011; Harvey, 2005). It has spread in advanced and emerging economies to varying degrees since the 1970s, and especially since the 1980s, and is characterised by market deregulation, freer capital flows worldwide, monetarism, privatisation, commodification, the weakening of labour's bargaining position and working conditions and attacks on the welfare state. It has also been marked by the financialisation of Western economies and the relocation of manufacturing to Asia and elsewhere to capture cheaper pools of labour and cut production costs. Consequently, economic growth has come to depend to a larger extent on credit and debt accumulation (corporate, personal, governmental), given the deindustrialisation of the West and the stagnation of real wages during the last several decades (Magdoff & Foster, 2009). The effects can be seen in the rising levels of inequality between rich and poor that have characterised advanced economies since the 1980s (Bonesmo Fredriksen, 2012). While it is true that many of neoliberalism's features may be found in Western economies prior to the 1970s, the point is that neoliberalism marks a significant intensification of such features as marketisation, freer transnational capital flows, deregulation, commodification and financialisation.

Neoliberalism has also entailed a restructuring of the state to align it more closely with the needs and values of corporate power, whereas previously, the state played a more active role in the redistribution of income and the establishment of social welfare programmes (Bruff, 2014; Cahill, 2014; Gill, 2008; Konings, 2010; Mirowski, 2013). Therefore, contrary to neoliberal theoretical principles advocating a small state, it is more accurate to describe the neoliberal state as restructured and reorganised. There has been a simultaneous roll-back and roll-out of state functions, so that the national state does not become necessarily less powerful, but utilises its power differently (Peck, 2001). Thus, neoliberalism is characterised not always by free competition as idealised in neoclassical theory, but by "protection for the strong and a socialization of their risks" combined to "market discipline for the weak" (Gill, 1995, p. 405). There is also a significant ideological dimension to neoliberalism, so as to present policies and practices favourably to the public, especially when they are contrary to popular interest. This is accomplished by governmental and corporate public relations discourses, but also by a range of institutions like marketing and public relations firms, think tanks, universities and the media.

This paper conceives of Ireland as a prototypical neoliberal state, following a number of analysts (Allen, 2009; Allen & O'Boyle, 2013; Fraser, Murphy, & Kelly, 2013; Mercille & Murphy, 2015). For example, between the 1980s and the 2008 crash, Ireland deregulated its banking industry and planning system, setting the conditions in place for a housing bubble to grow and later collapse, plunging the country into an unprecedented period of economic turbulence. It also reduced its corporate tax rate to 12.5% and welcomed global financial capital, privatised a range of state-owned enterprises, embraced urban entrepreneurialism and established a "social partnership" designed to remove the threat of strike action by organised labour and in general mute the more militant segment or the trade union movement. There is no space to discuss at length the factors behind such developments, but it has been argued elsewhere (Mercille & Murphy, 2015) that they are the result of both domestic and foreign forces. In particular, the EU "rule regime" (Brenner, Peck, & Theodore, 2010) has shaped Irish political economy along neoliberal lines, especially since the Maastricht Treaty of 1993. The monetarism and fiscal discipline that characterise Eurozone institutions as well as the intensification of marketisation by European institutions through the European single market have acted as key factors pushing Ireland further along the path of neoliberalism. The result has been a relatively low level of government expenditure on social programmes in Ireland, light regulation of the financial system, large dependence on foreign capital and flexible labour markets.

The resolution of the economic crisis that began in 2008 may be interpreted as a deepening of neoliberalism (Allen & Boyle, 2013; Fraser et al., 2013; Mercille & Murphy, 2015). Indeed, corporate and political elites have sought to increase their power and transfer the costs of the crisis onto citizens. This can be seen most clearly in the massive bank bailouts that have socialised private debts and in the range of crisis resolution mechanisms and policies implemented under the rubric of austerity that have affected disproportionately the poorer and more vulnerable segments of the population, which depend to a greater extent on services provided by the state (Blyth, 2013). This has occurred through a paring down of public services from health care to welfare, in regressive taxation schemes to raise extra revenues, and by transferring state assets to investors through privatisation.

Globally and in Ireland, the drinks industry has undergone a transformation under neoliberalism that reflects that of the corporate world as a whole. Indeed, from the early 1980s onwards, the alcohol industry embarked on a new and reinvigorated phase of lobbying and promotion (Babor et al., 2010; Butler, 2002). One important motivation was an awareness that it faced a significant threat from the new "public health" approach to alcohol that was being developed by the World Health Organisation (WHO) and other health authorities. This approach replaced the "disease concept" of alcoholism, which essentially explained drinking problems by reference to some mysterious deficit or predisposition in a relatively small number of drinkers, and which required further scientific elucidation. This, of course, is the approach that has always been favoured by the drinks industry, because it ascribes responsibility for alcohol-related problems like alcoholism and violence to drinkers themselves and not to the availability of alcohol. In Ireland, the approach of the Irish National Council on Alcoholism, which existed from 1966 to 1987, was a classic example of the disease concept (Butler, 2002).

With the rise of the public health approach as the new consensus of health promotion bodies, the drinks industry stepped up its promotional and lobbying activities. The public health approach is directly opposed to the industry's interests because it seeks to limit the availability of alcohol for consumption (Butler, 2002). Moreover, the simultaneous restructuring of the world and Irish economies along neoliberal lines provided the context within which the drinks industry offensive took shape and was deployed, taking advantage of increased global flows of capital and investment, the commodification of new realms of life, a reassertion of "free" markets, trade and economic liberalisation, as well as deregulation.

Therefore, it is no coincidence that it is in the early 1980s (in 1981) that the Drinks Industry Group of Ireland (DIGI) was formed as a formal umbrella organisation representing both manufacturers and retailers "with a view to unifying and strengthening the voice of the industry" in Ireland (Butler, 2002, p. 68). The trade group "was determined to combat the negative image of alcohol now being portrayed by public health advocates, and to oppose the notion that the state should use fiscal or other measures to reduce consumption levels" (Butler, 2002, p. 68). Later, in 2002, MEAS (Mature Enjoyment of Alcohol in Society) was established by the drinks industry to promote corporate social responsibility.

The sections below illustrate how the transformations in the drinks industry and related regulation and legislation took place at the national, European and global scales. Nationally, a number of pieces of legislation have been enacted to facilitate profit accumulation by the industry, including favourable tax measures, support for voluntary regulatory guidelines, and the enactment of weak legal regulations to reduce alcohol consumption. At the global scale, multinational alcohol companies have been able to capture new markets for investment and sale of their products through "free" trade agreements. The EU has also implemented legislative and legal frameworks favourable to the industry (Babor et al., 2010).

3. National scale

Since the 1980s, analysts have noted how Irish legislation has been particularly favourable towards the drinks industry (Butler, 2009, 2015; Hope, 2006; Hope & Butler, 2010). This has happened through a combination of measures seeking to deregulate and liberalise alcohol legislation; to remove restrictive rules and laws constraining the drinks industry and sale of alcohol; and to commodify new realms of social life, in particular, by expanding alcohol marketing to sporting events. Ann Hope, who acted as the National Alcohol Policy Advisor to the Department of Health for a decade (1995–2005), has noted how over the last three or four decades, the Department of Enterprise "has consistently called for deregulation of the alcohol market" and that the Department of Justice has been "in favour of liberalisation of the licensing laws". These government departments' political orientation "reflect[s] a probusiness perspective" and believes that more competition will result in cheaper alcohol and expanded consumer choice (Hope, 2006, p. 469). Similarly, Butler (2009, p. 343) has noted the "neo-liberal policy climate" in which alcohol policy has been embedded over the last several decades, so that marketisation has been prioritised over regulation. Indeed, for the last three decades, there has been, at best, only "nominal political support" for public health principles on the part of successive Irish governments, which have tended to align themselves with the drinks industry's interests (Butler, 2009, p. 350; see also Butler, 2002).

The most important instances of deregulation, liberalisation and commodification include the following. Whereas the alcohol industry was composed traditionally of producers, distributers and vintners, in more recent years, it has become more competitive and dynamic due to the entry of new commercial entities. For example, between 1998 and 2010, there was a 161% increase in the number of off-licences, while the sale of alcohol, often at discounted prices by large Irish and international supermarkets (Aldi, Lidl, Tesco, Dunnes), petrol stations and convenience stores, has grown significantly. Also, when a parliamentary committee reviewed licensing laws in the late 1990s, the vintners, hospitality and tourism interest groups lobbied significantly for longer opening hours in premises where alcohol is served. Notwithstanding the public health risks, the minister for Justice, Equality and Law Reform stated that the proposed changes were "progressive and in line with public expectation and demand and on terms which were economically and socially acceptable" (Hope, 2006, p. 471). As a result, the Intoxicating Liquor Act of 2000 broadened the opening hours of pubs from 11h30 pm to 12h30 am. Moreover, the same legislation increased alcohol availability by raising the number of exemptions for late openings of pubs. The court-granted late openings surged from 6342 in 1967 to 55,290 in 1994 to 81,933 in 2002 (it has since decreased to 64,878 in 2010 and 45,869 in 2013) (Hope, 2006; Lucey, 2015).

There have also been a number of instances when regulatory restrictions on the drinks industry's freedom have been either struck down, diluted or never implemented. For example, in 1994, the Road Traffic Act included a reduction in permitted blood alcohol concentration for drivers from 100 to 80 mg per 100 ml of blood and a two-year mandatory license suspension and driving ban. However, following the enactment of the law, the vintners and the Irish Hotel Federation strongly lobbied against the measures, "provoking a public debate of unprecedented ferocity" (Hope, 2006, p. 470). The result was a new legislation that diluted the penalties, lowering the mandatory suspension from two years to three months. Proposals to further lower the blood alcohol concentration level to 50 mg per 100 ml of blood, in line with most other European countries, were strongly resisted by the drinks industry, although this new limit was introduced in 2011. Similarly, it is only in 2006 that random breath testing was introduced in the country, despite its proven effectiveness, while the government strategy had previously ruled it out (Hope, 2006).

In addition, some pieces of legislation have directly boosted drinks industry profits through public subsidies. For example, in 2006, the Restrictive Practices (Groceries) Order allowed alcohol to be sold below cost price, further facilitating the purchase of alcohol products (Royal College of Physicians of Ireland, 2013, p. 6). This means that when alcohol is sold below cost in retail establishments, the retailers are entitled to a VAT refund from the government on the difference between the cost price and the actual sale price. The rationale is that by selling below cost, the retailers incur a loss and therefore the VAT refund seeks to compensate them. Such tax refunds thus support higher alcohol consumption by allowing products to be sold more cheaply. As the chairman of the parliamentary Committee on Health and Children, Jerry Buttimer, said: "In effect, the Government and taxpayers are subsidising those large retailers who can afford to sell alcohol below cost price" (Oireachtas, n.d.). Minister of State Roisin Shortall stated that such tax refunds "facilitate below cost selling" (Oireachtas, n.d.). According to the drinks industry itself, a complete ban on below cost selling of alcohol could generate as much as €20 million in increased VAT (Alcohol companies goal, 2013).

The implementation of a relatively weak regulatory structure has continued up to the present. The government presented in early 2015 the Public Health (Alcohol) Bill 2015 which contains some public health measures, although it is not very ambitious with respect to curbing the drinks industry's interests, and it remains to be seen if it will be enacted into law by the Irish Parliament (Butler, 2015). Moreover, the fact that it took 15 months to present the bill from the time the proposals for it were made shows that "it did not reflect any sense of urgency on the part of government" in relation to public health legislation for alcohol (Butler, 2015, p. 9). Consequently, as a recent report by Irish physicians observes, "actions to reduce alcohol consumption and to address harmful drinking patterns have, to date, been limited" (Royal College of Physicians of Ireland, 2013, pp. 2–3). It points out that there does not exist in Ireland an integrated model of care for the treatment of alcohol-related health problems. Moreover, the state neglects to finance research into alcohol-related harm, as there is "very little funding available" for it, even though levies on the alcohol industry could be used to support this research (Royal College of Physicians of Ireland, 2013, pp. 2–3).

Another significant aspect of the drinks industry in recent years that can be at least partially explained with reference to neoliberalism is the industry's sponsorship of sports and cultural events. In Ireland, alcohol sports sponsorship began in the early 1990s and today, soccer, rugby, Gaelic football and horse racing are sponsored by drinks companies such as Heineken, Guinness and Carlsberg. This marks a deepening commodification of culture and sports that is typical under neoliberalisation, as the private sector extends itself to domains of life that had until then remained, to varying degrees, somewhat insulated from "the market". Sponsorship allows the drinks industry to increase market share, sales and profits, whereas its restriction has the opposite effect. Indeed, scholarly research has established that marketing, and in particular sponsorship of sports and cultural events by the drinks industry, helps to secure new consumers. In particular, a number of systematic reviews have demonstrated that alcohol advertising encourages young people to drink sooner and in larger quantities. For example, Anderson, de Bruijn, Angus, Gordon, and Hastings (2009, p. 229) concluded that "alcohol advertising and promotion increases the likelihood that adolescents will start to use alcohol, and to drink more if they are already using alcohol" (see also Babor et al., 2010; de Bruijn et al., 2012; Hastings, 2009; Smith & Foxcroft, 2009).

The drinks industry has been successful in watering down or preventing the enactment of legislation banning the sponsorship of sports events by lobbying the state. In 2009, the government set up a National Substance Misuse Strategy Steering Group, whose membership included industry representatives. The group published its report in 2012 (Department of Health, 2012), which contained recommendations including a ban on alcohol sponsorship of sporting events by 2016. The drinks industry bodies on the group dissented and published minority reports, one of which accused the Steering Group of bias (Mature Enjoyment of Alcohol in Society, 2011). Also, documents obtained under the Freedom of Information Act by *Irish Times* journalists (Beesley, 2014) reveal direct industry lobbying. In 2013, the government proposed to explore the possibility of introducing a ban on sponsorship by 2020. This was a step back from the Steering Group's recommendation for a ban by 2016, but the industry was still opposed. The documents released show that domestic and global industry leaders lobbied the government up to its highest levels. Moreover, the documents showed that the industry was kept informed of normally confidential legislative plans by the government. For example, Diageo sent letters to the prime minister explaining corporate concerns, in addition to lobbying from industry groups like the MEAS, the DIGI, the Irish Distillers and the Alcohol Beverage Federation of Ireland, a division of Ireland's main business group, IBEC (Irish Business and Employers Confederation). Ireland's Chambers of Commerce also lobbied the state, citing the economic value of the alcohol sector and claiming there was no evidence that banning sponsorship would benefit public health. The then Minister for Sport, Leo Varadkar (now Minister for Health), supported the drinks industry in this respect (Beesley, 2014; Transparency International, 2014, pp. 25–26). As a result, there is still no ban on alcohol sponsorship of sporting events, and the current proposed Public Health (Alcohol) Bill 2015 will not implement a ban, opting instead for a "voluntary code of conduct" allowing the industry to regulate itself (Kelly, 2015).

This was not the only instance of industry lobbying against advertising restrictions. In 2005, documents were released that showed that over a four-year period, senior representatives of the drinks, broadcasting and advertising industries lobbied the Department of Health regarding government plans to regulate alcohol advertising (Downes, 2005). They were granted meetings with senior government officials on several occasions. Letters from Diageo, DIGI, MEAS, Irish Distillers, and advertising and media companies were sent to the government to highlight the alleged benefits of a voluntary code for alcohol advertising. Letters from Diageo also let the government know that the company was "both surprised and dismayed that the Guinness sponsorship of the All-Ireland hurling championships" had once again been "singled out" by the Minister of Health as an example of "undesirable sponsorship of sports" (Downes, 2005). Following this lobbying campaign, the government controversially decided not to implement its proposed Alcohol Products Bill, a legislation that was expected to implement significant controls on alcohol advertising.

The sponsorship of sports and cultural events by the drinks industry illustrates another manifestation of the privatisation forces that characterise neoliberalism. The Irish government has implemented a policy of austerity since 2008, which has translated into tax hikes and drastic public expenditure cuts. The latter imply a relative displacement of the state by the private sector in economic life, as private firms progressively play a larger role in financing activities that could otherwise be supported by public funds, such as sports and recreation. Thus, a constant theme in the public debate about whether or not the drinks industry should finance sports and cultural events is the fact that governmental budgets are tight or have been slashed, and that the private sector has thus become vital to supporting recreational activities. For example, Diageo threatened to scale back its operations in Ireland if the sponsorship ban went ahead, while the business press underlined the many economic contributions made by the drinks industry, such as domestic investment and employment (McCaughren, 2012).

The drinks industry has also substituted itself for public spending in other ways during the crisis, further deepening neoliberalism (Allen & O'Boyle, 2013; Fraser et al., 2013; Mercille & Murphy, 2015). Indeed, austerity means that there is less aggregate demand in the economy, leading many small businesses to struggle or go bankrupt, increasing unemployment and underemployment. However, companies like Diageo may enter the picture and support businesses as part of marketing campaigns. For example, in 2009, within the context of the Guinness 250th anniversary celebrations, Diageo created the Arthur Guinness Fund, set up to help entrepreneurs. In its first three years, the fund awarded €1.65 million to various business projects, in addition to providing business mentoring across Ireland. The (neoliberal) state is supportive of this strategy: Minister for the Environment, Community and Local Government, Phil Hogan, said that the awardees are "hugely inspiring people" who "have the drive, determination and the skills required to make extraordinary differences to their communities", in the face of government withdrawal from those communities (Connolly, 2012). The point is not that the Irish government has fully relegated to the corporate sector the task of stimulating the economy, but rather that a climate of austerity opens the door to greater private sector involvement in the economy, in the wake of the state's withdrawal from specific sectors.

4. European and global scales

Over the last several decades, the global alcohol market has adapted to the neoliberal currents that have transformed the world economy. The industry has become dominated by a small number of large corporations that seek to capture overseas investment opportunities through a number of free trade agreements and liberalised global financial flows (Casswell & Thamarangsi, 2009). Those companies began to consolidate regionally and operate internationally in the 1980s, and then went global in the 1990s. There has been a rush to capture new profit opportunities in emerging markets, in what has been described as "a scramble for new markets in the deregulating countries of Eastern Europe and the growing economies of Latin America and Asia" (Babor et al., 2010, p. 78). Global alcohol firms have entered emerging markets by buying shares in local companies, building new production facilities, finding distribution partners, entering into joint ventures and by buying local competitors (Babor et al., 2010).

Global "free" trade agreements of the last several decades are neoliberal in nature in that they liberalise trade and investment while incorporating myriad deregulation measures with respect to the environment, labour, health and safety among others. (Of course, there were trade agreements before neoliberalism, but the scale and scope of deregulation and liberalisation they implemented were not as significant.) This gives more freedom to firms to conduct their business transnationally and unimpeded by regulatory constraints (Harvey, 2005; Peet, 2009). Global agreements fall under the purview of the World Trade Organisation (WTO), which seeks to liberalise commercial exchanges by reducing government control over market access and national restrictions on the circulation of goods and services. This is accomplished by preventing countries from discriminating against foreign goods through taxes or regulations. Foreign products must be treated equally relative to local ones, which reduces the ability of governments to protect local industries and allows foreign alcohol products to penetrate markets more easily. Trade agreements negotiated in close consultation with corporate lobbyists have thus facilitated the geographical expansion of the drinks industry by weakening national and local regulations seeking to restrict the sale, availability and consumption of alcohol (Grieshaber-Otto et al., 2000; Zeigler, 2006, 2009). This applies, in particular, to trade agreements currently under negotiations, such as the Trans-Pacific Partnership, which aims to remove barriers to the global alcohol (and tobacco) companies by giving them more leverage over domestic public health policies (Kelsey, 2012).

Thus, alcohol multinational companies have been "strong supporters of trade treaties that [have] expanded their access to rapidly emerging markets" (Casswell & Thamarangsi, 2009, p. 2249). For example, the World Spirits Alliance lobbied for the General Agreement on Trade in Services by seeking the elimination or liberalisation of tariff and non-tariff barriers, including restrictions on advertising and distribution (Casswell & Thamarangsi, 2009). As a result, trade agreements have benefitted the drinks industry (Babor et al., 2010; Baumberg & Anderson, 2008b; Grieshaber-Otto et al., 2000; Shaffer, Waitzkin, Brenner, & Jasso-Aguilar, 2005; Zeigler, 2006, 2009). For example, the WTO ruled against Chile that it could not tax at higher rates imported spirits with higher alcohol content than its national liquor *pisco* because this would unduly protect the domestic liquor industry. There have also been a number of other attacks within the WTO on public health alcohol (and tobacco) legislation in Brazil, Australia, Thailand and Kenya, among others (Kelsey, 2012). For instance, when India sought to enter the WTO, the EU put pressure on the Indian government to cut tariffs on alcoholic drinks to open the Indian market to European companies. The EU also raised concerns about Thailand's laws to introduce graphic warning labels on alcohol products, claiming that this would constitute interference in trade (Collin, Johnson, & Hill, 2014).

Europe has embraced neoliberalism, especially since the Maastricht Treaty of 1993. It has emphasised the market system, the reduction of state roles in redistributing income, as well as monetary and fiscal regulations that favour budgetary and monetary discipline over Keynesian policy (see Gill, 2008; Stockhammer, 2014; Van Apeldoorn, 2002). This is reflected in alcohol policies favourable to the drinks industry. In particular, the EU's Strategy on Alcohol is weak in that it endorses policies that have been shown to be ineffective to reduce alcohol harms, such as education and persuasion strategies, while measures to raise the price of alcohol products, which are effective, are given short shrift (Gordon & Anderson, 2011). In fact, the EU has just announced that it would not renew its Strategy on Alcohol and let it expire, which means that alcohol policy will lack coordination and direction across the continent (Jacobsen, 2015).

The *Lancet* (2006, p. 1875) summarised the situation thus:

> The truth is that Europe's commitment to a common market means the specific danger alcohol poses to health is difficult to take into account. States cannot discriminate against products from another European country on the grounds of health, which limits their freedom to design health-protecting tax laws.

The problem is that "as long as negotiations over alcohol policy are dominated by the vested interests of free trade and industry ... governments in the EU will continue to shirk their moral obligations to protect their populations from the preventable risk of alcohol-related harm" (*Lancet*, 2006, p. 1875; see also Baumberg & Anderson, 2008a; Chenet & McKee, 1998). For example, the single market has involved the abolition of travellers' import quotas for alcoholic beverages in 1993, in line with neoliberal principles of free trade and free movement of goods. This has led some countries to reduce their taxes on alcohol products in order to reduce travellers' imports from neighbouring EU member states. However, lowering alcohol taxes has been linked to increased consumption and harms. For example, when Finland reduced its alcohol excise duty rates by 33% in 2004, the price drop was linked to a 10% rise in total alcohol consumption and to increases in harms related to alcohol (Österberg, 2011, p. 128; see also Mäkelä & Österberg, 2009).

Moreover, European excise taxes on alcohol have been reduced in real terms over the last several decades in most European countries, in line with deregulation and to the benefit of alcohol firms (Österberg, 2011). This is because the minimum excise duty rates established in 1993 by the EU have since then not changed in nominal terms, so that inflation has eroded their real value by approximately one-third. Also, the minimum excise rate duty on wine is zero, and countries that produce wine set their excise rate to zero, which makes it difficult to argue for higher taxes on other alcoholic beverages. The result is that in "most European countries the share of alcohol taxes of the price of alcoholic beverages is quite low" (Österberg, 2011, p. 124).

The clearest examples of the ways in which EU-level deregulation has affected national policies have come from the Scandinavian countries, which traditionally had implemented strong public health safeguards on alcohol products but have had to dilute them under EU pressure. For example, in 2001 and 2008 Sweden lowered alcohol excise duty rates for wine because according to the European Commission, Swedish taxation favoured beer, a domestic product, over wine, which is imported. Beer and wine had to be treated as equivalents to avoid discrimination of foreign products. Also, Finland's state monopoly on the production, export, import and wholesale of alcohol was dissolved when it joined the EU in 1995. Public monopolies can regulate prices and keep them high enough to restrain consumption (Mäkelä & Österberg, 2009).

There have not been, to this author's knowledge, significant instances where the EU has shaped directly Irish alcohol regulations, as in Scandinavia. One reason is that Irish alcohol strategies and policies are relatively weak in challenging the drinks industry and do not oppose any of the EU regulations (single market rules, excise duty or marketing rules). Nevertheless, as an EU member state, Ireland's national policies on excise taxes, competition and market access are enacted within the legislative context of the EU, which poses limits and constraints on alcohol regulation, as seen above. For example, in 2001, the Irish tax rate on cider was almost doubled because the EU required Ireland not to offer "preferential treatment" to this product that is mostly produced domestically, but relatively speaking, this remains a minor policy adjustment. Another potentially more important example is provided by Scotland's attempt to introduce minimum unit pricing, an effective public health measure to limit alcohol consumption. The policy was appealed by the Scotch Whisky Association on the grounds that it was not "proportionate" and the case is currently before the European Court of Justice. Therefore, if Ireland wished to introduce minimum unit pricing through its Public Health (Alcohol) Bill 2015, presumably, the legislation would have to go through the European Court (Alcohol Action Ireland, 2014).

In Ireland, the operations of Diageo have reflected trends in the global alcohol market. Formed in 1997 from the merger of Guinness and Grand Metropolitan, Diageo is the world's largest producer of spirits and also has major stakes in the global beer and wine markets. It has a market capitalisation of £47 billion and sells products in over 180 countries, in addition to holding offices in about 80 countries. In 2013, its net sales amounted to £11.4 billion and it spent £1.8 billion on marketing, or 15.6% of net sales, while generating operating profits of £3.4 billion.

Significantly, 42% of Diageo's business now takes place in emerging markets in Latin America, Africa, Asia, and Eastern Europe and Turkey, a fact that its annual reports emphasise, seeking to convince shareholders and investors that significant profits will be generated by establishing a presence in new markets to capture the income of rising middle classes (Diageo, 2013). For example, in recent years, Diageo expanded geographically through the following transactions: in Latin America, it purchased Ypioca (a major spirits producer) in Brazil, in the Middle East, it bought Mey Icki in Turkey, in India, it purchased a majority share in United Spirits, in Africa, it entered into a joint venture with United National Breweries and purchased Meta Abo Brewery in Ethiopia, and in China, it purchased a controlling stake in the Chengdu Quanxing Group (Collin, Johnson, & Hill, 2014, p. 5).

The Irish state has assisted the alcohol industry, and in particular Diageo, as an exporter to global markets. For example, in September 2014, Diageo opened a €169 million state of the art brewery in Dublin. The Prime Minister, Enda Kenny, was present and reiterated his strong backing for the business. He said:

> I'm delighted to open the new Diageo brewery ... this new €169 million investment in the heart of Dublin will help contribute to our export led recovery ... The Government's plan for recovery will see continued support for our indigenous export orientated food and drink sector ... I know that Government Departments and Enterprise Ireland are on hand and willing to assist where possible to ensure future investment of your brand in Ireland are successful. (Kenny, 2014)

Previously, in 2011, Diageo had made another investment of €153 million in a "brewing centre of excellence" in Dublin. The Minister for Jobs, Enterprise and Innovation, Richard Bruton, welcomed the investment and stated that

> High-tech manufacturing must be at the centre of our jobs recovery ... Every pint of Guinness sold throughout Europe and the United States is currently brewed in Dublin ... With this month's Action Plan for Jobs I am determined to ensure that high-growth Irish and international companies have the necessary supports to create the jobs and growth we so badly need. (Diageo, 2012)

The drinks industry is also an important source of exports due to the revenues it generates by attracting tourists to Ireland through the promotion of alcohol products, pubs and breweries. In this respect, the Irish state's economic strategy is also aligned with the drinks industry. Indeed, Ireland is perhaps the only country in the world to have placed a commercial drink brand (Guinness) at the very centre of its national identity. Thus, the Irish National Tourism Board "knows that promoting Guinness goes hand in hand with showcasing Ireland abroad", and as Sean McGrave, chief executive of the Institute of Advertising Practitioners in Ireland, put it: "Guinness is still the brand most associated with Ireland ... Guinness is synonymous with Ireland in the way the royal Family is with London" (Creaton, 2011). The Prime Minister, Enda Kenny, recently declared at a Diageo event: "And of course, Diageo plays a major role in our tourism sector. The Guinness Storehouse, which opened to the public in 2000, is a hugely-impressive facility attracting over 1 million visitors a year", making it the largest fee-charging visitor attraction in the country (Kenny, 2014). Similarly, the drinks industry states proudly that it provides a "major boost to Irish international image through brands such as Guinness, Baileys, Jameson and other Irish Whiskies", in addition to being an "important element of the tourism product of Ireland" (Foley, 2013, pp. 4–5).

The government also provides significant marketing support to the drinks industry by bringing foreign officials who visit Ireland to taste, in front of cameras and journalists, either a pint of Guinness or another Irish alcoholic beverage. For example, when President Obama came to Ireland in 2011, an important news story that stood out in media coverage was his sampling of a pint of Guinness. Likewise, when Queen Elizabeth visited Ireland at about the same time, she attended a demonstration to show her how to pour a perfect pint of Guinness. These two events have been estimated to have been worth €23 million of free global publicity for Guinness and Siobhan McAleer, a senior marketing and sales management specialist at the Irish Management Institute, said that "the fact that President Obama, who is seen as 'cool', drank a pint was so positive in terms of branding for younger people". She then stated that "what is good for Guinness should ultimately also be good for Ireland and its tourism industry" (Creaton, 2011).

Perhaps the most significant event that illustrates the extent to which state interests and economic strategy have been structured around the drinks industry is Arthur's Day, an annual series of music, drinking and cultural events taking place both in Ireland and worldwide and first organised by Diageo to mark the 250th anniversary of its Guinness brewing company. The event serves as a marketing tool in global markets and in 2013, events took place in 55 countries, including Malaysia, Singapore, Italy, Germany, United Arab Emirates and in the Caribbean. Diageo hopes to use such a celebratory event to establish and solidify its presence in emerging economies.[1] This event is implicitly linked to the promotion of Ireland globally and has been intertwined with the government's policies under the austerity programme, in particular the "Gathering" initiative. The latter was a year-long initiative that took place in 2013 and that sought to attract more visitors to Ireland by welcoming the Irish diaspora back to the country for visits that would hopefully raise tourism spending in the domestic economy. According to officials involved in the programme, the Gathering attracted some 250,000 tourists who would not otherwise have visited Ireland, generating revenues of €170 million (Fáilte Ireland, 2013).

The synergies between Irish government and drinks industry objectives were made explicit by the Gathering and Arthur's Day. Indeed, Diageo stated that it was "using the magic and excitement of Arthur's Day in 2012 to promote Ireland as a tourist destination during 2013, the

Gathering year, to millions of potential tourists in the key markets" (Guinness, 2012). Ireland's then Minister for Transport, Tourism and Sport, Leo Varadkar, declared:

> I'm delighted that a global brand like Guinness is getting on board with the Gathering Ireland. Arthur's Day is a great platform to spread the word about the Gathering, and encourage people around the world to visit Ireland in 2013. (Guinness, 2012)

In the same speech, the minister also announced a collaboration involving Guinness, Tourism Ireland and Aer Lingus (the national airline) "to bring some of the most influential international media to Ireland for Arthur's Day to showcase Dublin and Ireland as the tourist destination" (Guinness, 2012). The government thus cooperated with corporate objectives of profit maximisation and overseas expansion, while simultaneously seeking to attract overseas tourists as a small step to stimulate the economy under its neoliberal austerity programme.

5. Conclusion

Alcohol studies have only begun to pay close attention to critical political economy, let alone theorising its relevance to the drinks industry's evolving structure, addiction, and related subjects. This paper made a preliminary contribution in this direction and could act as a template for further research. The development of the alcohol industry and its regulation in Ireland since the 1980s were situated within the politico-economic context of neoliberalism. It was argued that at the national, European and global scales, key features of the restructuring of the drinks industry and related legislation are linked to central aspects of the neoliberalisation of the Irish and world economies.

Nationally, a range of measures have supported the drinks industry, including longer opening hours for pubs, the growth of sales through outlets such as off-licences and supermarkets, favourable tax measures, support for voluntary regulatory guidelines and the enactment of weak legal regulations to reduce alcohol consumption. Also, alcohol marketing was expanded to sporting events and attempts at constraining it were resisted, partially due to direct industry lobbying of the state.

The EU was shown to have enacted alcohol strategies favourable to the drinks industry as well, within the context of the continent's shift towards neoliberalism since the 1980s. This has prevented member states from adopting forceful policies to restrict the availability of alcohol and protect public health, which has been particularly evident in Scandinavia. Although the EU has not explicitly constrained Ireland to alter its laws because the latter already converge with European directives, it nevertheless sets the framework within which national regulations must operate. The EU's potential to restrict public health measures may soon become apparent if Ireland attempts to introduce minimum unit pricing for its alcohol products.

At the global scale, in recent decades, multinational alcohol companies have scrambled to capture new markets for investment and sale of their products through free trade agreements. The Irish state has explicitly backed Diageo in this process, considering the export revenues it generates as important to the domestic economy. Moreover, the Irish government supports the industry due to the large number of tourists it attracts to the country. Accordingly, the agendas of the drinks industry and the Irish state have meshed on more than one occasion, in particular during the Gathering initiative and Arthur's Day celebrations, which both aimed at promoting and branding Ireland internationally partly in order to attract more visitors to the country.

Acknowledgements

The author wishes to thank Joe Barry, Shane Butler and Ann Hope for helpful discussions during the research for this article.

Disclosure statement

No potential conflict of interest was reported by the author.

Note

1. See the website describing the cultural events taking place as part of Arthur's Day worldwide: http://www.guinness.com/en-ie/arthursday/ (retrieved April 15, 2014).

References

Alavaikko, M., & Österberg, E. (2000). The influence of economic interests on alcohol control policy: A case study from Finland. *Addiction*, *95*(Supplement 4), S565–S579.

Alcohol companies goal is to recruit young drinkers. (2013, June 29). *Irish Times*.

Alcohol Action Ireland. (2014). *Minimum unit pricing is to be referred to the Court of Justice of the European Union*. Retrieved May 20, 2015, from http://alcoholireland.ie/home_news/minimum-unit-pricing-is-to-be-referred-to-the-court-of-justice-of-the-european-union/

Allen, K. (2009). *Ireland's economic crash: A radical agenda for change*. Dublin: Liffey Press.

Allen, K., & O'Boyle, B. (2013). *Austerity Ireland: The failure of Irish capitalism*. London: Pluto.

Anderson, P., de Bruijn, A., Angus, K., Gordon, R., & Hastings, G. (2009). Impact of alcohol advertising and media exposure on adolescent alcohol use: A systematic review of longitudinal studies. *Alcohol & Alcoholism*, *44*(3), 229–243.

Babor, T. F., Caetano, R., Casswell, S., Edwards, G., Giesbrecht, N., Graham, K., ... Rossow, I. (2010). *Alcohol: No ordinary commodity. Research and public policy* (2nd ed.). Oxford: Oxford University Press.

Baumberg, B., & Anderson, P. (2008a). Health, alcohol and EU law: Understanding the impact of European single market law on alcohol policies. *European Journal of Public Health*, *18*(4), 392–398.

Baumberg, B., & Anderson, P. (2008b). Trade and health: How World Trade Organization (WTO) law affects alcohol and public health. *Addiction*, *103*, 1952–1958.

Beesley, A. (2014, January 5). Powerful play by drinks sector to block ban on sponsorship of major sporting events. *Irish Times*.

Blyth, M. (2013). *Austerity: The history of a dangerous idea*. Oxford: Oxford University Press.

Boas, T. C., & Gans-Morse, J. (2009). Neoliberalism: From new liberal philosophy to anti-liberal slogan. *Studies in Comparative International Development*, *44*(2), 137–161.

Bonesmo Fredriksen, K. (2012). *Income inequality in the European Union*. Economics department working papers no. 952, Paris: OECD. Retrieved April 1, 2014, from http://dx.doi.org/10.1787/5k9bdt47q5zt-en

Brenner, N., Peck, J., & Theodore, N. (2010). Variegated neoliberalization: Geographies, modalities, pathways. *Global Networks*, *10*, 182–222.

Bruff, I. (2014). The rise of authoritarian neoliberalism. *Rethinking Marxism*, *26*(1), 113–129.

Butler, S. (2002). *Alcohol, drugs and health promotion in modern Ireland*. Dublin: Institute of Public Administration.

Butler, S. (2009). Obstacles to the implementation of an integrated national alcohol policy in Ireland: Nannies, neo-liberals and joined-up government. *Journal of Social Policy*, *38*(2), 343–359.

Butler, S. (2015). Ireland's public health (alcohol) bill: Policy window or political sop? *Contemporary Drug Problems*, 1–12. doi:10.1177/0091450915579873

Cahill, D. (2014). *The end of laissez-faire? On the durability of embedded neoliberalism*. Cheltenham: Edward Elgar.

Casswell, S., & Thamarangsi, T. (2009). Reducing harm from alcohol: Call to action. *Lancet*, *373*, June 27, 2247–2257.

Chenet, L., & McKee, M. (1998). Down the road to deregulation. *Alcohol & Alcoholism*, *33*(4), 337–340.

Collin, J., Johnson, E., & Hill, S. (2014). Government support for alcohol industry: Promoting exports, jeopardising global health? BMJ, *6* June, 348, g3648. doi: 10.1136/bmj.g3648

Connolly, P. (2012, May 23). Ten social entrepreneurs share €750,000 Guinness fund. *Sunday Business Post*.

Creaton, S. (2011, May 26). Ireland did its bit for Guinness – but Diageo responds with job cuts, *Irish Independent*. Retrieved May 20, 2015, from http://www.independent.ie/business/irish/ireland-did-its-bit-for-guinness-but-diageo-responds-with-job-cuts-26736498.html

De Bruijn, A., Tanghe, J., Beccaria, F., Bujalski, M., Celata, C., Gosselt, J., … Slowdonik, L. (2012). *Report on the impact of European alcohol marketing exposure on youth alcohol expectancies and youth drinking*. AMPHORA Project. Retrieved April 18, 2014, from http://amphoraproject.net/files/AMPHORA_WP4_longitudinal_advertising_survey.pdf

Department of Health. (2012). *Steering group report on a national substance misuse strategy.* February. Retrieved May 20, 2015, from http://health.gov.ie/wp-content/uploads/2014/03/Steering_Group_Report_NSMS.pdf

Diageo. (2012). *Diageo announces brewing investment plans in Ireland.* Press release, 12 January. Retrieved May 20, 2015, from http://www.diageo.com/en-ie/investor/pages/resource.aspx?resourceid=1174

Diageo. (2013). *Annual report 2013.* Retrieved April 12, 2014, from http://www.diageo.com/EN-ROW/INVESTOR/Pages/resource.aspx?resourceid=1520

Downes, J. (2005, December 3). Documents reveal extent of lobbying on drink law. Irish Times, p. 9.

Draus, P., Roddy, J., & Greenwald, M. (2010). "A hell of a life": Addiction and marginality in post-industrial Detroit. *Social & Cultural Geography, 11*, 663–680.

Duménil, G., & Lévy, J. (2011). *The crisis of neoliberalism.* Cambridge, MA: Harvard University Press.

Fáilte Ireland. (2013). *The gathering, final report.* Retrieved April 18, 2014, from http://www.failteireland.ie/FailteIreland/media/WebsiteStructure/Documents/eZine/TheGathering_FinalReport_JimMiley_December2013.pdf

Foley, A. (2013). *The economic contribution of the drinks industry 2013.* Drinks Industry Group of Ireland. Retrieved July 10, 2015, from http://www.drinksindustry.ie/assets/Documents/The%20Economic%20Contribution%20of%20the%20Drinks%20Industry%202013x.pdf

Fraser, A., Murphy, E., & Kelly, S. (2013). Deepening neoliberalism via austerity and "reform": The case of Ireland. *Human Geography, 6*(2), 38–53.

Giesbrecht, N. (2000). Roles of commercial interests in alcohol policies: Recent developments in North America. *Addiction, 95*(Supplement 4), S581–S595.

Gill, S. (1995). Globalisation, market civilisation, and disciplinary neoliberalism. *Millennium – Journal of International Studies, 24*, 399–423.

Gill, S. (2008). *Power and resistance in the New World Order* (2nd ed.). London: Palgrave Macmillan.

Gordon, R., & Anderson, P. (2011). Science and alcohol policy: A case study of the EU strategy on alcohol. *Addiction, 106*(Suppl. 1), 55–66.

Grieshaber-Otto, J., Sinclair, S., & Schacter, N. (2000). Impacts of international trade, services and investment treaties on alcohol regulation. *Addiction, 95*, 491–504.

Guinness. (2012). *Arthur Guinness raises a glass for the gathering.* Retrieved April 18, 2014, from http://www.guinness-storehouse.com/en/PressRelease.aspx?prid=50

Harvey, D. (2005). *A brief history of neoliberalism.* Oxford: Oxford University Press.

Hastings, G. (2009). *"They'll drink bucket loads of the stuff": An analysis of internal alcohol industry advertising documents.* The Alcohol Education and Research Council. Retrieved April 18, 2014, from http://oro.open.ac.uk/22913/1/AERC_FinalReport_0060.pdf

Hawkins, B., Holden, C., & McCambridge, J. (2012). Alcohol industry influence on UK alcohol policy: A new research agenda for public health. *Critical Public Health, 22*(3), 297–305.

Haydock, W. (2014). The rise and fall of the "nudge" of minimum unit pricing: The continuity of neoliberalism in alcohol policy in England. *Critical Social Policy.* doi:10.1177/0261018313514804

Hope, A. (2006). The influence of the alcohol industry on alcohol policy in Ireland. *Nordic Studies on Alcohol and Drugs, 23*, 467–481.

Hope, A., & Butler, S. (2010). Changes in consumption and harms, yet little policy progress. *Nordic Studies on Alcohol and Drugs, 27*, 479–495.

Jacobsen, H. (2015). Commission set to dump EU alcohol strategy. *Euractiv*, 22 May. Retrieved May 23, 2015, from http://www.euractiv.com/sections/health-consumers/commission-set-dump-eu-alcohol-strategy-314782

Jayne, M., Valentine, G., & Holloway, S. (2008a). Geographies of alcohol, drinking and drunkenness: A review of progress. *Progress in Human Geography, 32*(2), 247–263.

Jayne, M., Valentine, G., & Holloway, S. (2008b). The place of drink: Geographical contributions to alcohol studies. *Drugs: Education, Prevention, and Policy, 15*(3), 219–232.

Jayne, M., Valentine, G., & Holloway, S. (2010). Emotional, embodied and affective geographies of alcohol, drinking and drunkenness. *Transactions, Institute of British Geographers, 35*, 540–554.

Jayne, M., Valentine, G., & Holloway, S. (2011). What use are units? Critical geographies of alcohol policy. *Antipode, 44*(3), 828–846.

Kelly, F. (2015). Alcohol sponsorship bill dropped. *Irish Times*, 24 January. Retrieved May 23, 2015, from http://www.irishtimes.com/news/politics/alcohol-sponsorship-bill-dropped-1.2077768

Kelsey, J. (2012). New-generation free trade agreements threaten progressive tobacco and alcohol policies. *Addiction, 107*, 1719–1721.

Kenny, E. (2014). *Speech by the Taoiseach, Mr. Enda Kenny T.D. at the formal opening of the new Diageo Brewhouse, Guinness Brewery, St. James's Gate Wednesday 10th September 2014, 2pm.* Retrieved May 20, 2015, from, http://www.merrionstreet.ie/en/category-index/economy/business/speech-by-the-taoiseach-mr-enda-kenny-t-d-at-the-formal-opening-of-the-new-diageo-brewhouse-guinness-brewery-st-jamess-gate-wednesday-10th-september-2014–2pm.html

Kneale, J., & French, S. (2008). Mapping alcohol: Health, policy and the geographies of problem drinking in Britain. *Drugs: Education, Prevention and Policy, 15*, 233–249.

Konings, M. (2010). Neoliberalism and the American state. *Critical Sociology, 36*(5), 741–765.

Lancet. (2006). Free trade rules exacerbate alcohol-related harm. *Lancet, 367*, June 10, 1875.

Love, M., Wilton, R., & DeVerteuil, G. (2012). 'You have to make a new way of life': Women's drug treatment programmes as therapeutic landscapes in Canada. *Gender, Place and Culture, 19*(3), 382–396.

Lucey, A. (2015). Fall in public order offences linked to fewer late bars, *Irish Times*, 18 May. Retrieved May 20, 2015, from http://www.irishtimes.com/news/crime-and-law/fall-in-public-order-offences-linked-to-fewer-late-bars-1.2215986

Magdoff, F., & Foster, J. B. (2009). *The great financial crisis: Causes and consequences.* New York, NY: Monthly Review.

Mäkelä, P., & Österberg, E. L. (2009). Weakening of one more alcohol control pillar: A review of the effects of the alcohol tax cuts in Finland in 2004. *Addiction, 104*, 554–563.

Martin, J., Barry, J., Goggin, D., Morgan, K., Ward, M., & O'Suilleabhain, T. (2010). Alcohol-attributable mortality in Ireland. *Alcohol and Alcoholism, 45*(4), 379–386.

Mature Enjoyment of Alcohol in Society. (2011). *National substance misuse strategy 2009–2016, minority report.* Retrieved May 20, 2015, from http://www.drugsandalcohol.ie/16912/2/Nat_Substance_Misuse_Strategy_2009–2016.pdf

McCaughren, S. (2012, October 28). Diageo chief's warning on sponsorship ban. *Sunday Business Post.*

Mercille, J., & Murphy, E. (2015). *Deepening neoliberalism, austerity, and crisis: Europe's treasure Ireland.* London: Palgrave Macmillan.

Mirowski, P. (2013). *Never let a serious crisis go to waste: How neoliberalism survived the financial meltdown.* London: Verso.

OECD. (2015). *Non-medical determinants of health: Alcohol consumption.* Retrieved May 20, 2015, from http://stats.oecd.org/Index.aspx?DataSetCode=HEALTH_LVNG#

Oireachtas. (n.d.). *Health committee chairman calls for end to VAT refunds on below cost sales.* Retrieved from http://www.oireachtas.ie/parliament/mediazone/pressreleases/name-2861-en.html

Österberg, E. L. (2011). Alcohol tax changes and the use of alcohol in Europe. *Drug and Alcohol Review, 30*, 124–129.

Peck, J. (2001). Neoliberalizing states: Thin policies/hard outcomes. *Progress in Human Geography*, 25(3), 445–455.

Peet, R. (2009). *Unholy Trinity: The IMF, World Bank and WTO.* London: Zed Books.

Royal College of Physicians of Ireland (RCPI). (2013). *Reducing alcohol health harm policy statement.* Retrieved April 18, 2014, from http://www.rcpi.ie/content/docs/000001/782_5_media.pdf

Saad-Filho, A., & Johnston, D. (eds.) (2005). *Neoliberalism: A critical reader.* London: Pluto Press.

Shaffer, E. R., Waitzkin, H., Brenner, J., & Jasso-Aguilar, R. (2005). Global trade and public health. *American Journal of Public Health, 95*(1), 23–34.

Smith, L. A., & Foxcroft, D. R. (2009). The effect of alcohol advertising, marketing and portrayal on drinking behaviour in young people: Systematic review of prospective cohort studies. *BMC Public Health*, 9, 51. Retrieved from http://www.biomedcentral.com/1471-2458/9/51

Stockhammer, E. (2014). *The Euro crisis and contradictions of neoliberalism in Europe, post Keynesian economics study group working paper 1401.* Retrieved May 23, 2015, from https://www.postkeynesian.net/downloads/wpaper/PKWP1401.pdf

Transparency International Ireland. (2014). *Influence and integrity: Lobbying and its regulation in Ireland.* Retrieved May 20, 2015, from http://transparency.ie/sites/default/files/TI%20Ireland_LLL_Final28%2011%2014.pdf

Van Apeldoorn, B. (2002). *Transnational capitalism and the struggle over European integration.* London: Routledge.

Wilton, R., & DeVerteuil, G. (2006). Spaces of sobriety/sites of power: Examining social model alcohol recovery programs as therapeutic landscapes. *Social Science and Medicine*, *63*, 649–661.

Wilton, R., & Moreno, C. M. (2012). Critical geographies of drugs and alcohol. *Social & Cultural Geography*, *13*(2), 99–108.

Zeigler, D. W. (2006). International trade agreements challenge tobacco and alcohol control policies. *Drug and Alcohol Review*, *25*, 567–579.

Zeigler, D. W. (2009). The alcohol industry and trade agreements: A preliminary assessment. *Addiction*, *104* (Suppl. 1), 13–26.

Colliding intervention in the spatial management of street-based injecting and drug-related litter within settings of public convenience (UK)

Stephen Parkin

Centre for Primary Care, Institute for Population Health, University of Manchester, Manchester, UK

This paper considers the structural production and amplification of tensions surrounding the issue of street-based injecting drug use and drug-related litter (injecting paraphernalia) discarded in public settings. These tensions, it is argued, is a consequence of colliding intervention (policy and practice) brought about by conflicting connections between national/local drug strategy and micro-level forms of governance regarding the spatial management of public space. These colliding interventions have negative consequences upon harm reduction and the formation of enabling environments. The paper draws upon data obtained from a five-year (multi-site) ethnographic study of street-based injecting conducted throughout the south of England during 2006–2011.

Shopper finds needles in Taunton public toilets.[1] (*Somerset County Gazette*, 27 December 2012)

Drug users arrested in Cambridge's "health hazard" loos.[2] (*Cambridge News*, 3 April 2013)

Ely's public toilets "rife" with drug activity.[3] (*Ely Weekly News*, 19 April 2013)

Council cleaner's HIV-test wait after drug needle stab in Sunderland toilets.[4] (*Sunderland Echo*, 30 July 2013)

Call for "drug haven" conveniences to be closed.[5] (*Hastings and St Leonard's Observer*, 14 December 2013)

Presented above are examples of local news headlines that have been reproduced from online versions of various provincial English newspapers. These articles report upon events located throughout the length and breadth of England during a 12-month period from 2012 to 2013. These selected items, however, *do not* adequately represent the full extent of similar reportage that occurs throughout the UK on a weekly basis. Nonetheless, the above headlines *do* provide an indication of the key issues underlying this paper. Namely, the relationship between street-based injecting drug use; the UK's policy of harm reduction, the appropriation of public toilets as settings for episodes of injecting drug use and the statutory (mis)management of drug-related litter. As will be demonstrated throughout this paper, the relationship between these features of UK urban environments is one defined by colliding and clashing policy perspectives at a *structural* level.

In essence, the colliding relationship that exists between the aforementioned topics perhaps reflects flawed strategies within national drug policy frameworks (of the UK). More specifically, although street-based injecting undoubtedly occurs throughout urban and rural locations of the UK (as indicated by the above headlines) there is currently no formal national policy (and/or good practice guidelines) that provides direction, guidance or advice on how such matters may be best managed by the relevant authorities/services at a local/frontline level. Instead, local authorities are expected to implement and deliver a regionalized version of a generic, national policy known as the government's Drug Strategy. In the absence of a specific policy relating to street-based injecting, local authorities therefore have to adapt and respond in accordance with the current strategy in addition to applying the enforcement procedures attached to policing "criminal" behaviour associated with possession of illicit substances. Accordingly, local responses to street-based injecting may typically involve spontaneous, reactive, interventions that lack strategic vision and/or planning in which harm reduction approaches may receive only limited attention. Such ad hoc procedures typically involve the coercive management of public places by physical manipulation (involving the closure, removal or limiting of access to affected areas) or the environmental re-design of communal spaces (using blue lights, barriers, CCTV, removal of flora/screens, etc.).[6] One plausible explanation for this *reactive* response to street-based injecting possibly relates to the *thematic* design of successive Drug Strategies since their initial inception over three decades ago.

Single-issue drug strategies in the UK: harm reduction, treatment, abstinence and recovery

Since the 1980s, various elected UK governments have typically prioritized a *single-issue theme* that characterizes the relevant Drug Strategy of successive public health policy frameworks (Berridge, 2012). Similarly, each single-issue theme has typically rested upon the "four pillars" (of enforcement, education, prevention and treatment) that characterize international drug policy (Heed, 2006; MacPherson, Mulla, & Richardson, 2006; Room, 2006). In the UK, initial responses to the HIV/AIDS epidemic during the mid-1980s adopted a significant *harm reduction* approach to drug policy in an attempt to curtail the epidemic (Stimson, 2000). In fact, it was during this particular period that "needle exchanges" were formally introduced to the British high street as part of attempts to reduce the spread of HIV. Successive strategies from 1995 to 2008 (Cabinet Office, HMSO, 1998; Department of Health, 1995; HM Government, 2008), however, have typically adopted a more punitive and coercive ethos, in which drugs and related harms were situated within a specific drugs–crime nexus (Monaghan, 2012; Stimson, 2000; Strang & Gossop, 2005). In this regard, the overriding policy issue became one of *treatment* for drug use, in which a society metaphorically "sick" with crime and drug use may be best treated by clinical intervention. Similarly, the introduction of a more *abstinence*-orientated Drug Strategy (HM Government, 2008; Scottish Government, 2008) was a strategy that mainly prioritized drug-free lifestyles. Indeed, the latter was almost certainly the forerunner of the present day Strategy that is dominated by the single issue of *recovery* from dependence (Galvani, 2012; Monaghan, 2012). Throughout each of these phases, harm reduction has consistently been included as a complementary and necessary intervention that typically supports the overriding theme of the relevant Strategy. However, in the most current period (2010–) *recovery* (from drug dependence) is often (explicitly and implicitly) associated with "economic productivity" and a more "aspirational nation" (Cameron, 2012). Indeed, the diminished and diminishing role of harm reduction within the current Strategy is made explicit by the Home Secretary. More precisely, Theresa May MP states:

> A fundamental difference between this strategy and those that have gone before is that *instead of focusing primarily on reducing the harms caused by drug misuse*, our approach will be to go much further and offer every support for people to *choose recovery* as an achievable way out of dependency. … The solutions need to be holistic and centred around each individual, with *the expectation that full recovery is possible and desirable*. (HM Government, 2010, p. 2, emphases added)

As harm reduction may not have the prominence in UK policy as in previous years, it is perhaps necessary to contextualize the centrality of this *global* paradigm in public health initiatives.

Harm reduction as public health policy framework

Following an epidemic of HIV identified in an area of Edinburgh (Robertson, 1990), the government's Advisory Council on the Misuse of Drugs (ACMD, 1988) advocated that management of the virus be given greater priority than the prevention of injecting drug use per se. Towards such public health goals, decisions were taken to introduce basic harm reduction initiatives[7] that have since become embedded within various national Drug Strategies by the successive governments of England, Northern Ireland, Scotland and Wales (Monaghan, 2012).

Since their formal introduction in 1987 (Stimson, Alldritt, Dolan, & Donoghoe, 1988), British-based NSPs continue to operate from drug services, primary care settings, community pharmacies or as part of outreach initiatives directed at specific populations (such as sex workers, homeless/roofless). As noted by the National Institute for Health and Care Excellence[8] (NICE, 2014), the original purpose of NSP initiatives continue to be the foundation of current service provision. For example, the primary aim of providing free, sterile injecting equipment (including paraphernalia such as swabs, filters and cookers) is to reduce the transmission of blood-borne infection caused by the shared use of injecting equipment. However, NSPs also continue to provide advice and information on safer injecting technique, avoiding overdose; access to facilities for disposing used equipment and provide a street-based gateway to services such as blood-testing, vaccination and treatment options (such as opioid substitution therapy).

Statutory support for NSPs is further *acknowledged* in the 2010 Drug Strategy (HM Government, 2010). More specifically, within a strategy that prioritizes recovery from drug dependence and the goal of drug-free lifestyles, NSPs are acknowledged as initiatives that may *facilitate* this goal in reducing drug-related harm and the spread of blood-borne viruses (NICE, 2014). Indeed, this recognition and support of NSPs as an essential public health initiative is perhaps confirmed by the ongoing shared use of needles and syringes in addition to the sharing of filters, cookers and water by people who inject drugs (NICE, 2014; Public Health England [PHE], 2013b). Furthermore, national (UK) estimates of blood-borne virus amongst people who inject drugs report of almost 50% prevalence for hepatitis C (approximately 215,000 individuals) and approximately 1% for HIV (Health Protection Agency, 2012; PHE, 2013a, 2013b). As such, there is a *recognized* need to sustain the development of NSPs as a legitimate form of public health intervention and as a valid response to the street-based injecting drug use that occurs (often unreported) in towns and cities throughout the UK on a daily basis.

Street-based injecting: an overview

Street-based (or "public") injecting typically involves the preparation and injection of controlled substances (such as amphetamine sulphate, cocaine, crack cocaine and heroin) within environments that are generally accessible to (and/or frequented by) members of the general public. Street-based injecting environments may be located within community spaces and temporarily appropriated by people who use drugs for the purposes of preparing and injecting drugs. Such locations may be further categorized as either "public" or "semi-public"; with toilets, parkland and alleyways exemplifying the former – and parking lots, abandoned buildings, wasteland and stairwells comprising the latter.

Academic studies of street-based injecting has intensified and expanded at a rapid pace since 2001. Most notably, a substantial body of work from Australia, Canada and the UK has considered the impact of "place" upon injecting practice and related harm (DeBeck et al., 2009; Dovey, Fitzgerald, & Choi, 2001; Fitzgerald, 2005; Fitzgerald, Dovey, Dietze, & Rumbold, 2004; Fry, 2002; Green, Hankins, Palmer, Boivin, & Platt, 2003; Hunt, Lloyd, Kimber, & Tompkins, 2007; Marshall, Kerr, Qi, Montaner, & Wood, 2010; McKnight et al., 2007; Navarro & Leonard, 2004; Parkin, 2009, 2011b, 2013, 2014, Parkin & Coomber, 2009a, 2009b, 2010, 2011a, 2011b; Pearson, Parkin, & Coomber, 2011; Rhodes et al., 2006, 2007; Small, Rhodes, Wood, & Kerr, 2007; Taylor et al., 2006). This collective international interest in street-based injecting drug use has provided a range of shared qualitative findings regarding the appropriation of public space and injecting-related hazard that typically prioritize the perspectives of people who inject drugs. For example, it is now widely accepted that street-based injecting emerges from various "situational necessities" (Rhodes et al., 2007, p. 276). That is, the inter-relationship of influences such as homelessness, socio-economic disadvantage, drug dependence, drug-cravings and various spontaneous "opportunities" (unexpected access to drugs and/or injecting space).

In addition, the above studies have noted that street-based injecting episodes are characterized by "urgency" and a desire for "privacy" whilst accessing public locations. Urgency is a requirement that avoids detection and interruption (by authority figures such as police, security guards in addition to members of the public). An urgency to inject quickly often influences inappropriately prepared drug solutes and a hurried administration of the actual injection (Parkin, 2011b, 2013, 2014; Small et al., 2007). Privacy is regarded as essential for concealing an intimate act whilst in possession of an illicit substance (Parkin, 2013; Small et al., 2007). For each of the above reasons, free-to-access public toilets that provide cubicles (with doors that can be locked from within) have been noted as popular and preferred environments by people regularly involved in street-based injecting drug use (Parkin, 2013; Small et al., 2007).

Tackling drug-related litter: a British response to street-based injecting

As a consequence of increased reports of needlestick injuries within community settings, in addition to increasing levels of discarded injecting equipment "in the general environment", Philipp (1993) comments that these concerns mark the emergence of a "new public health problem". The newspaper headlines at the onset of this paper demonstrate that this continues to be a contemporary and controversial issue within British communities over two decades later.

Despite concerns surrounding discarded injecting equipment, it was not until October 2005, that the UK government's Department for Environment, Food, and Rural Affairs (Defra) published a report titled *Tackling drug-related litter*. This document is dedicated to the issue of managing drug-related paraphernalia that may be found in street-based settings. In essence, *Tackling drug-related litter* was produced in recognition that discarded injecting equipment in public settings may "create a very real fear of infection and disease, (and) acts as a stark reminder of the wider harm caused by the misuse of drugs" (Department for Environment, Food and Rural Affairs [Defra], 2005, p. ii).

Tackling drug-related litter also provides a series of recommendations for managing and reducing the "growing problem" (Defra, 2005, p. 1) of discarded paraphernalia in various locations; the concomitant "fear, anger, disgust and frustration" (p. 1) such items may generate, in addition to the perceived and actual harms attached to discarded injecting equipment in community/public settings. Similarly, throughout the report, Defra continuously advocates the formation of *local partnerships* and *joint-working initiatives* as a means of implementing a locally coordinated and effective response to the management of discarded drug-related paraphernalia (and by inference, street-based injecting). As such, Defra's (2005) *statutory* vision of a joined-up approach to public health and community safety prioritizes on-going liaison and intervention between *local authorities, community organizations, police constabularies, drug/alcohol services* and all *frontline employees* that may have contact with discarded equipment (whether in the public or private business sectors).

Of further import is that whilst *Tackling drug-related litter* and its various recommendations seek to promote community safety and public health, there is also underlying support for the practice and principles of harm reduction throughout the report. For example, the benefits of harm reduction intervention as part of the UK Drug Strategy is made explicit, particularly with regard to needle and syringe distribution and the relationship between drug use and sex work (Defra, 2005, pp. 3–4). Similarly, many of Defra's recommendations for "tackling" drug-related litter in community settings are premised upon pre-existing examples of "good practice" noted throughout the UK, in which public health, community safety and *harm reduction* are often central tenets of the interventions cited.

A total of 14 recommendations regarding the management of drug-related litter are made by Defra. Of these, almost all emphasize the importance of co-ordinated responses to the surveillance, management, collection and disposal of drug-related litter. Similarly, at least 11 of these 14 recommendations endorse some form of harm reduction intervention. For example, Defra suggests that local authorities and community organizations may be more proactive in formalizing agreements regarding positive policing of *used* needle possession, the siting of sharps bins in public toilets, avoiding the installation of blue lights[9] in public settings and providing training for all people who may encounter discarded equipment during the course of their employment. Indeed, the specific intervention described later in this paper (safer toilet design via the "Cambridge Model") is one that has been promoted and supported by central government policy-makers as an example of best practice – as it is one that *proactively* seeks to minimize drug-related hazard within community settings (Defra, 2005, p. 37). Each of the aforementioned activities may be described as those that seek to alter the physical environment in which they are located for the benefit of affected communities. Indeed, such projects may be further regarded as exemplars of "enabling environments" (Duff, 2009, Moore & Dietze, 2005) that purposely seek to remove obstacles at a situational/structural level in order to facilitate the practice of harm reduction (Rhodes, 2002, p. 91).

At this point, it should also be noted that Defra is *not* a body responsible for any government policy regarding illicit drug use. Nevertheless, it is a *statutory* body that works in conjunction with other central government departments (namely the Home Office and Department for Health) in promoting the current Drug Strategy (Defra, 2005, p. i). As such, *Tackling drug-related litter* may be regarded, at best, as an advisory document that provides a recommended template for good practice guidance, to be considered by all local authorities throughout the UK. Accordingly, Defra's (2005) recommendations provide *options* for local authorities and should not necessarily be interpreted as a template for national implementation.

The "Cambridge Model" of safer public toilet design

An explicit illustration of good practice in the management of drug-related litter relates to an initiative identified by Defra (2005) in the city of Cambridge (UK) and implemented by the local authority of that location. In this example, the provision of public conveniences, (similar to that contained within Figure 1[10]), is applauded and commended as an environment that appropriately "tackles" drug-related litter in community settings. More accurately, the relevant toilet

Figure 1. The "Cambridge Model" of safer public toilet design.

design aims to minimize incidents of needlestick injury (via spatial planning and spatial management) and simultaneously provides opportunities for the discrete disposal of assorted sharp items in public places whilst concealed from public view. It is especially due to the latter reasons that the overall design is regarded as a model of good practice in the *environmental* management of public health and community safety.[11]

Elsewhere, the author (Parkin, 2014) presents a series of photographic images that visualize and demonstrate the "Cambridge Model"[12] as "gold standard" design in the management of drug-related litter within public conveniences as suggested by Defra (2005). However, in the absence of such images here, the design in summary consists of several stand-alone, unisex, toilet cubicles grouped together as a single unit in a prominent "high street" location. In addition, the overtly public location and noticeable "chalet" design of the unit aims to maximize naturally occurring surveillance of any "suspect" behaviour associated within or around the immediate vicinity of the unit. These design features are applauded by Defra, as they facilitate the provision of public amenity where formalized supervision (by local authority employees or other frontline service personnel) may not necessarily be available.

The commendable design of the chalet-unit continues *within* each individual cubicle, in which discrete signage notifies patrons of the location of "sharps bins" adjacent and above washbasins. Furthermore, these notices feature *visual* icons of objects deemed suitable for disposal within the "birdhouse" opening located upon the internal fascia unit (see Figure 1). As such, appropriate items for disposal include needles and syringes in addition to other objects associated with washroom attendance (such as razor blades and safety pins). In some settings, Braille-notification also accompanies these icons in order to inform those experiencing visually impaired difficulties of the relevant disposal facilities. Overall, the symbolic, textual, tactile and visual ambiguity of the signage is a further demonstration of creditable design. This is because the non-specific notice advises the public of facilities designed for the discarding of sharp items per se rather than identify specific objects relating explicitly to injecting drug use. Accordingly, this more neutral and impartial notification possibly minimizes concerns relating to any community unease associated with the immediate community, environmental, social and physical setting (pertaining specifically to drug issues and illustrated in the newspaper headlines above).

Other commendable features within the unit that contribute to "safer toilet design" include self-contained hand-washing facilities (providing access to hot, running water, soap and drying facilities); comparatively more comfortable and more hygienic space in private settings and the provision of alarms in the event of emergency. Moreover, the absence of flat surfaces, ledges and shelves further minimize the amount of littering spaces available for the discarding of injecting paraphernalia. As such, the overall design *within* these toilet units is viewed positively by Defra (2005), as the spatial minimalism within aims to purposely reduce opportunities for needle-stick injury to occur amongst all patrons who attend public toilets (including those who may work there).

Although bespoke public conveniences such as that described above have been designed specifically with community safety in mind, they also (perhaps inadvertently) provide amenity for housing opportunities for harm reduction practice (due to safe, private, concealed space containing adequate lighting as well as cleansing and disposal facilities). At this point, it is perhaps crucial to emphasize that it would be irresponsible for any professional body to advocate toilet environments as "recommended" sites of safer injecting drug use. However, in the context of street-based injecting, (in which lifestyles are often characterized by transience, homelessness, rooflessness, unemployment and poverty), public conveniences per se do provide temporary injecting-niches that facilitate attempts at reducing drug-related harm (Parkin, 2013). Similarly, as noted earlier, episodes of street-based injecting regularly take place within public toilets on an international scale and are spatially related to "situated necessities" of those typically participant in street-based injecting.

As such, the use of toilet facilities as settings for episodes injecting drug use is a topic that is bookended by particular policy frameworks. That is, on one side, NSP settings provide the means and equipment to conduct "safer" injecting (but not the "space" to do so); and on the other a series of guidelines and recommendations dedicated to the clearance of the same items when discarded in public settings (i.e. spatial management of people and place). Street-based injecting episodes within public conveniences therefore bridge these particular concerns. However, what actually happens at "ground zero" with regard to the policies of harm reduction and the management of street-based injecting is not necessarily consistent with these particular policy designs. This latter issue is addressed in the following section that summarizes relevant findings from empirical ethnographic research located in the south of England during 2006–2011.

The research

The account described below emerged from a series of ethnographic studies of street-based injecting that were each located in various urban centres (×4) throughout the south of England (Parkin, 2009, 2011b, 2013, 2014; Parkin & Coomber, 2007, 2008, 2009a, 2009b, 2009c, 2010, 2011a, 2011b; Pearson et al., 2011).[13] All studies attached to this project were examples of applied action research that were commissioned (in full or in part) by assorted local authorities as part of rapid appraisal responses to street-based injecting drug use. All research and associated methods were ethically approved by the relevant committees.

Throughout the 5-year period of research a total of 71 people with experience of injecting drugs within a street-based setting ("in the last month") were interviewed (predominantly within NSP settings). Throughout the collapsed cohort, a typical male respondent ($n = 54$)

was aged 36, white British and originated from the immediate local area. This person would be currently unemployed; have experience of rooflessness, report current homeless and have spent time in prison as a result of drug-related offences. Similarly, a typical female respondent (n = 17) was aged 30, white British and also from the immediate local setting. This person would also have experience of rooflessness, report current homeless, be unemployed and have some experience of sex work. The average injecting career across the cohort was 11 years (although 13.5 years for male respondents and 6 years for female respondents). The overall profile of this particular cohort was therefore characterized by mid-adulthood, long-term drug dependence with widespread experience of socio-economic exclusion and unstable housing.

Furthermore, 169 frontline service personnel (e.g. toilet attendants, car park attendants, police officers, drug workers, outreach teams, security guards, etc.) were also interviewed regarding their experiences of managing street-based injecting. In addition, over 400 street-based injecting environments were attended by the author, accompanied by people who inject drugs and/or by frontline service personnel. Also attached to the various studies was a significant visual research component in which the author attempted to "picture harm reduction" with the use of photography and video (collecting over 1000 images of injecting environments and over one hour of video material).

Due to the qualitative design of this ethnographic project, methods of data generation included various forms of interviewing (unstructured, structured and semi-structured), participant observation, direct observation and observant-participation, as well as the use of the aforementioned visual methods. More detailed accounts of the above (including the epistemology, ontology and rationale underlying each study) are documented in the relevant texts (Parkin, 2013, 2014).

Presented below are findings relevant to the above discussion that relate specifically to harm reduction, public conveniences (the "Cambridge Model" in particular) and the management (by various authorities) of street-based settings appropriated for injecting episodes as noted in one particular setting.[14]

The views of people who inject drugs within the "Cambridge Model" of safer toilet design

The following section summarizes the views, opinions and experiences of people who inject drugs that relate exclusively to the "Cambridge Model" of safer toilet design as portrayed in Figures 1 and 2. These views were obtained from one of four settings during the multi-site ethnography described above. In addition, the urban centre concerned was the only location in the study where the "Cambridge Model" was made available by statutory authority. The respondent cohort (×20 individuals) relevant to the location in question was familiar with the various units that were located throughout the relevant urban centre (consisting of approximately 20 toilet cubicles within three stand-alone units). In addition, most of those interviewed had direct experience of using the toilet cubicles as a location for conducting injecting episodes. Similarly, consensus amongst those interviewed was that the drug-related litter bins within the toilets were a positive attempt by local authorities to proactively address *street-based injecting* in the urban centre concerned. Of these respondents, several individuals recognized the public health and community-safety agenda that typically underlies such initiatives. For example:

> I've noticed in some places they are putting sharps boxes and I think, "well, that's not encouraging (street-based injecting)". I think it's realistic. They know (street-based injecting) is happening. And, it's better than people leaving (injecting paraphernalia) on the floor, because, like, Hep C virus can stay alive for 90 days (outside of the body) ... (Respondent 08, Male)

> I think it's a great idea. I thought it was very well thought out because obviously there are people that are injecting and they don't want (to keep) needles on them ... and not everyone is of the state of mind

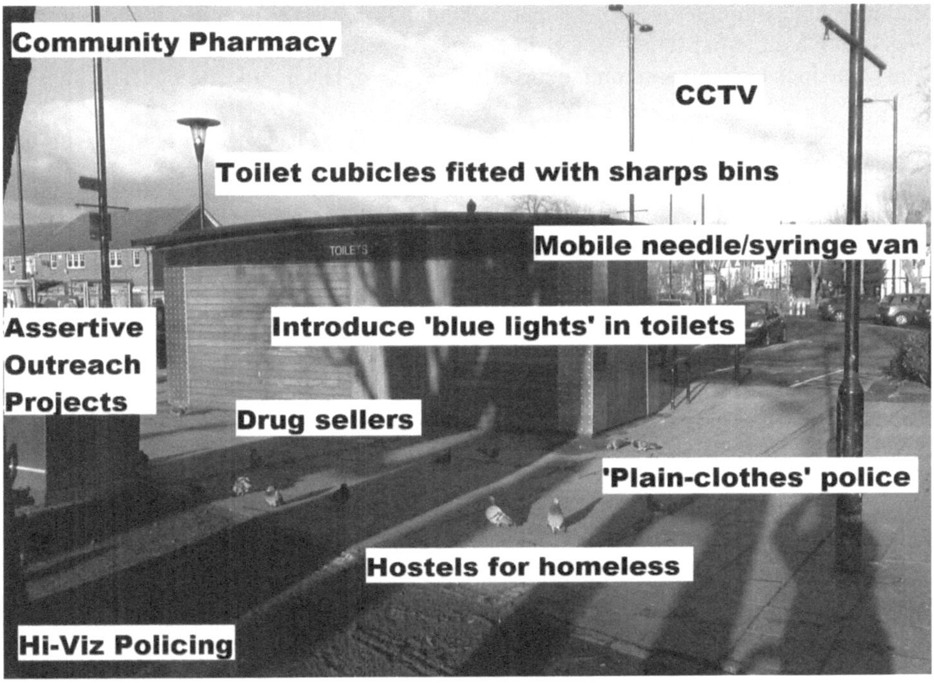

Figure 2. A visualization of colliding intervention in the spatial management of street-based injecting and drug-related litter within settings of public convenience (UK).

> just to put the lid back on. So you don't want people coming across (discarded sharps) and getting it in the foot or whatever. I think it's a great idea that there is a place where they can be disposed of safely ... (Respondent 20, Male)

However, the presence of public toilets equipped with facilities for depositing injecting paraphernalia was also viewed with some confusion relating to an "operational ambiguity". For example, some respondents were of the belief that the relevant local council were explicitly "catering for" street-based drug users in providing informal, locally sanctioned, *environments of injecting drug use*. In these particular responses, the term "safety" was not used in the context of public health. Instead, "safety" was used as an indigenous expression to describe the absence of police intervention, in settings (toilets with sharps bins) which appeared to offer a temporary sanctuary from possible arrest. For example:

> I don't know if it's because they've (injecting drug users) been told it's a safer place, but what I've noticed in them toilets is you've got a hole for sharps and stuff like that. So I don't know if they've like ... they probably like seen that in the past and thought, "Yeah you can go there (to inject) ... it's a *safe* place to come and go" because of that. (Respondent 18, Male, emphasis added)

Similarly:

> Well it's *safe* I suppose because if you didn't have a 'cin bin (portable sharps container) on you, you can at least discard your needle safely (in there). (And) because you can lock the (toilet door) and if people are sort of like "pee-ing" in there when they (inject), they'd be able to discard everything anyway. So nobody would know that they had been (injecting) there anyway. (Respondent 16, Female, emphasis added)

Indeed, this spatial ambiguity is further supported in the following extract in which the respondent perceives the "Cambridge Model" of toilet design as a semi-formal injecting setting that is simultaneously the focus of increased police surveillance of people who inject drugs (and their arrest).

> I've been arrested in a few toilets as well, when I've been standing (injecting) in the toilets (cubicles). I've used them a lot of the time (for injecting heroin). And there's also toilets which are the same (design at a nearby location). And … on the wall they've got the needle bin … where you put needle disposals and all sorts like that. So really … (street based injecting) is sort of, like, being catered for, isn't it? It is, isn't it? Really, it is. If you've got them amenities in there. (Respondent 03, Female)

Similarly:

> In public toilets, the (sharps) facilities some of them have, I think, should be made more widespread … but only on the basis that we can go to these places discretely, with discretion and without the fear of having that *bang, bang, bang*. "We're (police) outside waiting for you". (Respondent 01, Male)

Nevertheless, the ambiguity and function of settings equipped with sharps bins is perhaps superfluous in the context of *street-based* injecting, especially when considered alongside associative issues such as drug dependence, homelessness, avoiding arrest and addressing withdrawal symptoms. Indeed, when situated within these particular experiences of injecting drug use, any environmental ambiguity associated with places of shelter is diminished in the pursuit of "feeling well again". For example:

> … put it this way, if you're feeling that rough and you've got a bag (of heroin), you've got your works on you, you'll find a way of doing it and you *will* find a place to do it. And obviously if those toilets are there and they've got sharps facilities to be used then I think it's probably better for everyone concerned to (inject there) … . but I don't think it's promoting you to do it there because (street-based injecting) is not everyone's cup of tea. (Respondent 07, Male)

Similar sentiments to each of the aforementioned points may be noted in the following extract in which the individual recognizes the value attached to the safer design features within the relevant public toilets. However, the added inference regarding an absence of more "specialized" harm reduction provision for people who inject drugs ("us") and who may continue to inject within public conveniences adds poignancy to this particular observation.

> I'm assuming it's the council that have obviously put this all into process. But when the toilets were going to be built, (they must have said) "Right, well let's put this into the equation to make it better". I don't think it's better for *us* ((laughs)) but it is better for the general public. (Respondent 12, Male, emphasis added)

Indeed, the limited harm reduction value afforded by toilet cubicles per se is further noted in the following comment. In this extract, the respondent articulates how the immediate and positive benefits afforded by "place" may be forever reduced by the negative consequences of injecting drugs behind locked doors of public conveniences (whether they are equipped with sharps bins or not).

> ((*sighs*)) … (the toilets are) a good thing as in that you've got somewhere to go. But it's a bad thing because if you lock yourself in, and you go over (overdose), then you're fucked … (Respondent 17, Male)

Ethnographic observations

Whilst the above views typify those from a cohort of street-involved, mainly homeless people who report long-term dependence to heroin and/or crack cocaine, it is evident that the "Cambridge Model" of toilet provision is viewed positively *and* with suspicion by those who inject drugs. In short, the spatial ambiguity and operational rationale of providing public toilets equipped with drug-related litter bins appears to raise confusion regarding the "official" intent and purpose of the receptacles.

As a means to further comprehend this confusion, suspicion and uncertainty one perhaps needs to fully appreciate the immediate environmental setting in which one of the units was situated at the time of fieldwork (2011). Figure 2 presents a visual depiction of ethnographic observation conducted at the site concerned during a three-month period of fieldwork (by the author; conducted alone and/or whilst accompanied by frontline service personnel). In the relevant environment, multiple injecting episodes were known to take place (by numerous services) on a regular basis. The figure presents a rear view of the toilet block (located adjacent a parking lot in a "high street" location) and is surrounded by textblocks that aim to "map" a variety of (drug-related) services and interventions that surrounded this particular setting on a daily basis.

Accordingly, the immediate environment adjacent the toilet block was frequented by street-based drug sellers as well as by people who inject drugs. Nearby was a hostel that provided short-term accommodation for those reporting homelessness and/or multiple dependence issues (in which staff were reported to enforce penalties and sanctions for ownership of injecting paraphernalia whilst on the premises). Opposite the toilet block was a community pharmacist that dispensed methadone prescriptions for those attending a drug treatment centre in the town centre; a mobile NSP visited the parking lot at specific times of the week and (statutory and third sector) outreach workers regularly patrolled the area due to known associations with rough sleeping. In addition to the above, the immediate environment was under constant surveillance by CCTV cameras that were positioned immediately outside (and focused upon) the toilet block; "hi-viz" policing regularly occurred around the area (with patrol cars/vans often stationed nearby) and "plain-clothes" ("undercover") police officers were known to operate throughout the vicinity. Finally, despite the constant presence of policing and/or surveillance, the installation of fluorescent blue lights within the toilets was also considered as a possible "solution" to prevent future episodes of injecting drug use in the relevant toilet unit. (It later became evident to the author that the relevant body was also aware that such installations were the antithesis of Defra recommendations and contrary to the recommended design of public toilets per se).

Upon awareness of the various forms of environmental management employed by various bodies of local and statutory authority within this setting is made apparent, the confusion and suspicion held by people who inject drugs in this location is perhaps further clarified. Indeed, from the perspective of those who do *not* inject drugs, it is perhaps unclear what is to be achieved by the implementation and availability of multiple interventions in the vicinity that both enable and problematize harm reduction within such a concentrated and contained area. As such, it is feasible to suggest that this uncertainty relates to a conflict of interest associated with the four pillars of (UK) drug policy, in which "prevention", "treatment" and "enforcement" services collide within and around a particular environmental setting known for injecting drug use (the toilet cubicles). However, the overall effect of this "colliding intervention" is the delegitimizing and disconnecting of attempts to influence harm reduction intervention/practice within that specific location. Whilst this generalization may initially appear somewhat sensationalist, it may be further validated by events noted in *Cambridge* both during and after the collection of all data during the author's fieldwork. This is described in full detail in the following section.

The rise and fall of the "Cambridge Model"

Although the author did not conduct any fieldwork in the city of Cambridge at any point during the study, communications were exchanged with a Manager of street services in connection with discussions regarding the implementation and operation of the toilets described in the Defra (2005) report. For example, with regard to the perceived impact the "Cambridge Model" had upon drug-related litter and street-based injecting in Cambridge itself, the aforementioned Manager wrote the following to the author (circa 2009 emphases added):

> We have 60 toilet cubicles with this type of disposal. I can say these disposal facilities are heavily used. We use 7 litre sharps containers and in some high use toilets we can change a bin once a week. We have never counted the number of syringes but know that the majority of syringes seem to be 1 or 2 mil (barrels) but there are also a significant number of 5 mil (barrels). *What (the bins have) done is greatly reduce the number of needles found in the area around the toilets.*
>
> In one case, where the toilets are in a multi-storey car park, prior to the toilets being modernised, used needles were regularly found in the car park. Since the toilets now have needle disposal, *it is rare for a used needle to be found in the car park.* The approach taken (by the relevant local authority) in providing needle disposal in public toilets was quite controversial. However, our legal advice and risk assessment at the time put public – *and staff*- safety first and therefore needle disposal was introduced in the toilets. It was also recognised that the legitimate users of needles (diabetics) may want to dispose of used equipment.
>
> *(We have) never taken the view to use so called (blue) "lights" in public toilets to deter drug users.* (Name deleted) has always taken the view that public toilets are for everybody to use and that the public and our cleaning staff should feel safe and confident to use them. I must admit that our experience is that our drug users respect this approach and leave the facilities as they found them. We have never had complaints from the public that they have been put off using our toilets because they are used by drug users.
>
> I have campaigned for a number of years with colleagues in other agencies that public toilets are not provided as safe injecting rooms. *But in the absence of anything else ... I would rather needle users access a clean and well lit public toilet; inject safely, and leave rather than go into the bushes, car park or dimly lit alley with no washing provision or proper disposal for needles.* (Manager, personnel communication via email)

From the above testimony, an enabling approach to harm reduction, street-based injecting and the environmental management of injecting environments is evident. This may be noted in decisions to avoid blue light installations; the decrease in discarded injecting paraphernalia in the immediate public area and a desire to provide an appropriate, hygienic and illuminated setting for injecting purposes.

It is also worthwhile to reiterate that it was precisely this project in Cambridge (and its approach to drug-related litter management) that received commendation from within a *department of central government* (Defra, 2005). However, divergence from this support for harm reduction may be noticed in an analysis of online media reports of the same setting several years later. For example, four years later in 2013, the exact same facilities were branded as a "health hazard" (see opening headlines) and the same toilet facilities appear to have been a site of targeted enforcement by the local constabulary. More specifically, as reported in the *Cambridge News*:

> The (police) officer said: "Daily patrols have been undertaken at varied times throughout the day. Police officers have arrested two males for possession and use of drugs in the toilets." He went on to report that police found two men sleeping rough in the toilets and in possession of stolen goods, adding both were arrested. But addicts using the toilet claim they are getting a mixed message. One addict, who did not wish to be named, told the News: "I don't get why they have facilities in the toilets to dispose of our needles after we inject if they are going to arrest us for that very thing. It's a Catch 22."

This strategic shift noted in Cambridge over a four-year period appears consistent with the environmental management of the location visualized in Figure 2. More accurately, it demonstrates the way in which a collision of enforcement and harm reduction procedures establishes environmental uncertainty that is emphasized by conflicting intervention (underpinned by the "addict's" comment above). Furthermore, the shift towards enforcement procedures in Cambridge (in 2013) would appear *inconsistent* to the reportage below describing events in 2011 (provided by the same newspaper regarding the same initiative).

> Council bosses hope the huge boost in syringes put into sharps bins means addicts are getting the message about disposing of needles safely.
>
> There has been a *56 per cent rise* in syringes put into bins or dumped in the city's council-run toilets, new data obtained by the News has revealed.
>
> In 2008, 3,721 needles were collected from the 20 conveniences but that number increased to 4,088 the following year, 5,025 in 2010 and 5,806 so far this year.
>
> Cambridge MP (Name) met police and held an emergency meeting last year on how to tackle the number of dirty syringes discarded in the streets of Cambridge.
>
> (Name) (title of post), said: "I think addicts are getting the message and *we welcome the fact that more needles are being disposed of in the correct way.* We have been campaigning hard for this and working closely with our partners. *This is good news.*"[15] (Cambridge News, 02 December 2011, emphases added)

Discussion

Presented above are two case studies of a public health and community-safety initiative (located in two different English towns/cities) that has been here termed the "Cambridge Model". Both projects attempted to establish enabling environments for the practice and principles of harm reduction to occur and were housed within bespoke, stand-alone public toilets in "high street" settings. Furthermore, the design and intent of the initiative in question has been previously applauded by Defra, a body within central government dedicated to environmental concerns (such as drug-related litter in community settings). However, despite the well-intended introduction of the initiative by particular sectors of local authority in the relevant settings, any *harm reduction* value attached to the scheme appears to have gradually eroded over time. Indeed, it is perhaps more accurate to state that all harm reduction value of the safer toilet scheme (in these settings) appears to have been *undermined* by enforcement procedures including the targeted policing of injecting drug users.

Accordingly, one may conclude that statutory guidelines pertaining to harm reduction at a national (macro) level are challenged by opposing authorities at a local (micro) level. In this regard, good practice guidelines relating to harm reduction are disregarded in the interests of the *environmental management* of drug-related litter, street-based injecting and people who inject drugs.

Indeed, this situation does not appear unique to the two the urban settings described above. Findings from Blenkharn's (2008) online audit of drug-related litter management strategies by services *throughout the UK* describe inconsistent collection procedures conducted by over 500 organizations (including statutory bodies). Blenkharn notes that some organizations promoted "confused, inadequate and misleading information" with materials disseminated to the general public regarding the appropriate collection and discarding of drug-related litter. Similarly, the audit noted only limited evidence of dedicated drug-related litter bins made available in "high risk areas" of street-based injecting drug use. Given the direction and assistance available from central government (Defra, 2005), these inconsistent approaches to the management of discarded injecting paraphernalia at a unitary level appear to further support the conclusion above. In addition, the apparent lack of dedicated drug-related litter bins installed in public settings for "safer" disposal of injecting paraphernalia appears equally disconcerting given the positive evaluation such low-threshold intervention has previously received in numerous international settings (Defra, 2005; de Montigney, Moudon, Leigh, & Young, 2010; Parkin, 2013; Riley et al., 1998).

Colliding intervention in public spaces: an empirical demonstration of "risk environment"

Despite a history of demonstrable impact upon public health and community safety, many harm reduction initiatives are consistently viewed with caution, controversy and/or objection (Colon & Marston, 1999; Drucker, 2006; Forte, 2015; Korner & Treloar, 2003; Smith, 2010; Strike, Myers, & Millson, 2004; Takahashi, 1997; Ti & Kerr, 2014; Treloar & Fraser, 2007). This hesitancy is typically shared at micro-levels of society, especially by local authority, provincial media outlets and the general public. This resistance to harm reduction in community settings therefore appears to establish a policy-related paradox; as the practice and principles of such initiatives are typically supported within national policy frameworks as part of strategic intervention to protect public health and reduce drug-related harm and hazard.

A demonstration of this paradox has been presented above, in which an environmentally based initiative (designed to protect public health and reduce discarded injecting equipment in street-based/community settings) within sites of public convenience is regarded from a variety of conflicting perspectives. From a local authority perspective, the initiative may be regarded as an attempt to establish enabling environments for harm reduction to occur in a manner that is consistent with central government guidelines regarding the proactive, environmental, management of drug-related litter. Furthermore, the explicit aim of drug-related litter bins in toilet cubicles is to provide discrete locations for the anonymous and concealed disposal of used injecting equipment. However, this aim has also been interpreted as the implicit creation of informal injecting cubicles from the perspective of people who inject drugs. Accordingly, when such locations become the focus of a third perspective, (that of increased policing and enforcement procedures by local constabularies), street-involved individuals view the initiative with suspicion and caution. A fourth perspective lies in (mainly pejorative and/or moralistic) reports published online and in local media outlets that typically portray public toilets affected by injecting episodes as environments despoiled and corrupted by dirt, danger and/or disease. Collectively, these various micro-level perspectives concerning enabling environments, harm reduction, law enforcement and stigma collide to establish a socially constructed "risk environment" in which it appears uncertain to the central protagonists whether street-based injecting drug use is a *public health* issue, a *community-safety* issue, a *criminal* issue or a *moral* issue.

For the above reasons, this paper provides an empirical assessment of the "risk environment" thesis advocated by Rhodes (2002, 2009) which seeks to provide a sociological framework for understanding (and reducing) drug-related harm. According to Rhodes, this framework defines the risk environment as the physical and social spaces in which a variety of micro-/macro-level factors interact to increase opportunities for drug-related harm to be *reduced* and/or *produced*. Consequently, consideration of the risk environment thesis seeks to "understand the environmental determinants of harm as a means to creating 'enabling environments' for harm reduction" (Rhodes, 2002, p. 91). However, as noted throughout this paper, the establishment of enabling environments (the "Cambridge Model") in various community settings does not always have the desired effect of reducing drug-related harm. Instead, the colliding interventions; including the micro-level interpretation of macro-level policies and continued episodes of street-based injecting highlight the difficulties raised by competing social/structural factors that may increase vulnerability to drug-related harm. These factors relate to the informal establishment of street-based injecting environments by people who use drugs; the role of policing and targeted enforcement by local constabularies and the negative portrayal of enabling environments and street-based injecting environments within provincial media reports.

Whereas the appropriation of street-based injecting environments (within toilet cubicles) should be regarded as an outcome of assorted situated necessities by people who use drugs (relating to disadvantage and inequity), the surrounding environmental pressures brought about by increased policing provides opportunities for drug-related harm to continue. This harm may include detention and arrest; rushed preparation/injection; displacement of injecting to more concealed locations and may subsequently diminish the efforts of NSP, outreach workers and municipal authority in minimizing such hazards. At the very least, these conflicting practices of applied drug policy and spatial management suggest that a micro-level interpretation of each is somehow *disconnected* from macro-level strategies. Furthermore, local level intervention does not necessarily reflect a strategic, joined-up approach and/or politically integrated response to *street-based injecting drug use*.

A European approach to local intervention?

As noted elsewhere (Chheng, Leang, Thomson, Moore, & Crofts, 2012) successful components of harm reduction initiatives prioritize the coordination and cooperation of various stakeholder organizations and their relevant policies and practice. This principle is advocated consistently throughout *Tackling Drug-related Litter* (Defra, 2005), especially with regard to the formation of *local partnerships* and *joint-working initiatives* (between *local authorities*, *community organizations*, *police constabularies*, *drug/alcohol services* and *frontline personnel*) seek to provide meaningful responses to issues surrounding street-based injecting. However, as emphasized throughout this paper, such approaches to street-based injecting/drug-related litter do not appear standard responses throughout areas of local authority in England. Indeed, the evidence of colliding intervention noted above suggests there is a need for local authorities and national governments (throughout the UK) to adopt a more inspired, innovative and pragmatic approach to the *spatial management* of street-based injecting drug use.

One possible approach to reducing drug-related harm in street-based settings may be the introduction of Safer Injecting Facilities[16] (SIF), especially in locations where concentrated episodes of street-based injecting may frequently occur. Facilities of this nature have been widely available throughout Europe since 1986 (Hedrich, 2004; Stoever, 2002) and, according to the Drug Policy Alliance, 92 SIF operated in 62 international cities in 2012. SIF are defined as legally sanctioned, medically supervised health-care facilities designed primarily to reduce harm associated with drug use (Kimber, Dolan, & Wodak, 2005; Wright & Tompkins, 2004). The principal aim of SIF is to provide hygienic environments for individuals to use drugs in a safe and supervised manner and to physically remove them (if only temporarily) from harms associated with injecting in public locations (Hall & Kimber, 2005, Wright & Tompkins, 2004). In addition, SIF provide low-threshold opportunities that reduce the sharing and discarding of injecting equipment in an environment that prioritizes hygiene and risk management. In 2015, no similar amenity exists (or has ever existed) in any location throughout the UK – as they are generally considered too politically controversial to implement (Strathdee & Pollini, 2007). Nevertheless, support for such initiatives has been made public by various figures of local authority. For example, both the Chief Constable of Durham Constabulary and the Police and Crime Commissioner for the same region have each advocated[17] the harm reduction and crime reduction benefits associated with such intervention, as well as highlighting the impact such facilities may have upon the local authority management of drug-related litter. Despite support from such influential individuals, SIF are unlikely to feature in national drug strategies of current/future government. This pessimism may be explained with the emphasis placed upon the *single-issue* currently at the heart of the national Drug Strategy (HM Government, 2010): namely, *recovery* from dependent drug use (that overtly emphasizes a structural shift away from harm reduction policies).

Although SIF may not currently be a viable option in the UK, the spatial management of drug-related issues may be informed by equally pragmatic and innovative models of policy design also noted throughout continental Europe. For example, a European Monitoring Centre for Drugs and Drug Addiction report regarding "drugs policy and the city" acknowledges that "the adoption of drugs strategies at national level has become a standard feature of the public administrative response to drug problems in Europe, (but) a more *unclear and complex situation exists at city level*" (2015, p. 3, emphasis added). In short, different cities have different drug issues to address in which a generic national strategy is not always appropriate. For this reason a number of European cities have developed "city-level policies" that provide bespoke responses to issues (such as open drug scenes, proactive outreach, drug tourism) considered environmentally and spatially specific to those settings. Perhaps most significantly, city-level policies "can mirror or depart from the concerns of national ones" (2015, p. 13) in which city authorities formulate a strategic response that runs parallel the interests of the state.

Accordingly, the introduction of a "city-level policy" by unitary and municipal authorities throughout the UK may provide a framework for more networked and complementary responses to locally relevant concerns. Such an approach would unite key stakeholders in providing a co-ordinated and synchronized response to local issues (such as street-based injecting and drug-related litter management) with the aim of avoiding the various collisions identified above. Indeed, the necessary structures to implement a city-level policy appear to already exist in the form of local authority resources, drug and alcohol services and locally elected Police and Crime Commissioners. In an idealistic setting, these various actors would formulate local policy dedicated to solution-focused, harm reduction responses to geographically relevant issues within their particular administrative area. Indeed, a micro-level partnership of this design would also appear consistent with attempts to reduce drug-related harm within a *local* framework that prioritizes the underlying constructions of *indigenous* "risk environments". Furthermore, a micro-level policy of this design may actually *complement* any macro-level national drug strategy (and may even *facilitate* the aims and objectives of single-themes within the latter).

Finally, in the absence of such innovative approaches to drug policy, it is perhaps worth noting that "public health and harm reduction are parallel social movements" (Rhodes, 2002, p. 85) that share common ground with regard to the reduction of health-related risk and harm via *individual, community, policy and environmental change*. However, such goals may not be achieved if attempts at creating environments for enabling harm reduction are disrupted by intervention that is characterized by collision.

Acknowledgements

The views, opinions and academic content in this paper are those of the author. These views, opinions and interpretations should not necessarily be associated with any previous/current body/people associated with the research described throughout this text. In addition, these views and opinions are not necessarily shared or held by any institution to which the author has been previously or currently attached (especially those associated with the author's current position at the University of Manchester). The author acknowledges the support of Mr G. Halksworth for this paper. The author thanks the relevant authority for its permission to reproduce visual data obtained from the relevant study described in this work (which must remain anonymous to be consistent with the text). Selected paragraphs in this paper have been reproduced with permission (in an amended and edited form) from Parkin, S. (2014). *An applied visual sociology: Picturing harm reduction*. Farnham: Ashgate/Gower, Copyright © 2014.

Disclosure statement

No potential conflict of interest was reported by the author.

Notes

1. http://www.somersetcountygazette.co.uk/news/10129034.Shopper_finds_needles_in_Taunton_public_toilets/?ref=rss (accessed 1 July 2014).
2. http://www.cambridge-news.co.uk/Cambridge/Drug-users-arrested-in-Cambridges-health-hazard-loos-20130405151852.htm#ixzz2nqMgEoRz (accessed 1 July 2014).
3. http://www.ely-news.co.uk/News/Elys-public-toilets-rife-with-drug-activity-20130419095033.htm#ixzz2nqV9xVmY (accessed 1 July 2014).
4. http://www.sunderlandecho.com/news/crime/council-cleaner-s-hiv-test-wait-after-drug-needle-stab-in-sunderland-toilets-1-5901925 (accessed 1 July 2014).
5. http://www.hastingsobserver.co.uk/news/local/call-for-drug-haven-conveniences-to-be-closed-1-5745846 (accessed 1 July 2014).
6. The wider ethnographic research attached to this work has noted that attempts to manage street-based injecting in this manner do not necessarily remove the activity from the built environment. Instead such coercive practice typically tends to displace and disperse people who use drugs to more marginalised, more concealed settings of *harm production* (Parkin, 2008, 2011a, 2013).
7. Needle and syringe programmes (NSPs) and opioid substitution therapy.
8. According to the NICE website, this is a Non-departmental Public Body independent of government, but sponsored by the Department of Health. It is an organisation that provides advice and guidance to improve health and social care (see www.nice.org.uk).
9. Researchers in England and Canada (Crabtree et al., 2013; Parkin, 2009, 2013, 2014; Parkin & Coomber, 2010) have each concluded that the installation of fluorescent blue lights designed to prevent injecting drug use can contribute to participation in more *harmful* injecting practice by those involved in more regular street-based injecting episodes.
10. Figures 1 and 2 are ***not*** of the public toilets in Cambridge described in the Defra (2005) report. Instead, they are photographs taken during the author's fieldwork of public toilets that may be regarded as 'almost identical' to the 'Cambridge model' advocated by Defra (i.e. same toilet, different location).
11. Such facilities are ***not*** purposely designed to house-injecting episodes.
12. The actual design is that of a Swedish public toilet manufacturer who produce bespoke, stand-alone conveniences in a variety of European countries (see www.danfo.com), whereas the 'Cambridge Model' is a term coined by the author for purposes of convenience [*sic*] only.
13. The initial study (2006–2009) was conducted as the author's doctoral research and was funded by a Collaborative Award in Science and Engineering Studentship provided by the Economic and Social Research Council of Great Britain as well as by a relevant body within local government of the setting concerned (a body formerly known as a Drug and Alcohol Action Team that was responsible for the implementation of the national Drug Strategy at a local level). Research conducted during the period 2010–2011 may be regarded as 'postdoctoral' and furthered studies of the same topic.
14. Purposely not identified for reasons relating to 'anonymity' of setting.
15. http://www.cambridge-news.co.uk/News/Almost-6000-drugs-needles-disposed-of-in-Cambridge-public-toilets-02122011.htm#ixzz2nqOYLrHp. *Postscript*: Events in Cambridge surrounding drug-related litter continue to make local news. In April 2015, the *Cambridge News* provided a map of '16 top hotspots where dirty needles are found' in various public settings during the first quarter of 2015. See http://www.cambridge-news.co.uk/16-hotspots-dirty-needles-Cambridge-map/story-26410740-detail/story.html#ixzz3g8m2h84t (accessed 17 July 2015).
16. also known as Drug Consumption Rooms.
17. http://www.bbc.co.uk/news/uk-england-29566218 (accessed 17 July 2015) and http://www.bbc.co.uk/news/uk-england-24730381 (accessed 17 July 2015).

References

ACMD. (1988). *AIDS and drug misuse*. Part 1 (Report by Advisory Council on the Misuse of Drugs). HMSO: London.

Berridge, V. (2012). The rise, fall, and revival of recovery in drug policy. *Lancet*, *379*(9810), 22–23.

Blenkharn, J. I. (2008). Clinical wastes in the community: Local authority management of discarded drug litter. *Public Health, 122*, 725–728.

Cabinet Office, HMSO. (1998). *Tackling drugs to build a better Britain*. London: Author.

Cameron, D. (2012, October 10). *Conservative Party conference keynote speech*. Conservative Party annual conference, Birmingham. Retrieved April 5, 2014, from http://www.theguardian.com/news/datablog/2012/oct/10/david-cameron-conservative-party-conference-speech

Chheng, K., Leang, S., Thomson, N., Moore, T., & Crofts, N. (2012). Harm reduction in Cambodia: A disconnect between policy and practice. *Harm Reduction Journal, 9*, 30. Retrieved from http://www.harmreductionjournal.com/content/9/1/30

Colon, I., & Marston, B. (1999). Resistance to a residential AIDS home. *Journal of Homosexuality, 37*, 135–145.

Crabtree, A., Mercer, G., Horan, R., Grant, S., Tan, T., & Buxton, J. A. (2013). A qualitative study of the perceived effects of blue lights in washrooms on people who use injection drugs. *Harm Reduction Journal, 10*, 22. Retrieved from http://www.harmreductionjournal.com/content/10/1/22

DeBeck, K., Small, W., Wood, E., Li, K., Montaner, J. S. G., & Kerr, T. (2009). Public injecting among a cohort of injecting drug users in Vancouver, Canada. *Journal of Epidemiology and Community Health, 63*, 81–86.

Department for Environment, Food and Rural Affairs. (2005). *Tackling drug-related litter: Guidance and good practice*. London: Author.

Department of Health. (1995). *Tackling drugs together*. London: Author.

Dovey, K., Fitzgerald, J., & Choi, Y. (2001). Safety becomes danger: Dilemmas of drug-use in public space. *Health and Place, 7*, 319–331.

Drucker, E. (2006). Insite: Canada's landmark safe injecting program at risk. *Harm Reduction Journal, 3*. Retrieved from http://www.harmreductionjournal.com/content/3/1/24

Drug Policy Alliance. (2012). *Supervised injection facilities: Resource sheet*. New York: Author.

Duff, C. (2009). The drifting city: The role of affect and repair in the development of 'enabling environments'. *International Journal of Drug Policy, 20*, 202–208.

European Monitoring Centre for Drugs and Drug Addiction. (2015). *Drugs policy and the city in Europe*. Lisbon: Author.

Fitzgerald, J. L. (2005). Policing as public health menace in the policy struggles over public injecting. *International Journal of Drug Policy, 16*, 203–206.

Fitzgerald, J., Dovey, K., Dietze, P., & Rumbold, G. (2004). Health outcomes and quasi-supervised settings for street injecting drug use. *International Journal on Drug Policy, 15*, 247–257.

Forte, J. A. (2015). Not in my social world: A cultural analysis of media representations, contested spaces, and sympathy for the homeless. *The Journal of Sociology & Social Welfare, 29*(4), Article 9. Retrieved from: http://scholarworks.wmich.edu/jssw/vol29/iss4/9

Fry, C. L. (2002). Injecting drug user attitudes towards rules for supervised injecting rooms: Implications for uptake. *International Journal of Drug Policy, 13*, 471–476.

Galvani, S. (2012). *Supporting people with alcohol and drug problems*. Bristol: Policy Press.

Green, T., Hankins, C., Palmer, D., Boivin, J.-F., & Platt, R. (2003, July). Ascertaining the need for a Safer Injecting Facility (SIF): The burden of public injecting in Montreal, Canada. *Journal of Drug Issues, 33*(3), 713–731.

Hall, W., & Kimber, J. (2005, March 18). Being realistic about benefits of supervised injecting facilities. *The Lancet*.

Health Protection Agency. (2012). *Shooting up: Infections among people who inject drugs in the United Kingdom 2011*. Health Protection Agency, Health Protection Scotland, Public Health Wales, and Public Health Agency Northern Ireland, London.

Hedrich, D. (2004). *European report on drug consumption rooms*. Luxemburg: European Monitoring Centre for Drugs and Drug Addiction.

Heed, K. (2006). Response: If enforcement is not working, what are the alternatives? *International Journal of Drug Policy, 17*(2), 104–106.

HM Government. (2008). *Drugs: Protecting families and communities: The 2008 drug strategy*. London: Home Office.

HM Government. (2010). *Drug strategy 2010: Reducing demand, restricting supply, building recovery: Supporting people to live a drug free life*. London: HMSO.

Hunt, N., Lloyd, C., Kimber, J., & Tompkins, C. (2007). Public injecting and willingness to use a drug consumption room among needle exchange programme attendees in the UK. *International Journal of Drug Policy, 18*, 62–65.

Kimber, J., Dolan, K., & Wodak, A. (2005). Survey of drug consumption rooms: Service delivery and perceived public health and amenity impact. *Drug and Alcohol Review, 24*, 21–24.

Korner, H., & Treloar, C. (2003). Needle and syringe programmes in the local media: 'Needle anger' versus 'effective education in the community'. *International Journal of Drug Policy, 15*, 46–55.

MacPherson, D., Mulla, Z., & Richardson, L. (2006). The evolution of drug policy in Vancouver, Canada: Strategies for preventing harm from psychoactive substance use. *International Journal of Drug Policy, 17*(2), 85–95.

Marshall, B. D., Kerr, T., Qi, J., Montaner, J. S. G., & Wood, E. (2010). Public injecting and HIV risk behaviour among street-involved youth. *Drug and Alcohol Dependence, 110*, 254–258.

McKnight, I., Maas, B., Wood, E., Tyndall, M. W., Small, W., Lai, C., ... Kerr, T. (2007). Factors associated with public injecting among users of Vancouver's Supervised Injecting Facility. *American Journal of Drug and Alcohol Abuse, 33*, 319–326.

Monaghan, M. (2012). The recent evolution of UK drug strategies: From maintenance to behaviour change. *People, Place and Policy Online, 6*, 29–40.

de Montigney, L., Moudon, A. V., Leigh, B., & Young, K. (2010). Assessing a drop box programme: A spatial analysis of discarded needles. *International Journal of Drug Policy, 21*, 208–214.

Moore, D., & Dietze, P. (2005). Enabling environments and the reduction of drug-related harm: Reframing Australian policy and practice. *Drug and Alcohol Review, 24*, 275–284.

Navarro, C., & Leonard, L. (2004). Prevalence and factors related to public injecting in Ottawa, Canada: Implications for the development of a trial safer injecting facility. *International Journal of Drug Policy, 15*, 275–284.

NICE. (2014). *Needle and syringe programmes: NICE public health guidance 52.*

Parkin, S. (2008, June 17–18). *From one space to another. The displacement of risk behaviour (injecting drug use) in an urban environment.* Ways of living: Inequalities, risks and choices, 1st annual ENQUIRE conference, University of Nottingham.

Parkin, S. (2009). *The effect of place on health risk: A qualitative study of micro-injecting environments* (Unpublished PhD thesis). University of Plymouth.

Parkin, S. (2011a, October 3–5). *Colliding interventions: The problematising of public injecting drug use.* Contemporary drug problems conference: Beyond the buzzword: Problematising 'drugs', Prato, Italy.

Parkin, S. (2011b). Identifying and predicting drug-related harm with applied qualitative research. In J. Katz, S. Peace, & S. Spurr (Eds.), *Adult lives: A life course perspective* (pp. 439–448). Bristol: Policy Press.

Parkin, S. (2013). *Habitus and drug using environments: Health, place and lived experience.* Farnham: Ashgate.

Parkin, S. (2014). *An applied visual sociology: Picturing harm reduction.* Farnham: Ashgate.

Parkin, S., & Coomber, R. (2007). *A rapid appraisal of public injecting sites and drug related litter in Plymouth* (Unpublished Report for Plymouth Drug and Alcohol Action Team). University of Plymouth.

Parkin, S., & Coomber, R. (2008). *A comparative study of drug related litter collected in Plymouth during 2006–2007 and 2007–2008* (Unpublished Report for Plymouth Drug and Alcohol Team). University of Plymouth.

Parkin, S., & Coomber, R. (2009a). 'Informal sorter houses': A qualitative insight of the 'shooting gallery' phenomenon in a UK setting. *Health and Place, 15*, 981–989.

Parkin, S., & Coomber, R. (2009b). Public injecting and symbolic violence. *Addiction Research and Theory, 17*(4), 390–405.

Parkin, S., & Coomber, R. (2009c). *An informal evaluation of drug-related litter bins in Plymouth City Centre* (Unpublished Report for Plymouth Drug and Alcohol Action Team). University of Plymouth.

Parkin, S., & Coomber, R. (2010). Fluorescent blue lights, injecting drug use and related health risk in public conveniences: Findings from a qualitative study of micro-injecting environments. *Health and Place, 16*, 629–637.

Parkin, S., & Coomber, R. (2011a). Public injecting drug use and the social production of harmful practice in high-rise tower blocks (London, UK): A Lefebvrian analysis. *Health and Place, 17*, 717–726.

Parkin, S., & Coomber, R. (2011b). Injecting drug user views (and experiences) of drug-related litter bins in public places: A comparative study of qualitative research findings obtained from UK settings. *Health & Place, 17*, 1218–1227.

Pearson, M., Parkin, S., & Coomber, R. (2011). Generalizing applied qualitative research on harm reduction: The example of a public injecting typology. *Contemporary Drug Problems, 38*, 61–91.

Philipp, R. (1993). Community needlestick accident data and trends in environmental quality. *Public Health, 107*, 363–369.

Public Health England. (2013a). *Hepatitis C in the UK.* London: Author.

Public Health England. (2013b). *Shooting up: Infections among people who inject drugs in the UK (2012)*. London: Author.

Rhodes, T. (2002). The 'risk environment': A framework for understanding and reducing drug-related harm. *International Journal of Drug Policy, 13*, 85–94.

Rhodes, T. (2009). Risk environments and drug harms: A social science for harm reduction approach. *International Journal of Drug Policy, 20*, 193–201.

Rhodes, T., Kimber, J., Small, W., Fitzgerald, J., Kerr, T., Hickman, M., & Holloway, G. (2006). Public injecting and the need for 'safer environment interventions' in the reduction of drug-related harm. *Addiction, 101*, 1384–1393.

Rhodes, T., Watts, L., Davies, S., Martin, A., Smith, J., Clark, D., … Lyons, M. (2007). Risk, shame and the public injector: A qualitative study of drug injecting in South Wales. *Social Science and Medicine, 65*, 572–585.

Riley, E., Beilenson, P., Vlahov, D., Smith, L., Koenig, M., Jones, T. S., & Doherty, M. (1998). Operation Red Box: A pilot project of needle and syringe drop boxes for injection drug users in East Baltimore. *Journal of Acquired Immune Deficiency Syndrome Human Retrovirology, 18*, S120–S125.

Robertson, R. (1990). The Edinburgh epidemic: A case study. In J. Strang & G. V. Stimson (Eds.), *AIDS and drug misuse: The challenge for policy and practice in the 1990s* (pp. 95–107). London: Routledge.

Room, R. (2006). Response. Drug policy and the city. *International Journal of Drug Policy, 17*(2), 136.

Scottish Government. (2008). *The road to recovery: A new approach to tackling Scotland's drug problem*. Edinburgh: Author.

Small, W., Rhodes, T., Wood, E., & Kerr, T. (2007). Public injection settings in Vancouver: Physical environment, social context and risk. *International Journal of Drug Policy, 18*, 27–36.

Smith, C. B. R. (2010). Socio-spatial stigmatization and the contested space of addiction treatment: Remapping strategies of opposition to the disorder of drugs. *Social Science and Medicine, 70*, 859–866.

Stimson, G. V. (2000). Blair declares war: The unhealthy state of British drug policy. *International Journal of Drug Policy, 11*, 259–264.

Stimson, G. V., Alldritt, L., Dolan, K., & Donoghoe, M. (1988). Syringe exchange schemes for drug users in England and Scotland. *British Medical Journal, 296*, 1717–1719.

Stoever, H. (2002). Crack cocaine in Germany: Current state of affairs. *Journal of Drug Issues, 32*, 413–421.

Strang, J., & Gossop, M. (2005). The 'British system' of drug policy: Extraordinary individual freedom, but to what end? In J. Strang & M. Gossop (Eds.), *Heroin addiction and the British system: Volume 2: Treatment and policy responses* (pp. 206–219). Abingdon: Routledge.

Strathdee, S. A., & Pollini, R. A. (2007). A 21st-century Lazarus: The role of safer injection sites in harm reduction and recovery. *Addiction, 102*, 848–849.

Strike, C. J., Myers, T., & Millson, M. (2004). Finding a place for needle exchange programs. *Critical Public Health, 14*, 261–275.

Takahashi, L. M. (1997). The socio-spatial stigmatization of homelessness and HIV/AIDS: Toward an explanation of the NIMBY syndrome. *Social Science and Medicine, 45*, 903–914.

Taylor, A., Cusick, L., Kimber, J., Rutherford, J., Hickman, M., & Rhodes, T. (2006). *The social impact of public injecting* (Independent Working Group on Drug Consumption Rooms). Joseph Rowntree Foundation, p. Paper D.

Ti, L., & Kerr, T. (2014). The impact of harm reduction on HIV and illicit drug use. *Harm Reduction Journal, 11*, 7. Retrieved from http://www.harmreductionjournal

Treloar, C., & Fraser, S. (2007). Public opinion on needle and syringe programmes: Avoiding assumptions for policy and practice. *Drug and Alcohol Review, 26*, 355–361.

Wright, N. M. J., & Tompkins, C. N. E. (2004). Supervised injecting centres. *British Medical Journal, 328*, 100–102.

Space, scale and jurisdiction in health service provision for drug users: the legal geography of a supervised injecting facility

Stewart Williams

School of Land and Food (Geography and Spatial Sciences Discipline), University of Tasmania, Hobart, Australia

Sydney's Medically Supervised Injecting Centre delivers the significant benefits of harm reduction, but has been controversial regards the law. Its contested history is examined here through the lens of legal geography. Narrative analysis reveals that the arguments for and against the centre's establishment referenced matters ranging from international treaties through to municipal governance. These arguments and their outcome were variously shaped by the different spaces and scales of jurisdiction but not simply in a zero sum game of law played out through the hierarchically ordered nesting of container-like territories. The implications for legal geography and for public health are discussed.

Introduction

In most countries the possession and use of drugs such as heroin, methamphetamines and cocaine is illegal. However, there are places inside the nation-state where this prohibition is lifted. For people who inject drugs (PWID), the provision of supervised injection facilities (SIFs) allows consumption of what otherwise remain prohibited substances.[1] Since the first of these legally sanctioned facilities opened in Switzerland in 1986 their number has continued to grow.[2] While spurred by public health arguments, the delivery of such services to PWID has been hampered because it has also been influenced in significant ways in terms of law, crime and policing.

The Medically Supervised Injecting Centre (MSIC) in Sydney, Australia, is the only official SIF in the southern hemisphere. It has been contentious despite operating within the law since 2001 and gaining more permanence as it moved beyond trial status in 2010. The story behind the trials and tribulations of this service holds insights into the challenges and opportunities for delivering health services to PWID. Our analysis focuses on the protracted debate over the establishment of the MSIC as we look at how the key stakeholders and their arguments have linked different places from which the law is variously spoken and enacted.

In the first section (SIFs, public health and the law) of this paper, we situate our case study with respect to the relationships among SIFs, public health and law. We then describe in the second section (The legal geography approach) our analytical framework as that of legal geography, outlining the focus of inquiry and methods used. The third section (Case study: the contested history of the MSIC's establishment) provides an overview of the MSIC's contested history involving diverse and variously placed stakeholders. In the fourth section (Discussion: the role of jurisdictional space and scale), we discuss how the different spaces and scales of the MSIC's legal framing influenced the debate about its proposed and ongoing delivery. In sum, the paper makes important contributions to both legal geography and public health literatures. Firstly, it illustrates the complexities of jurisdiction as evinced in the actual practice of law; secondly, it then reveals the value of these insights with potential application advancing the delivery of harm reduction, notably health services for PWID.

SIFs, public health and the law

In the 1980s and 1990s SIFs began operating in Switzerland, Germany and the Netherlands in response to increased levels of injecting drug use and HIV infection. Recognition of the role of injecting drug use in blood-borne virus (BBV) transmission then figured in combating the spread of hepatitis C among PWID. Efforts to establish services such as needle and syringe programmes (NSPs) as well as SIFs intensified at this time as the quality, affordability and availability of heroin and hence its use and adverse health impacts were at a peak in Europe, North America and Australia. A substantial body of research links SIFs to reductions in the rates of fatal overdose and BBV transmission and improvements in the health and wellbeing of PWID including referral into treatment programmes (Fry, Cvetkovski, & Cameron, 2006; Hedrich, 2004; Hedrich, Kerr, & Dubois-Arber, 2010; IWG, 2006; Kimber, Dolan, Van Beek, Hedrich, & Zurhold, 2003).

Given their success, SIFs are becoming more numerous mostly in Europe. The exceptions are the MSIC, which opened in Sydney in 2001, and InSite, which opened in Vancouver in 2003. Proposals for establishing these SIFs have been based on public health arguments, especially those of harm reduction which aims "to reduce the adverse health, social and economic consequences of the use of legal and illegal psychoactive drugs without necessarily reducing drug consumption" (IHRA, 2010, n.p.). Those opposing such services for PWID, including in Australia, have typically taken the illegality of drugs as a founding premise.

Decisions about health service provision tend to be devolved from the federal level to state and territory governments in Australia. Since the early 1990s, three such governments have attempted on several occasions to establish SIFs. While proposals for the MSIC in Sydney (in New South Wales or NSW) eventually garnered enough support to proceed, those advanced for Canberra (in the Australian Capital Territory or ACT) and Melbourne (in Victoria) have been consistently quashed including most recently in 2003 and 2011, respectively (Fitzgerald, 2013; Gunaratnam, 2005; Mendes, 2002). One early international comparison noted that Australian proposals were "the subject of considerable controversy and debate, and have been met with some resistance" (Elliot et al., 2002, p. 20). A persistent intractability has rendered the MSIC's existence in NSW fraught, and encouraged policy reversals by the governments of Victoria and the ACT (Bessant 2008; Fitzgerald, 2013; Schatz & Nougier, 2012).

Health service provision for PWID is highly contentious and politicized because of the moral ambiguity that emerges with illicit drugs and the clear-cut stance held by the police on their possession and use. Opposition from communities and governments to proposed services such as NSPs as well as SIFs has often succeeded in North America, Australia and even Europe through alignment with the dominant legal position (Bernstein & Bennett, 2013; Bessant, 2008; Davidson & Howe, 2013; Fitzgerald, 2013; Houborg & Frank, 2014; Tempalski, Friedman, Keem, Cooper, & Friedman, 2007; Zampini, 2014). While arguments about establishing SIFs are often finally determined on legal rather than public health grounds, the outcomes vary among and within nation-states because the law's interpretation and application is spatially contingent.

A legal geography approach is therefore useful for examining how particular decisions get made about such services in light of their jurisdictional framing.

The legal geography approach

Legal geography is a substantive area of research conducted for over two decades from diverse disciplinary perspectives (see, e.g. Blomley, 1994, 2011; Blomley, Delaney, & Ford, 2001; Cooper, 1998; Delaney, 1998, 2003; Holder & Harrison, 2003). It has increasingly evinced how law and space warrant closer attention because of a mutual constitution that is powerful and reaches everywhere. In an introductory overview of legal geography's corpus, some of its key contributors note how "nearly every aspect of law is either located, takes place, is in motion, or has some spatial frame of reference. ... Likewise, every bit of social space, lived places and landscapes are inscribed with legal significance" (Braverman, Blomley, Delaney, & Kedar, 2014, p. 1).

However, Braverman et al. (2014) do not simply celebrate legal geography. In a constructive critique, they identify weaknesses in the bulk of scholarship undertaken to date, including its focus on *where* but not *how* law happens. Still, advances in recent work have explored legal geography's variously material and discursive, performative and relational assemblages (e.g. Blomley, 2013, 2014; Delaney, 2010; Graham, 2011; Riles, 2011; Valverde, 2009, 2011). The continuous making and remaking of different legal realities subsequently invites a scholarly reorientation to include, for example, a focus on variations over time as well as space, and an embrace of more diverse empirical materials and sophisticated theorisations (Bartel et al., 2013; Braverman et al., 2014; Graham, 2011).

Such developments are exemplified here with this investigation into the MSIC in Australia. SIFs have been examined in terms of their geographic location and legal determination, but not explicitly using a legal geography framework.[3] Here we look at the MSIC's provision as the historically and geographically complex and contingent result of a contest among diverse stakeholders with assorted views on drugs and drug treatment. Notably, these stakeholders, the debates had, decision-making processes used and outcomes reached were always already situated in relation to laws variously holding sway over different places. So, in this analysis, we focus on the role of jurisdiction understood in terms of administering legal governance territorially and thus as a problem of space and scale.

Early work in legal geography was at pains to elucidate law's power to shape legal subjects and practices dependent on their location. It therefore focused on identifying the enunciation of law and its impacts within those bounded spaces of jurisdiction where a court is empowered to hear and determine legal disputes. This interest in the law's territorialisation was useful for explaining what is allowed to happen where, for example, in terms of property rights and judgments (see, for example, Clark, 1982, 1985; Ford, 1999; Frug, 1996; Neuman, 1987). Yet such work is problematic, despite reflecting the law's geographical imaginary, as its conceptual foundation relies on an overly simplistic nesting of spaces that are assumed to be tightly bound units, mutually exclusive and hierarchically ordered. In reality, the practice of law is quite different. Legal scholarship and jurisprudence have therefore entertained endless debate in Australia, for example, about the High Court's capacity to impose on state and territory judicial function via judicial review, advisory opinion and protection of the rule of law (Fearis, 2012; Goldsworthy, 2014; Irving, 2004), and elsewhere, for example, regards the power of local legislatures and officials to challenge a country's exercising its national laws and meeting international obligations (Butt, 2010) or the scope for extra-territorial jurisdiction in regional conventions (Miller, 2010)

More accurate and nuanced interpretations of how space and scale function in the actual practice as well as geographical imaginary of law have likewise been informing the legal geography literature. One early but important observation, for example, states:

> sociolegal life is constituted by different legal spaces operating simultaneously on different scales and from different interpretive standpoints. So much is this so that in phenomenological terms and as a result of interaction and intersection among legal spaces one cannot properly speak of law and legality but rather of interlaw and interlegality. […] Interlegality is a highly dynamic process because the different legal spaces are non-synchronic and thus result in uneven and unstable mixings of legal codes. (de Sousa Santos, 1987, p. 288)

That socio-legal life is constituted through heterogeneous assemblages reinforces the need to see space less as reified in the fixed, container-like objects of territory and more as networks momentarily connecting phenomena in open, dynamic relations of force and flow, proximity and distance. It also challenges the traditional scalar architecture of hierarchically nested, areal units which situates the local and its supposedly lesser matters inside provinces and regions subsumed by the "bigger" concerns and powers of national and transnational spheres. Indeed, "legal powers and legal knowledges appear to us as always already distinguished by scale [… as it] organizes legal governance, initially, by sorting and separating" (Valverde, 2009, p. 141). Scale is not an ontological reality but an epistemological device manifesting in legal practice as jurisdiction, and thus best understood through empirical studies:

> Rather than treating it as a thing in the world, our task should become that of tracing the ways in which scale solidifies and is made "real", and under what conditions, and making sense of the work such solidifications do. (Blomley, 2013, p. 8)

In this paper, we look at how different geographical imaginaries and legal practices have shaped the MSIC's establishment in Australia. Methodologically, we follow Braverman (2014) and Watkins and Burton (2013) in using a multi-disciplinary approach to examine the processes and outcomes obtained in this particular case. The materials available from archival research include public health policies and proposals, political statements, media reports, legislation, case law, drug service evaluations, organisation websites and research papers.

In addition to doctrinal research in law, the most suitable methods include the close textual reading and coding of narrative analysis. We deploy them in our case study, as have done Zadjow (2006) and Fitzgerald (2013), to examine the main arguments framing the debate over the establishment of the MSIC. Like these researchers, we recognize the dominance of legal narratives in the SIF debate, but we add new insights here by focusing on the role of jurisdictional spaces and scales.

Case study: the contested history of the MSIC's establishment

The MSIC was established after a SIF was proposed for Sydney's Kings Cross. This red light district was at the centre of Australia's 1990s heroin epidemic and infamous for its escalating levels of public injecting and drug overdose. Yet issues of policing, crime and law dominated the ensuing, highly politicized debate. Understanding what subsequently played out therefore requires attention to the country's juridico-political institutions and governance structure.

The Commonwealth of Australia is a federation of six states and two territories which are in turn made up of local government areas or councils. The *Customs Act 1901 (Commonwealth)* regulates the importation of drugs, enforced by the Australian Federal Police, but each of the states and territories has a judiciary and legislature hence its own police and laws governing the manufacture, possession, distribution and use of drugs both legal and illegal. They are likewise responsible for the delivery of health services albeit with funding mostly provided by the federal government. The MSIC's establishment was driven by stakeholders including the state government of NSW, but with connections to other jurisdictions reflecting the three levels of governance in Australia (see Figure 1). Levels of legal jurisdiction follow those of political governance in Australia with a similarly hierarchical system of courts and tribunals applying a single body of common law. Highest up are those superior courts comprising the High Court and Federal Court, and of which the former can hear appeals from all other courts in Australia and determines constitutional matters whereas the latter's original jurisdiction is to hear criminal and civil cases concerned with Commonwealth law. And then there is the Supreme Court, the highest court in each state and territory, which hears the most serious or complex of criminal offences and civil disputes with lesser cases devolved to the lowest inferior court of record, the Magistrates Court, although in some states there is also an intermediate County or District Court.

The first proposal to trial a SIF in Sydney resulted from the NSW state government's 1997 *Royal Commission into the NSW Police Service*. In his report, Justice James Wood condoned the closure of illegal shooting galleries in the Kings Cross area of inner Sydney because of their links to organized crime and police corruption. He also found that "health and public safety benefits [of establishing a SIF] outweigh the policy considerations against condoning otherwise unlawful behaviour" (Wood, 1997, p. 222). In his recommendation to trial a SIF, Wood delegated the licencing and supervision of such a facility to the NSW Department of Health pending an amendment to the *Drug Misuse and Trafficking Act 1985 (NSW)*.

The proposal was dismissed though in 1998 as the members of a Joint Select Committee into Safe Injecting Rooms, established in 1997 by NSW Premier Bob Carr, voted six to four against it. Their final report (Parliament of New South Wales, 1998) recognized that a SIF

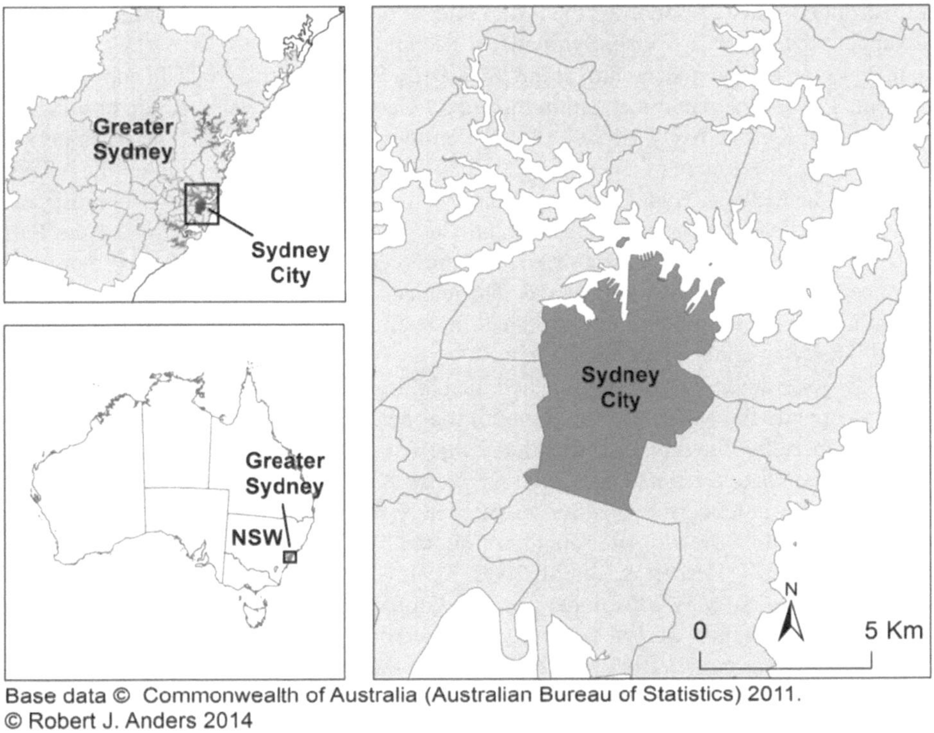

Figure 1. The Australian subnational jurisdictions of NSW and Sydney City.

would result in fewer charges of self-administration (of drugs), taking up less police and court time, but concerns arose around the problem of complicity as discretion would have to be exercised in policing the area around any such facility. In effect, the report "redefined the central rationale for SIFs and the deeper systemic links between the drug market and police corruption had all but disappeared" (Fitzgerald, 2013, p. 83). The law thus cleansed of any malfeasance in this context subsequently became available for framing the SIF debate in Australia in a very particular manner. It was readily used under the conservative rule of Prime Minister John Howard (1996–2007) as a time when prevention rather than treatment characterized national drug policy (Bessant, 2008).

Meanwhile, there was growing support for a SIF in King's Cross. A community group was formed in late 1998 by recovering drug users and parents of drug users (some whose children had died from drug overdoses) led by the Reverend Ray Richmond of the Uniting Church's Wayside Chapel in Kings Cross. Although spurred by the local manifestation of a worsening public health crisis, the group comprized some well-connected individuals. They included NSW Legislative Assembly member Clover Moore (later Lord Mayor of Sydney), former NSW parliamentarian Ann Symonds (chair of the 1998 parliamentary inquiry and cofounder of the Australian Parliamentary Group for Drug Law Reform), and two doctors of whom one was internationally respected harm reduction advocate Alex Wodak (director of the Alcohol and Drug Service, St Vincent's Hospital, Sydney).

The group was aware that a drug summit planned by the NSW government did not include SIFs on any agenda given the recent parliamentary inquiry outcome. Members therefore agreed to commence the temporary operation of an illegal SIF (called the Tolerance or T-Room) in the Wayside Chapel. It was opened in May 1999 as a public event coinciding with the drug summit. The room operated for a few days until closed by police with several arrests made, but all charges were subsequently dropped. Most importantly, the group's act of civil disobedience afforded a media presence advancing their cause (Wodak, Symonds, & Richmond, 2003).

There was then an unexpected turn at the *NSW Drug Summit* with a trial SIF supported (NSW Government, 1999). The recommendation moved by Clover Moore was seconded by Ingrid van Beek (Director of Kings Cross's Kirketon Road Centre which delivers health services for PWID, including a NSP). The Sisters of Charity, a religious organisation, were invited by the NSW government to run the MSIC as Sydney's first official SIF trial, but in October they were instructed to withdraw by Cardinal Ratzinger (Prefect of the Congregation for the Doctrine of the Faith in Rome). The directive seemed an unprecedented intervention into state affairs (Totaro, 1999), but its concerns were spiritual not political. The Vatican then decreed, after some deliberation, that no Catholic organisation should participate in such a trial as it involved cooperation with "grave evil" that was understandably illegal.

The NSW government instead approached the Uniting Church of Australia, which applied in June 2000 to operate the MSIC for an 18 month trial period. The NSW government granted the license in October 2000 having amended the *Drug Misuse and Trafficking Act 1985 (NSW)* via Schedule 1 of the *Drug Summit Legislative Response Act 1999 (NSW)*. Amid ongoing debate, the Uniting Church defended its position theologically on moral grounds (as had the Vatican). However, in "upholding the ultimate sanctity of human life" it was emphatic about "acting completely within the law" (Herbert & Talbot, 2000, n.p.).

The MSIC opened in May 2001 under trial conditions (on short-term basis subject to rigorous evaluations). The legislation was subsequently extended on three separate occasions until this trial status was lifted in November 2010 with enactment of the *Drug Misuse and Trafficking Amendment (Medically Supervised Injecting Centre) Bill 2010 (NSW)*. The MSIC operates now on a continuing basis without the uncertainty of having to reapply every four years for the legislative change needed to extend its duration as a trial.

Discussion: the role of jurisdictional space and scale

Policy decisions and legislation enabling the provision of SIFs have been enacted with little consistency in Australia.[4] Much remains the remit of states and territories but their exercise of jurisdictional power over one bounded geographical area is not total or mutually exclusive. With the MSIC, the NSW government was pitted against the Australian federal government but entwined stakeholders at all levels of governance. Arguments from "above" and "below" (in the traditional hierarchy of scale) had varying effect because their power and influence were not always limited to or determined by any one space or scale of jurisdiction.

Scalar interventions from above

State and territory governments wanting to initiate new health services for PWID in Australia have often faced federal government resistance on legal grounds, including the opposition to SIFs then led by Prime Minister John Howard. Continuing to promote his "Tough on Drugs" strategy adopted in 1997, he stated:

> The Federal Government also believes that the introduction of injecting rooms or a heroin trial or both would be damaging to the Australian community insofar as such a step would signal that illicit drug use is acceptable. (Howard, 2000, n.p.)

Under Howard, national drug policy favoured law enforcement over health programmes, and the funding level for prevention was and has since remained several times greater than for treatment (Bammer, Hall, Hamilton, & Ali, 2002; Gunaratnam, 2005; Moore, 2005; Ritter, McLeod, & Shanahan, 2013). The MSIC's establishment in such conservative times is remarkable. It eventuated because the contestation was reduced to legal arguments had across multiple jurisdictions, none of which necessarily had any greater reach or authority.

Supranational jurisdictions and powers did not over-rule others when the federal government linked its case to Australia's international obligations. Being a signatory to the three main international drug control treaties administered by the UN has complicated the SIF debate in Australia.[5] The UN's International Narcotics Control Board (INCB) is a quasi-judicial entity requiring these treaties to be observed, and its annual reports regularly criticize efforts to establish SIFs (Schatz & Nougier, 2012). In 2000, when the MSIC's trial operation was meant to commence, an INCB spokesperson reportedly stated:

> Any national, state, or local authority that permits the establishment and operation of such drug injection rooms also facilitates illicit drug trafficking. (Yamey, 2000, p. 667)

Also, Australia each year produces almost half the world's supply of licit opiates, which is regulated by the INCB (Williams, 2010, 2013). Therefore, when Prime Minister Howard berated NSW Premier Carr in the media for supporting the MSIC, he mentioned the INCB and possible UN sanctions on the Australian opiates industry (Nolan, 2003).

The UN encourages members to take a stance against SIFs, but contrary decisions at national and subnational jurisdictional levels do not necessarily contravene these international treaties (Elliott, Malkin, & Gold, 2002; Gunaratnam, 2005; Malkin, Elliott, & McRae, 2003). As the UN's own legal advice to the INCB (2002, p. 5) states:

> It might be claimed that [establishing SIFs] is incompatible with the obligations to prevent the abuse of drugs, derived from article 38 of the 1961 Convention and article 20 of the 1971 Convention. It

> should not be forgotten, however, that the same provisions create an obligation to treat, rehabilitate and reintegrate drug addicts, whose implementation depends largely on the interpretation by the Parties of the terms in question.

Indeed other international conventions can be taken as demanding such initiatives. Harm reduction advocates have long drawn on human rights law and jurisprudence to balance the drug conventions (Barrett, 2010; Bewley-Taylor, 2005; Bewley-Taylor & Jelsma, 2012; Elliott, Csete, Wood, & Kerr, 2005: Malkin, 2001). Bodies such as the UN Human Rights Commission and the World Health Organisation have enshrined in law those principles entitling individuals to the highest levels of health and wellbeing, but variations arise in how it gets interpreted and applied.

International law, whether it concerns drug control or human rights, permits some autonomy to the signatories as written into the overarching *Vienna Convention on the Law of Treaties 1969*. While every international treaty is binding under the *Vienna Convention*, this latter's articles provide the signatories with several escape clauses. For example, a nation-state "may not invoke the provisions of its internal law as justification for its failure to perform a treaty" (Article 27) but is to be interpreted and applied simply "in good faith" (Article 26). Likewise, a nation-state must apply a treaty to "its entire territory" unless, that is, "a different intention appears from the treaty or is otherwise established" (Article 29). So, international law need not always prevail with its power imagined as imposing comprehensively on the nation-state. On the other hand, legal arguments put forward nationally as well as internationally can still be challenged and overturned at subnational jurisdictional levels.

Scalar interventions from below

The MSIC's establishment was a state government initiative shaped by local factors. The spread of SIFs outwards from Europe to Australia and Canada via global networks and mobile policy circuits has always been contingent on the particularities of place (McCann, 2008; McCann & Temenos, 2015). Similarly, top-down approaches to drug regulation typified by international treaties and national prohibition can be enhanced by involving non-state or third-party actors (Ritter, 2010).

After the state drug summit, the NSW government decided to work with non-government organisations wanting SIFs established, "providing there is support for this at the community and local government level" (NSW Government, 1999, p. 46). The MSIC's establishment was therefore carefully managed here. For example, Part 5, 36Q (1) and (2) of the amended *Drug Misuse and Trafficking Act 1985 (NSW)* enabled the development to proceed outside the usual statutory planning processes that require approval from local authorities administering the *Environmental Planning and Assessment Act 1979 (NSW)*. A Community Consultation Committee was formed though, representing local residents, drug users and their families, the Kings Cross Chamber of Commerce and Tourism, local health and social welfare services, the police, and local and state governments.

The committee, charged with identifying the best location for a SIF, examined 39 sites over six months (MSIC, 2014). In 2000, a public presentation of two possible sites incited locals to form the Potts Point Community Action Group. The cry for a less residential location was answered when local businesses agreed to a site in the main thoroughfare of Kings Cross. Its location also made sense in being close to the Kirketon Road Centre's NSP outlet, as well as having the highest prevalence of heroin deaths in Australia (MSIC, 2014; Wodak et al., 2003).

While the MSIC's current location was thus decided, some local businesses were displeased and took action albeit unsuccessfully to the NSW Supreme Court. In *Kings Cross Chamber of*

Commerce and Tourism Inc v The Uniting Church of Australia Property Trust (NSW) & Ors [2001] NSWSC 245, representations for the plaintiff referred to state and federal law and even constitutional concerns based on the *Commonwealth of Australia Constitution Act 1900 (Imp)*. In practice, the case was confined to a far more parochial matter. In summing up the case (*Kings Cross Chamber of Commerce and Tourism Inc v The Uniting Church of Australia Property Trust (NSW) & Ors* [2001] NSWSC 245, p. 2), Justice Sully stated:

> The sole function and duty of the Court is to examine and construe the terms of the license as issued; and the procedures by means of which the application for the license was assessed and granted; and then to come to a reasoned answer to the question whether the license has been properly issued according to law.

The substance of this particular case was subordinate to other legal decisions made at state level, but it illustrates the importance of attending to the technicalities of law practiced on the ground where matters of local jurisdiction can be critical.

With Clover Moore elected Sydney Lord Mayor in 2004, the local government of Sydney City Council has long supported SIFs and now promotes itself as the MSIC's "home" (SCC, 2014a). Council acknowledges in its *Drug and Alcohol Strategy* objective of "Advocating to other levels of government … for the continued operation of the Medically Supervised Injecting Centre" (SCC, 2007, p. 26) that multiple spaces and scales of jurisdiction pertain here, but elsewhere highlights its own special jurisdictional position:

> Local governments are uniquely positioned to address drug harm with key partners because the impacts of drug use are felt at a community level the most. Councils can also respond to specific problems more swiftly than other levels of government. (SCC, 2014a, n.p.)

Sydney City Council's regulatory interests concern order and safety. These issues and their importance for the success of the MSIC are reflected in its first evaluation (MSIC Evaluation Committee, 2003). The MSIC's impacts on law and order (public injecting; drug-related loitering and property crime; and community attitudes) as well as public health (opioid overdoses; BBV incidence, prevalence and transmission; client health and service use) were found there to be positive, and increasingly so in subsequent evaluations.

The second of four evaluations administered by the National Centre in HIV Epidemiology and Clinical Research focused solely on community attitudes. It revealed from telephone surveys of Kings Cross conducted in 2000, 2002 and 2005 that the proportion of respondents agreeing with the MSIC's establishment had generally increased over this time to 73% of residents and 68% of business operators (NCHECR, 2006). Concerns persisted around crime and safety, negative image for the area and discarded syringes (NCHECR, 2006).

Fears that the MSIC's establishment would lead to more crime happening in its vicinity were not realized (Fitzgerald, Burgess, & Snowball, 2010). The final, most comprehensive evaluation of the MSIC thus focused on "public amenity" rather than crime per se, and the report detailed "substantial" decreases in (observed and self-reported) public injecting and "steady" declines in (observed and collected) amounts of discarded injecting equipment (KPMG, 2010).

Discarded syringes, like public injecting, pose broad health risks for society, but are best tackled locally. They are a priority for Sydney City Council, which exercises its "regulatory and enforcement actions … to improve the safety and amenity of residents and visitors" (SCC, 2014b, n.p.) and manages 65 community syringe disposal bins and a 24-hour needle clean-up hotline funded under the NSW government's Community Sharps Management Program (SCC, 2014a). Its support for the MSIC is understandable as discarded syringes pose one of council's "biggest problems" (SCC, n.d., n.p.)

Conclusion

In this case study, we have used a legal geography approach and the method of narrative analysis to examine how jurisdiction influenced the protracted contest over the MSIC's establishment in Sydney, Australia. We note the importance of attending to the socio-spatial imaginaries and empirical practices of law as our findings challenge the traditionally accepted reification of different jurisdictional spaces and scales into the hierarchically ordered nesting of discreet areal units.

In some countries, establishing SIFs is seen to have depended on a sympathetic government implementing change to national legislation (Houborg & Frank, 2014; Zampini, 2014). In the case of the MSIC, however, the Australian federal government's stance against SIFs even when calling on the supposedly higher authority of international treaties was resisted and beaten by the state government of NSW which supported such a trial. Furthermore, the lowest level of jurisdiction in the form of the Sydney City Council has been critical to the ongoing delivery of this health service. While the values of harm reduction and the lofty ideals of human rights to good health have informed the establishment of SIFs around the world, in this instance it is the municipal governance of such matters as public injecting and discarded syringes that has driven continuing support for the MSIC.

Our research demonstrates legal geography's utility as an approach eminently suitable for understanding how law is made manifest in space. It especially demands our rethinking the traditional architecture of space and scale with respect to the exercise of juridico-political power which, as our case study has shown, can be exerted sideways and upwards (and not simply or only downwards) from one jurisdiction to another. The territorialisation of legal power has long been envisaged as jurisdiction, but its hierarchical ordering of space and scale is in practice far more complex and even contradictory than has normally been conceded in the geographical imaginary of law.

There are also implications around health service provision for PWID. Local stakeholders play an important role in the fate of proposals for such services, and the North American experience has led other researchers to suggest that the proponents of NSPs and SIFs form coalitions with higher order (national and international) actors to progress their objectives (McCann, 2008; Tempalski et al., 2007). Efforts to establish and then optimize the delivery of such health initiatives on the grounds of harm reduction are often seen to be countered by the enactment of law or undermined by the juridico-political structures of government (Fischer, Turnbull, Poland, & Haydon, 2004; Houborg & Frank, 2014; Zampini, 2014). However, as we have shown in this Australian case, and Bernstein and Bennett (2013) intimate in the Canadian context, there are significant opportunities to progress the provision of health services for PWID through collaboration among local stakeholders, including not least those responsible for the regulation and enforcement of public order, amenity and safety. This is so, precisely if also perhaps surprisingly, because they have the capacity to intervene in legal processes at other jurisdictional levels as any one or more of the whole suite of laws along with its many actors, instruments and practices, variously described as being international, federal, state or local, can at any time influence what happens in a particular place or territory irrespective of its spatial extent and scalar position.

Acknowledgements

This paper has benefitted variously from conversations initially had with Associate Professor Jason Prior, feedback offered by participants at the *Inaugural Australian Legal Geography Symposium* held at the University of Technology, Sydney (12–13 February 2015), reviews received from two referees for *Space and Polity*, and the support of the Institute of Australian Geographers.

Disclosure statement

No potential conflict of interest was reported by the author.

Notes

1. SIFs are also called safe or safer (as well as supervised) injecting spaces, places, sites or centres. They are the main type of facility known as drug consumption rooms (DCRs) and distinct from alternatives such as safe or supervised inhalation rooms which cater for people who use drugs by means other than injecting.
2. Recent counts include that provided by Hedrich et al. (2010, p. 307) who state: "By the beginning of 2009 there were 92 operational DCRs in 61 cities, including in 16 cities in Germany, 30 cities in the Netherlands and 8 cities in Switzerland."
3. One exception is Prior and Crofts' (2015) analysis of the MSIC understood as a space of sanctuary.
4. The variation among states and territories regarding the provision of SIFs has also been apparent with NSPs, methadone maintenance treatment programmes and funding for drug user organisations in Australia.
5. These treaties comprise the *Single Convention on Narcotic Drugs of 1961 as amended by the 1972 Protocol*, the *Convention on Psychotropic Substances of 1971*, and the *Convention against Illicit Traffic in Narcotic Drugs and Psychotropic Substances of 1988.*

References

Bammer, G., Hall, W., Hamilton, M., & Ali, R. (2002). Harm minimisation in a prohibition context – Australia. *Annals of the Academy of Political and Social Sciences*, *582*, 80–98.

Barrett, D. (2010). Security, development and human rights: Normative, legal and policy challenges for the international drug control system. *International Journal of Drug Policy*, *21*, 140–144.

Bartel, R. Graham, N. Jackson, S. Prior, J. H. Robinson, D. F. Sherval, M. & Williams, S. (2013). Legal geography: An Australian perspective.*Geographical Research*, *51*, 339–353.

Bernstein, S. E., & Bennett, D. (2013). Zoned out: 'NIMBYism', addiction services and municipal governance in British Columbia. *International Journal of Drug Policy*, 24, e61–e65.

Bessant, J.. (2008). From 'harm minimization' to 'zero tolerance' drugs policy in Australia: How the Howard government changed its mind. *Policy Studies*, *29*, 197–214.

Bewley-Taylor, D. (2005). Emerging policy contradictions between the United Nations drug control system and the core values of the United Nations. *International Journal of Drug Policy*, *16*, 423–431.

Bewley-Taylor, D., & Jelsma, M. (2012). *The UN drug control conventions: The limits of latitude. Series on legislative reform of drug policies No. 18*. Amsterdam: Trans National Institute.

Blomley, N. (1994). *Law, space and the geographies of power*. New York, NY: Guilford Press.

Blomley, N. (2011). *Rights of passage: Sidewalks and the regulation of public flow*. Oxford: Routledge.

Blomley, N. (2013). Performing property, making the world. *Canadian Journal of Law and Jurisprudence*, *26*, 23–48.

Blomley, N. (2014). What sort of legal space is a city? In A. M. Brighenti (Ed.), *Interstices: The aesthetics and politics of urban in-betweens* (pp. 1–20). Farnham: Ashgate.

Blomley, N., Delaney, D., & Ford, R. (2001). *The legal geographies reader: Law, power, and space*. Oxford: Blackwell.

Braverman, I. (2014). Who's afraid of methodology? Advocating a methodological turn in legal geography. In I. Braverman, N. Blomley, D. Delaney, & A. Kedar (Eds.), *The expanding spaces of law: A timely legal geography* (pp. 120–141). Stanford: Stanford University Press.

Braverman, I., Blomley, N., Delaney, D., & Kedar, A. (2014). Expanding the spaces of law. In I. Braverman, N. Blomley, D. Delaney, & A. Kedar (Eds.), *The expanding spaces of law: A timely legal geography* (pp. 1–29). Stanford: Stanford University Press.

Butt, A. (2010). Regional autonomy and legal disorder: The proliferation of local laws in Indonesia. *Sydney Law Review, 32*, 177–191.

Clark, G. (1982). Rights, property, and community. *Economic Geography, 58*, 120–138.

Clark, G. (1985). *Judges and the cities: Interpreting local autonomy.* Chicago, IL: University of Chicago Press.

Cooper, D. (1998). *Governing out of order: Space, law and the politics of belonging.* London: Rivers Oram Press.

Davidson, P. J., & Howe, M. (2013). Beyond NIMBYism: Understanding community antipathy toward needle distribution services. *International Journal of Drug Policy, 25*, 624–632.

Delaney, D. (1998). *Race, place and the law: 1836–1948.* Austin: University of Texas Press.

Delaney, D. (2003). *Law and nature.* New York, NY: Cambridge University Press.

Delaney, D. (2010). *The spatial, the legal and the pragmatics of world-making: Nomospheric investigations.* Abingdon: Routledge.

Elliott, R., Csete, J., Wood, E., & Kerr, T. (2005). Harm reduction, HIV/AIDS, and the human rights challenge to global drug control policy. *Health and Human Rights, 8*, 104–138.

Elliott, R., Malkin, I., & Gold, J. (2002). *Establishing safe injection facilities in Canada: Legal and ethical issues.* Toronto: Canadian HIV/AIDS Legal Network.

Fearis, E. (2012). Kirk's new mission: Upholding the rule of law at the state level. *Western Australian Jurist, 3*, 61–101.

Fischer, B., Turnbull, S., Poland, B., & Haydon, E. (2004). Drug use, risk and urban order: Examining supervised injection sites (SISs) as 'governmentality'. *International Journal of Drug Policy, 15*, 357–365.

Fitzgerald, J. L. (2013). Supervised injecting facilities: A case study of contrasting narratives in a contested health policy arena. *Critical Public Health, 23*, 77–94.

Fitzgerald, J. L., Burgess, M., & Snowball, L. (2010). *Trends in property and illicit drug crime around the Medically Supervised Injecting Centre: An update* (Crime and Justice Statistics: Bureau Brief 51). Sydney: NSW Bureau of Crime Statistics and Research.

Ford, R. (1999). Law's territory (a history of jurisdiction). *Michigan Law Review, 97*, 843–930.

Frug, J. (1996). The geography of community. *Stanford Law Review, 48*, 1047–1108.

Fry, C., Cvetkovski, S., & Cameron, J. (2006). The place of supervised injecting facilities within harm reduction: Evidence, ethics and policy. *Addiction, 101*, 465–467.

Goldsworthy, J. (2014). Kable, Kirk and judicial statesmanship. *Monash Law Review, 40*, 75–114.

Graham, N. (2011). *Lawscape.* New York, NY: Routledge.

Gunaratnam, P. (2005). *Drug policy in Australia: The supervised injecting facilities debate* (Asia Pacific School of Economics and Government Discussion Papers). Canberra: Australian National University.

Hedrich, D. (2004). *European report on drug consumption rooms.* Lisbon: European Monitoring Centre for Drugs and Drug Addiction.

Hedrich, D., Kerr, T., & Dubois-Arber, F. (2010). Drug consumption facilities in Europe and beyond. In T. Rhodes & D. Hedrich (Eds.), *Harm reduction: Evidence, impacts, and challenges* (pp. 306–331). Lisbon: European Monitoring Centre for Drugs and Drug Addiction.

Herbert, H., & Talbot, W. (2000). *Theological perspectives on the Medically Supervised Injecting Centre to be operated by the uniting church board for social responsibility.* Sydney: Uniting Church of Australia.

Holder, J. & Harrison, C. (2003). *Law and geography.* Oxford: Oxford University Press.

Houborg, E. & Frank, V. A. (2014). Drug consumption rooms and the role of politics and governance in policy processes. *International Journal of Drug Policy, 25*, 972–977.

Howard, J. W. (2000, December 13). *Illicit drugs policy. Media release.* Retrieved from http://pmtranscripts.dpmc.gov.au/browse.php?did=11562

IHRA. (2010). *What is harm reduction?* International Harm Reduction Association. Retrieved from http://www.ihra.net/files/2010/08/10/Briefing_What_is_HR_English.pdf

INCB. (2002, September 30). *Flexibility of treaty provisions as regards harm reduction approaches*, prepared by the Legal Affairs Section of the United Nations Drug Control Programme, E/INCB/2002/W.13/SS.5.

Irving, H. (2004). Advisory opinions, the rule of law, and the separation of powers. *Macquarie Law Journal, 6*, 105–34.

IWG. (2006). *The report of the Independent Working Group on drug consumption rooms.* York: Joseph Rowntree Foundation.

Kimber, J., Dolan, K., Van Beek, I., Hedrich, D., & Zurhold, H. (2003). Drug consumption facilities: An update since 2000. *Drug and Alcohol Review/Harm Reduction Digest, 22*, 227–233.

KPMG. (2010). *Further evaluation of the Medically Supervised Injecting Centre during its extended trial period (2007–2011) final report*. Sydney: Author.

Malkin, I. (2001). Establishing supervised injecting facilities: A responsible way to help minimise harm. *Melbourne University Law Review, 25*, 680–756.

Malkin, I., Elliott, R. & McRae, R. (2003). Supervised injection facilities and international law. *Journal of Drug Issues, 33*, 539–578.

McCann, E. (2008). Expertise, truth, and urban policy mobilities: Global circuits of knowledge in the development of Vancouver, Canada's 'four pillar' drug strategy. *Environment and Planning A, 40*, 885–904.

McCann, E., & Temenos, C. (2015). Mobilizing drug consumption rooms: Inter-place connections and the politics of harm reduction drug policy. *Health & Place*, 31, 216–223.

Mendes, P. (2002). Drug wars down under: The ill-fated struggle for safe injecting facilities in Victoria, Australia. *International Journal of Social Welfare, 11*, 140–149.

Miller, S. (2010). Revisiting extraterritorial jurisdiction: A territorial justification for extraterritorial jurisdiction under the European Convention. *European Journal of International Law, 20*, 1223–1246.

Moore, T. J. (2005). *Monograph No. 01: What is Australia's 'drug budget'? The policy mix of illicit drug-related government spending in Australia* (DPMP monograph series). Melbourne: Turning Point Alcohol and Drug Centre.

MSIC. (2014). *Background and evaluation*. Medically Supervised Injecting Centre. Retrieved from http://www.sydneymsic.com/background-and-evaluation

MSIC Evaluation Committee. (2003). *Final report of the evaluation of the Sydney Medically Supervised Injecting Centre*. Sydney: Author.

NCHECR. (2006). *Sydney Medically Supervised Injecting Centre interim evaluation report no. 2: Evaluation of community attitudes towards the Sydney MSIC*. Sydney: Author.

Neuman, G. (1987). Territorial discrimination, equal protection, and self-determination. *University of Pennsylvania Law Review, 135*, 261–382.

Nolan, T. (2003, December 1). Bob Carr attacks John Howard over heroin injecting room politics. *ABC Radio*.

NSW Government. (1999). *NSW Drug Summit 1999: Government plan of action*. Sydney: Author.

Parliament of New South Wales. (1998). *Report on the establishment or trial of safe injecting rooms*. Joint Select Committee into safe injecting rooms. Sydney: Author.

Prior, J. H., & Crofts, P. (2015). Shooting up illicit drugs with God and the State: The legal–spatial constitution of Sydney's Medically Supervised Injecting Centre as a sanctuary. *Geographical Research* Advance online publication. doi:10.1111/1745-5871.12171

Riles, A. (2011). *Collateral knowledge: Legal reasoning in the global financial markets*. Chicago, IL: University of Chicago Press.

Ritter, A. (2010). Illicit drugs policy through the lens of regulation. *International Journal of Drug Policy, 21*, 265–270.

Ritter, A., McLeod, R., & Shanahan, M. (2013). *Monograph no. 24: Government drug policy expenditure in Australia – 2009/10* (DPMP monograph series). Melbourne: Turning Point Alcohol and Drug Centre.

SCC. (2007). *Drug and alcohol strategy*. Sydney: Author.

SCC. (2014a). *Drug safety*. Sydney: Author. Retrieved from http://www.cityofsydney.nsw.gov.au/community/health-and-safety/alcohol-and-drugs/drug-safety

SCC. (2014b). *Compliance policy*. Sydney: Author. Retrieved from http://www.cityofsydney.nsw.gov.au/council/our-responsibilities/policies

SCC. (n.d.). *Clean streets*. Sydney: Author. Retrieved from http://www.cityofsydney.nsw.gov.au/live/waste-and-recycling/clean-streets

Schatz, E., & Nougier, M. (2012). *Drug consumption rooms: Evidence and practice*. London: International Drug Policy Consortium.

de Sousa Santos, B. (1987). Law: A map of misreading: Toward a postmodern conception of law. *Journal of Law and Society, 14*, 279–99.

Tempalski, B., Friedman, R., Keem, M., Cooper, H. J., & Friedman, S. R. (2007). NIMBY localism and national inequitable exclusion alliances: The case of syringe exchange programs in the United States. *Geoforum, 38*, 1250–1263.

Totaro, P. (1999, October 29). Pope Vetoes Nuns' injecting room role. *Sydney Morning Herald*.

Valverde, M. (2009). Jurisdiction and scale: Legal 'Technicalities' as resources for theory. *Social and Legal Studies*, 18, 139–157.

Valverde, M. (2011). Seeing like a city: The dialectic of modern and premodern ways of seeing in urban governance. *Law and Society Review, 45*, 247–312.

Watkins, D., & Burton, M. (2013). *Research methods in law*. London: Routledge.
Williams, S. (2010). On islands, insularity and opium poppies: Australia's secret pharmacy. *Environment and Planning D: Society and Space*, *28*, 290–310.
Williams, S. (2013). Licit narcotics production in Australia: Geographies nomospheric and topological. *Geographical Research*, *51*, 364–374.
Wodak, A., Symonds, A., & Richmond, R. (2003). The role of civil disobedience in drug policy reform: How an illegal safer injection room led to a sanctioned Medically Supervised Injecting Centre. *Journal of Drug Issues*, *33*, 609–623.
Wood, J. R. T. (1997). *Royal Commission into the NSW Police Service final report. Volume II: Reform*. Sydney: Government of New South Wales.
Yamey, G. (2000). UN condemns Australian plans for 'safe injecting rooms'. *British Medical Journal*, *320*, 667.
Zadjow, G. (2006). The narrative of evaluations: Medically supervised injecting centers. *Contemporary Drug Problems*, *33*, 399–426.
Zampini, G. F. (2014). Governance versus government: Drug consumption rooms in Australia and the UK. *International Journal of Drug Policy*, *25*, 978–984.

Political struggles on a frontier of harm reduction drug policy: geographies of constrained policy mobility

Andrew Longhurst and Eugene McCann

Department of Geography, Simon Fraser University, Burnaby, Canada

This article contributes to the conceptualization of how policy models circulate by analysing the 'frontier politics' that occurs when a mobile policy meets resistance and constraint. We argue that advocates of harm reduction drug policy operate within a constrained political–institutional environment, but one that is not closed or predetermined. We make the argument in reference to struggles over harm reduction drug policy in Surrey, BC, a suburban municipality in Greater Vancouver. Thus, even at frontiers, policy change may occur, even if slowly, incrementally, or cautiously. In conclusion, we reconsider questions of constrained mobility, policy assemblages, and frontier politics to reflect on the character of, and possibilities for, policy change.

Introduction

In 2001, Vancouver, British Columbia (BC) adopted its landmark Four Pillars Drug Strategy, intended to comprehensively respond to the harms of illicit drug use through not only law enforcement, but also education, prevention, and harm reduction. Harm reduction – often the most contentious pillar – is a public health approach to illicit drug use that seeks to reduce its harms to individuals and society without necessarily reducing drug consumption or enforcing abstinence as a goal. Policy actors, including people who use drugs (PWUD), public health workers, non-profit organizations, health researchers, policy professionals, and politicians, reformulated models from Europe and Australia to produce a local response to overdose deaths, epidemic levels of HIV and hepatitis C infection, public street disorder, and crime in Vancouver's Downtown Eastside neighbourhood (McCann, 2008). A key part of the new approach was the opening, in 2003, of North America's first Supervised Injection Facility, 'Insite', where people who use drugs may inject street-bought substances with clean needles under the supervision of trained staff, but harm reduction also includes the provision of clean needles, other necessary equipment, opioid substitution therapies, and access to low-threshold services for PWUD. Harm reduction is an official part of BC provincial health policy. Yet, more than a decade after its adoption, the geography of harm reduction implementation remains uneven and politically contested, especially in suburban and exurban municipalities across the Greater Vancouver region. Harm reduction's mobility, after reaching Greater Vancouver, has been significantly constrained.

Our purpose is to detail and analyse the city-regional political geographies of constrained policy mobility in Greater Vancouver. Specifically, we focus on the 'frontier politics' of policy mobilization across an urban region: struggles that occur when the harm reduction model is resisted in suburban jurisdictions. Through a case study of Surrey, BC, a rapidly growing suburban municipality, we examine the politics of this policy frontier. We argue that, as in the case of many other policy models, harm reduction advocates operate within a constrained political–institutional environment and advance their policy model cautiously and incrementally – neither fully successfully nor unsuccessfully – within spaces of contest. In this regard, 'policy mobility' can be seen to be a fundamentally political–geographical process and analytical perspective.

We follow the travels of harm reduction drug policy through policy-making sites and situations in order to understand the motivations, contexts, and effects of its mobilization and mutation (McCann & Ward, 2012; Peck & Theodore, 2010a, 2012). The study is based on one year of mixed-method research (2014–2015), including 45 semi-structured key-informant interviews (43 unique interviewees, including policymakers, business elites, non-profit service providers, and activists), observation of 15 meetings (14 business community or police-convened neighbourhood stakeholder meetings and one of a peer group of PWUD). These methods were coupled with a descriptive statistical analysis of the suburbanization of poverty in the region from government welfare data. Methods also included substantial archival research into government records (primarily correspondence and internal memos) obtained through 5 Freedom of Information requests, 315 media articles, and over 100 policy and planning documents and meeting minutes. Interviews and documents were coded, analysed, and triangulated for recurrent and divergent discourses and themes (Flowerdew & Martin, 2005).

We begin by situating our discussion within contemporary literatures on the geographies of policy and by elaborating our notion of policy frontiers and assemblages. Subsequently, we outline the socio-economic and drug policy contexts of Greater Vancouver, specifically focusing on Surrey. The case of Surrey is then used to discuss three aspects of the politics of drug policy in Surrey: how certain actors promote a more punitive crime reduction agenda in opposition to harm reduction; how other actors advocate for increased harm reduction services as an alternative to a criminalization and abstinence-oriented agenda; and how the negotiation between the two approaches is expressed in Surrey's built environment. In conclusion, we return to questions of constrained mobility, policy assemblages, and frontier politics to reflect on the character of policy change across regions.

Urban and regional policy, policy mobility, and policy frontiers

For critical human geographers, space is not simply a bounded territorial entity but relationally constituted through the diverse flows and movements of people, ideas, and resources from close-by and far-afield. The policy mobilities approach conceptualizes the spatialities and relationalities of 'making up' (Ward, 2006) or 'worlding' (McCann, Roy, & Ward, 2013; Roy & Ong, 2011) cities through the global–local circulation of policy models, their mutation as they travel, and the politics of fixing or assembling them in place (Baker, Cook, McCann, Temenos, & Ward, in press; Baker & Ruming, 2014; Gonzalez, 2011; McCann, 2011b; McCann & Ward, 2011, 2012; Peck, 2002; Peck & Theodore, 2010a, 2010b, 2010c).

Policy mobilization is, then, a fundamentally political and power-laden process, shaped by the political–economic and historical contexts in which it operates, and by the situated practices of various policy actors. Thus, the policy mobilities approach provides a grammar with which to discuss the productive tension between inter-local relationalities and local and regional territorialities (McCann & Ward, 2010). The approach has, nonetheless, been criticized for, among other things, its tendency to focus on policies that have actually moved (Jacobs, 2012). This concern has always been recognized (McCann, 2008) and the policy mobilities literature has addressed the critique (McCann & Ward, 2015) and has begun to engage questions of policy immobility and differential rates of policy mobility to some extent (Clarke, 2012; Jacobs, 2012; Temenos, 2014; Temenos & McCann, 2013, p. 253). This paper contributes to the discussion on policy mobility with reference to drug policy in Canada's third most populous urban region.

The policy mobilities approach understands policy to move among places through the work of a range of 'policy actors', including politicians, bureaucrats, and activists. These actors engage in various forms of learning, comparison, translation, and education as they identify, package, and promote particular policy models through persuasive narratives about their capacities and effectiveness. Through this process, policy ideas and models are drawn from elsewhere or from global information 'clearing houses' and reshaped to address particular definitions of local problems. The approach draws inspiration from, and complements, the critical policy studies literature, which is similarly concerned with questions of power and state transformation. Critical policy studies scholars understand policy as a social organizing principle and means of framing social relations (Shore, Wright, & Pero, 2011), as an activity that defines problems to be 'fixed' (Bacchi, 2009; Ball, 1993), and as written but also contested and reworked through everyday practices (Lipsky, 1980; Proudfoot & McCann, 2008). Thus, the study of how policies are made and moved illuminates how power relations are organized and reproduced. The notion of 'assemblage' helps highlight and conceptualize the related making and moving of policies. Policies are developed in reference to and through the mobilization of elements and resources from nearby and elsewhere. They are often then purposively moulded to new local contexts by a wide range of policy actors, still with reference to more widely dominant ideologies (McCann & Ward, 2011a; Peck & Theodore, 2015).

More specifically, 'policy activists' – officials and bureaucrats working within state institutions who are committed to the implementation of a policy agenda (Yeatman, 1998) – are often key to the mobilization and assemblage of policies and, as Allen and Cochrane (2007, p. 1171) argue, the making of city-regions themselves. Crucially, the notion of 'regional assemblages' (Allen & Cochrane, 2007, p. 1171) illuminates how policies are produced across city-regional territories and how the work of assembling them interrelates with a region's scaled political and institutional architecture. Assemblages are products of the work of various policy actors who draw ideas, models, and knowledge from close by and elsewhere and knit them together into a regionally specific, often uneven, policy approach. This is a thoroughly political process, at the nexus of space and polity. It involves a politics of the exemplar (McCann, 2011c), in which debates and struggles revolve around differing policy models and their attendant ideologies, evidence, and interests.

The idea of a 'policy frontier' is a useful addition to the policy mobilities lexicon because it speaks to the politicized barriers that can slow down or stop the moving and making of (certain) policies, especially ones that contradict dominant ideologies. The term 'frontier' brings a great deal of conceptual and political baggage with it, not least in its colonial connotations. Therefore, it must be deployed advisedly. Nonetheless, the idea helps in thinking about how mobile policies encounter resistance, barriers, and challenges as they are mobilized. 'Frontier politics' is not predetermined and remains politically open:

> [F]rontiers are liminal zones of struggle between different groups for power and influence – each seeking to expand their influence by shaping these zones on their own terms. In this view, the frontier is a fuzzy geographic space where outcomes are uncertain. Whereas borders and walls create well-defined barriers to be breached or defended, frontiers have a complex geography whose very outlines are the products of contestation. Contestation may break out within seemingly stable localities, threatening to fracture frontier zones from within or to extend them to new territories. (Leitner, Peck, & Sheppard, 2007, pp. 311–312)

Therefore, a policy frontier can be defined as a 'fuzzy geographic space' where the future of policy change is neither certain nor predetermined. Policy frontiers, and practices that encounter resistance (e.g. needle exchanges), are themselves part of wider city-regional struggles over social justice (Jonas, 2012) and are central to understanding 'new expressions of territorial cooperation and conflict' within metropolitan governance (Harrison & Hoyler, 2014, p. 2249).

Surrey and Vancouver in relational context

As the region's two largest cities, Vancouver and Surrey are often discussed in tandem. Surrey's population in 2011 was 468,250 (compared to Vancouver's population of 603,502) and is the fastest growing municipality in the region. The median household income in Surrey was $60,168, and the median individual income was $23,983 in 2005 (Statistics Canada, 2007).[1] Surrey's growth machine – a loose alliance of actors with coinciding interests in increasing the market value of local land – seeks to emulate Vancouver's development model by attracting investment in high-end, high-rise downtown condos. On the other hand, while Vancouver has combined its entrepreneurialism with an innovative harm reduction approach to open-air drug scenes, Surrey's elites speak of Vancouver's harm reduction approach, and particularly its Downtown Eastside neighbourhood with its concentration of social and health services, as a model to be avoided (Longhurst, 2015). North Surrey's Whalley neighbourhood is similar to Vancouver's Downtown Eastside socially and economically, with visible homelessness and an open-air drug scene. Surrey as a whole exhibits the highest percentage increase in the regional share of income assistance (welfare) recipients, rising from 17% to 22% between 1995 and 2013, while Vancouver's share has decreased from 35% to 29%.[2] Whalley, meanwhile, is being redeveloped to resemble downtown Vancouver physically, but Surrey's social and health strategy stands in marked contrast to its regional rival, despite similarities in its social problems (Figure 1).

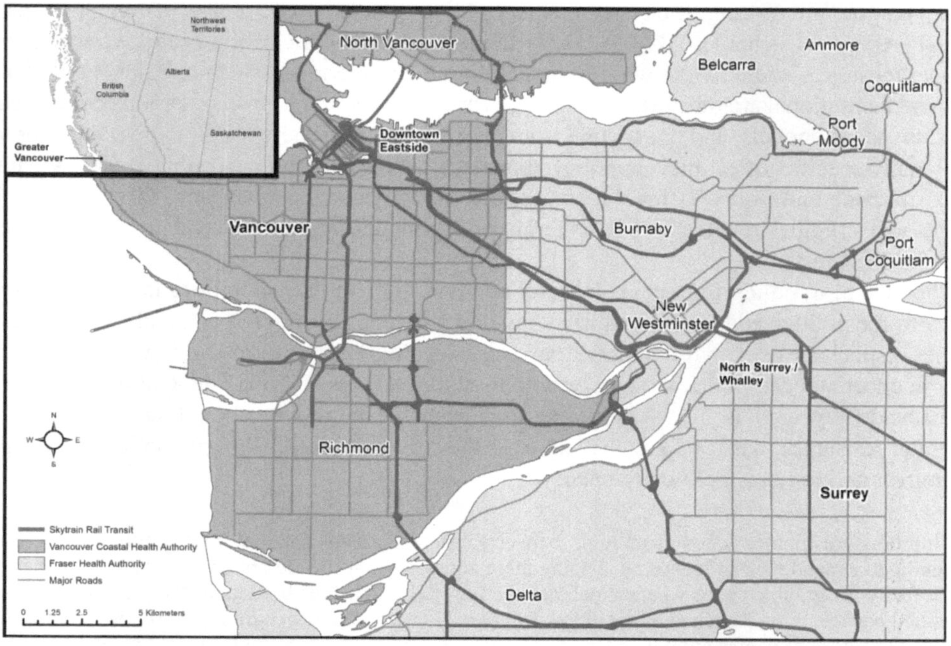

Figure 1. Vancouver and Surrey. Cartography: John Ng, Department of Geography, Simon Fraser University.

Harm reduction is a public health approach to drug use – in our study, particularly the consumption of illicit drugs by low-income people, often in public spaces. It focuses on the mitigation of drug-related harms, not the prevention of drug use itself. Harm reduction practitioners do not oppose abstinence as a goal for some participants in their programmes, but they contend that it is only one point on a continuum of care and that it should not be a litmus test for admission into programmes, nor should it be the only goal of such services. Neither should drug use be criminalized, they argue (Erickson, Riley, Cheung, & O'Hare, 1997). Harm reduction is commonly associated with needle and syringe exchange programmes, methadone treatment, pill testing at music festivals, and more controversially, with supervised injection facilities. It is a mobile policy model, travelling among certain locations around the world (McCann, 2008, 2011a; McCann & Temenos, 2015) and a social movement, with a human rights and social justice orientation recognizing PWUD's right to health care and inclusion in society and in decisions about their own care (Temenos, 2014, 2015).

The City of Surrey's discomfort with this model sits awkwardly within the institutional organization of health care in BC. Harm reduction is embedded in official provincial health policy in BC (Ministry of Health, 2005), which delegates regional health authorities to deliver harm reduction programmes. Nonetheless, harm reduction principles are not accepted equally among municipalities across the province. A case in point is the Greater Vancouver region, which straddles two health authority jurisdictions: the Fraser Health Authority (FHA), including Surrey, and the Vancouver Coastal Health Authority (VCHA), including Vancouver. The health authorities are responsible for working with municipal (local) governments to ensure programmes are available and equitably distributed across their jurisdictions. Written policies do not always match on-the-ground practice within specific political contexts, and numerous municipal governments in the suburban FHA region, including Surrey, have used zoning bylaws to either prohibit or geographically constrain needle exchange programmes and methadone dispensaries (Bernstein & Bennett, 2013). In the period 1995–2009, FHA recorded the highest hepatitis C rates in the province (Katic & Fenn, 2014), suggesting that harm reduction programmes are problematically limited. While programmes have been improving, increasing needle distribution is understood by the FHA as necessary to reduce the spread of blood-borne infections. One health authority official pointed to significant improvements, but conceded, 'We have a lot of work to do' (Interview, health authority official, 2014).

Thus, while harm reduction services are available in Surrey, they operate in a constrained political and institutional context without official acknowledgement or support from the local government (Geddes, 2010). In Surrey, criminalization and abstinence models define most politicians' understandings of illicit drug use and PWUD. During the early 2000s, when key Vancouver politicians were successfully advocating for the inclusion of harm reduction into their drug strategy, Surrey's policy-makers expressed strong disapproval of Vancouver's approach (Reevely, 2002). As Surrey's then-mayor put it, 'We don't believe in harm reduction, and we don't believe in safe-injection sites' (quoted in McMartin, 2003). Over the years, Surrey's political elites have remained opposed to harm reduction policy interventions and often invoke an imaginary of Vancouver's Downtown Eastside as a place of concentrated inner city poverty, addiction, and criminality and, therefore, as a problem that Surrey must avoid if it is to successfully redevelop its new City Centre.

Nonetheless, opposition to harm reduction in Surrey, while dominant, is not complete. Frontline health and social service workers, health officials, and anti-poverty and drug policy activists continue to advocate for harm reduction services. They see the resistance to harm reduction approaches as detrimental to the welfare of marginalized citizens, particularly homeless PWUD, who they feel should be provided services in their own neighbourhood. As one staff member from an advocacy organization noted, ' … there's an awful reflex in the hinterlands to say all drug problems are [Vancouver] Downtown Eastside problems, and people should go downtown for services' (Interview, advocacy organization staff, 2014).

Political struggles on the drug policy frontier

Surrey, then, is a policy frontier: a complex, mutable zone shaping and being shaped by struggles over the policy responses to illicit drug use among people who are often low-income. These struggles involve a range of individuals and institutions on both sides of the harm reduction and crime reduction 'divide', with some working across the two perspectives. Those working to institutionalize harm reduction try to educate policy-makers and coordinate meetings among front-line harm reduction service providers, for example, but they are faced with an array of opposing forces and strategies. On the other hand, those intent on maintaining the institutional dominance of abstinence and criminalization approaches face few actors explicitly working to resist their efforts. Advocacy for policy change in Surrey operates in a severely constrained environment. Without the support of local politicians and police and a strong cadre of advocates in civil society – all key elements of drug policy change in Vancouver in the early 2000s – harm reduction advocates and practitioners in Surrey are primarily dedicated to promoting acceptance of their model within health and social services institutions (e.g. internally educating health authority nurses and staff). In the remainder of this section, we discuss the complexity of Surrey as a drug policy frontier, focusing first on the dominant political discourse of crime reduction, not harm reduction, then outlining attempts by harm reduction advocates to embed their model more firmly in Surrey. Subsequently, we briefly discuss the way in which these struggles are manifest in Surrey's built environment.

Emphasizing crime reduction, not harm reduction

In the fall of 2005, city councillor Dianne Watts became Surrey's mayor. She was elected on a bold crime-fighting and city-building agenda, intended to transform Surrey from a supposed suburban 'backwater', defined by poverty and crime, into the region's largest city with a sparkling new downtown (Luymes, 2008). For her, crime is reduced by addressing its 'root causes', specifically drug and alcohol addiction: 'The relationship between crime and drug addiction is complex and intertwined and must be dealt with together' (Watts quoted in City of Surrey, 2007b). Just as her counterpart in Vancouver had acted 'extrospectively' (McCann, 2013; Peck & Tickell, 2002) to find a harm reduction model a few years before, Watts engaged in a very public campaign to scan the global policy landscape for crime reduction best practices:

> We really needed to [go] … out and [find] what are the best practices out there? What can we make work for our city? Every city is unique. So if you know what is going to work you bring it back and begin to develop a strategy that you feel will speak to your community and the need of your community. (Watts quoted in Jenion, 2010, pp. 137–138)

Surrey's Crime Reduction Strategy (City of Surrey, 2007a) draws on UK crime reduction programmes and New York City's approach, including 'quality of life' policing and CCTV surveillance, specialized 'problem-solving' courts, drug testing upon arrest, court-ordered and private treatment programmes, and youth drug and crime prevention initiatives among other anti-crime policy innovations (The Leader, 2006, 2007a, 2007b). Yet, a number of the proposed policy initiatives have not been implemented since they require funding and implementation from provincial and federal levels of government. As one local politician conceded, political elites travelled to the UK as a political performance to demonstrate action on crime: 'The whole trip … it's to be able to demonstrate you are doing something, instead of just doing it' (Interview, city councillor, 2014). Nevertheless, the mobilization of models from elsewhere that were represented locally as global best practices reinforced and repackaged an ongoing ideological agenda favouring criminalization and abstinence approaches.

Long before Watts' mayoral tenure, drug use in Surrey, as in most places in North America including Vancouver until 2001, was understood as a criminal matter to be addressed through enforcement-oriented crime reduction policies. Surrey's Crime Reduction Strategy, and its 'therapeutic jurisprudence' (Kaye, 2010) approach was a criminal justice policy fix, intended to maintain a putative causal relationship between addiction and crime. As elsewhere, innovations like 'problem-solving courts' (Kaye, 2012) permit the 'drug addict [to be] constituted as an "anti-citizen", a person whose drug dependency is symbolically related to non-productive labour, a leaching of state resources, and criminality' (Kaye, 2012, p. 214; Proudfoot, 2011). Within Surrey itself, a cadre of politicians and policy activists – specifically senior bureaucrats working closely with elected politicians – mobilize criminalization and abstinence-based policy responses (Boyd & Carter, 2014; Carter, 2009, p. 372; Kerr & Wood, 2008; Parliament of Canada, 2009).

Surrey's policy approach to the issue of illicit drug use is, then, a strong criminalization and enforcement assemblage, bringing together an anti-harm reduction federal police agency, bylaw and fire departments, and local politicians with close ties to conservative provincial and federal political parties (Dhillon, 2015). These are key institutions constraining the movement and adoption of harm reduction into the city.

Advocating for harm reduction before crime reduction

In this context of dominant, institutionalized criminalization and abstinence-oriented approaches, how do advocates of an alternative harm reduction model gain a foothold in Surrey? Following our argument that policy frontiers are not clear and straightforward barriers but, rather, zones of contestation, it is perhaps not surprising that harm reduction approaches do exist in Surrey. FHA policy activists (front-line and mid-level staff), non-profit, FHA-funded service providers, and peer drug user[3] groups (that also receive FHA funds) practice harm reduction approaches. These policy advocates struggle to embed harm reduction policy learning within FHA by educating nurses, doctors, and substance use counsellors, and by advocating for harm reduction in meetings convened by local policymakers, police, and the business community. Additionally, in ways similar to the criminalization-oriented actors discussed above, these actors are connected to harm reduction networks that facilitate learning among practitioners and PWUD across Greater Vancouver, as well as through conferences and even experience working within HIV prevention/harm reduction advocacy organizations elsewhere, particularly, but not exclusively, in BC.

Furthermore, peer drug user groups play a significant role in political struggles to strengthen harm reduction in Surrey. This also involves attempts to educate policy actors and it includes advocacy for the rights of PWUD to access life-saving and life-enhancing health services. Practical efforts often include peer distribution of harm reduction supplies (e.g. sterile needles) and education and support intended to prevent overdoses and infections among fellow PWUD. FHA staff members and advocacy organizations emphasize the crucial role of drug user activism in the mobilization of harm reduction in Vancouver's Downtown Eastside (Boyd, MacPherson, & Osborn, 2009), but bemoan its absence in Surrey:

> A lot of users [in the Downtown Eastside] are advocates – strong advocates for the rights of drug users. We don't really have that here [in Surrey]. There's nobody here that has really been standing out and making a point, and having a following here. It's really kept under the thumb and kept down. (Interview, front-line FHA worker, 2014)

This assessment notwithstanding, there are two peer drug user groups advocating for harm reduction in Surrey. One group is closely associated with a Vancouver-based drug user group that played a key role in Vancouver's drug policy change. This organization often uses a somewhat adversarial approach to organizing, placing them at odds with the City of Surrey, police, senior FHA officials, and even sometimes potential allies including non-profit harm reduction service providers. Surrey's police force, the federal Royal Canadian Mounted Police (RCMP) view this drug user group as an 'advocacy organization', and have appeared not to welcome them at neighbourhood stakeholder meetings (Field notes, police-convened meeting, 2015).

After several years convening meetings with PWUD in civic facilities, including the public library, this group leased a commercial storefront for a meeting space and drop-in centre. The space was located in Whalley, adjacent to the homeless shelter and needle distribution facility in the heart of the neighbourhood's open drug market. In just over a month the lease was terminated and the organization was told to vacate the space (Katic & Fenn, 2014). Interviews and email correspondence obtained through a Freedom of Information request reveal that the City of Surrey pressured the landlord to terminate the lease because a prominent activist was from the Vancouver-based drug user group, and city councillors and senior bureaucrats feared they were distributing harm reduction materials, such as clean injecting equipment, and would operate a supervised injection facility (FOI request available from the authors). The significant concern and involvement by the City of Surrey's senior bureaucrats illustrate the degree to which a group associated with Vancouver's Downtown Eastside, in the minds of Surrey's political elites, was seen as a threat to the City of Surrey's drug policy approach. Even one of Surrey's more progressive councillors justified the City's response:

> [E]very city should have a harm reduction plan that the community buys into. Until you have that community buy-in, forget it. So if any harm reduction plan is willing to come in, and can see that it has to be a made-in-Surrey solution, I'm all up for that conversation … If you want to come into the community as a radical and say that you [Surrey people] are all bad human beings for not signing up for this [harm reduction approach], I don't want to talk to you then because … you're not being helpful to anyone … [and] I understand why local residents and businesses don't want it in their neighbourhood. (Interview, city councillor, 2014)

Emphasizing the strength of feeling on the issue at the City of Surrey, the politician went on to acknowledge that the City had pressured the private landlord to end the lease, even though the space was being used as just a space for PWUD to meet. For the city councillor, harm reduction initiatives must be,

> supervised by [the FHA and service should be provided] … in an area where there isn't impact on neighbourhoods, and where people who are brought in … are actually counselled to give up the habit. That has to be a part of it. (Interview, city councillor, 2014)

The City of Surrey's resistance to harm reduction services, learning, and advocacy, except within very tight limits, affirms the dominant criminalization/abstinence drug policy model. Harm reduction advocacy of the type favoured by this Vancouver-connected group is framed as 'radical' and '[coming] into the community' from outside, specifically Vancouver (Interview, city councillor, 2014, as quoted at length above). One member of an advocacy organization lamented, 'As much as we've gained ground in legitimizing harm reduction, have we legitimized anything really beyond one little injection room in Vancouver if drug users can't even rent a space [in Surrey] to meet? What kind of citizenship is that?' (Interview, advocacy organization official, 2014). Despite the setback, the peer drug user group continues to meet and search for a permanent meeting space and one activist from the group identifies the lack of a permanent meeting space for PWUD, similar to what exists in Vancouver's Downtown Eastside, as a significant barrier to drug policy change in Surrey (Interview, activist, 2014).

A second, more conciliatory, peer drug user group also advocates for a harm reduction drug policy approach in Surrey. This group is non-adversarial in its engagement with the City of Surrey, business community, police, and the non-profit harm reduction service provider. Mid-level and senior City of Surrey bureaucrats will engage with this group because of its non-confrontational approach. Although it is a newly established group, working to develop into a non-profit organization, it has contributed to incremental change. One of the group's activists attends stakeholder meetings convened by a predominately conservative business community, and there appears to be a general willingness to have the organization at the table, even if some business members are opposed. The financial and in-kind support provided by the City of Surrey, FHA, a non-profit service provider, and Simon Fraser University allowed this drug user group to organize a harm reduction public education lecture series, bringing in a leading public health expert with ties to VCHA and the University of BC. The drug user group opted for an arguably moderate title for the seven-lecture series – 'Drugs, Families, and Society'. Nonetheless, one activist from the Surrey-based drug user group noted that the barrier to harm reduction in Surrey is ' … the lack of 'open support' [from the] mayor and city council' but the group has 'begun to work with the City of Surrey … from the Social Planning Department to the Crime Prevention Department … to aid in the creation of a focused, [meaningful] foundation where necessary social changes can be spawned' (Email correspondence, drug user group activist, 2015).

As a policy frontier, Surrey is a complex place of negotiations, positionings, mobilizations, barriers, and differing strategies that do not simply cleave along criminalization/harm reduction lines but also have complex resonances across this divide. Some policy actors believe they can advance policy change through cautious incrementalism, and they have made some advances. Yet, interviews suggest that while the City of Surrey will not erect explicit barriers to harm reduction services – such as bylaws preventing clean needle distribution – it will use less explicit tactics to restrict the movement of harm reduction into Surrey. It must be remembered, of course, that these political negotiations have material effects, both on the health of PWUD in the city and on the character of the city's built environment. It is to this aspect of the policy frontier that we now turn.

'Spatial incrementalism' and the politics of harm reduction service visibility

The limited success of incrementally institutionalizing harm reduction services in Surrey seems to rely, at least in part, on their invisibility in the built environment, or on the services appearing to be abstinence-based, or to be serving existing crime reduction objectives (see Temenos, 2014, in the role of visibility and invisibility in the politics of harm reduction drug policy). Two examples of the harm reduction service infrastructure are illustrative: mobile needle distribution and a sobering centre.

In 2005, the City of Surrey attempted to force the closure of the local needle distribution programme by requiring the harm reduction service provider to conduct a costly 'community impact study'. The service provider successfully challenged the City in provincial court, but politically conservative local elites and politicians have long seen the city block where the needle distribution and low-barrier homeless shelter and drop-in centre are located as a 'communal hangout for druggies' (Interview, politician, 2014). Homeless camps, loitering, and open drug use are issues of significant concern for politicians and business groups, particularly because these activities are visible. Indeed, the service provider, which operates the services on leased City of Surrey-owned property, will soon be displaced to a different part of the city. A new purpose-built facility will be constructed only for the shelter in the new location, while condominium towers are planned for the existing site where the shelter, drop-in centre, and clinic and needle distribution are located (Interview, service provider senior staff, 2014). Research has not revealed any plans for the relocation of the clinic and needle distribution programme. Key politicians and senior bureaucrats intend for fixed-site needle distribution to cease, but the future of this service remains uncertain and is likely subject to political negotiations between the City, the Business Improvement Association, FHA, the service provider, and drug user groups.

In turn, the service provider has used FHA funding to begin operating a mobile needle distribution and health outreach van. This is also a pragmatic response to the expansive suburban geography and the dispersed nature of poverty and PWUD across the municipality, compared to a more concentrated geography in Vancouver. These mobile services are relatively invisible, compared to fixed-site needle distribution from a storefront, and are not subject to the same type of critique from politicians and the business community. In one way, the mobile van demonstrates a strategic attempt to institutionalize harm reduction service provision, and yet it escapes political contestation because of its relative invisibility, as opposed to using the visibility of PWUD and harm reduction services as a spatial strategy to raise awareness and spark debate (Temenos, 2014).

A second example of invisibility as a strategy for embedding harm reduction in Surrey is the city's sobering centre, an FHA-operated facility intended to divert intoxicated individuals – largely chronic substance users – out of emergency rooms or jail cells. For local political elites the sobering centre is primarily characterized as a crime reduction intervention, originating as a policy recommendation from the Crime Reduction Strategy (City of Surrey, 2007a, p. 26). While the facility is exactly what the name suggests – a place to sleep and sober up under medical supervision – it operates under a low-barrier, harm reduction philosophy aiming to provide non-judgemental care, counselling, and supports, including the informal distribution of needles and syringes, for those actively using substances. Additionally, while alcohol or illicit substances may not be consumed on-site, they can be stored there until people leave.

The sobering centre is located on the same site as an abstinence-based residential addiction recovery programme operated by an abstinence-based non-profit which is funded by FHA and strongly supported by local political elites. The non-profit service provider is uneasy about the sobering centre's harm reduction approach. Yet, in many ways, the co-location of abstinence-based and harm reduction services illustrates Surrey's drug policy assemblage: criminalization, abstinence, and harm reduction drug policy approaches drawn from disparate places co-exist in tension.[4] Abstinence is favoured by the City of Surrey, but nonetheless, harm reduction is cautiously and incrementally institutionalized by a scaled network of actors and institutional arrangements (i.e. FHA staff and funding from the provincial government for delivery of harm reduction services in partnership with a non-profit service provider). These services rely politically on limited visibility and the ability for local policymakers to publicly represent the sobering centre as an abstinence-based programme and crime reduction intervention, even when it functions otherwise. Nevertheless, a local politician expressed frustration with the philosophy of the low-barrier or harm reduction service approach, which allows – and encourages – repeat visits from chronic substance users who are at risk of harm:

> According to Fraser Health Authority, and they are the experts, I'm not, but every opportunity to interact with one of those folks is yet another opportunity to just sort of steer the ship just a little bit. So I've got to take them for their word on that. [But] I don't see the big success stories coming out of that at all. (Interview, city councillor, 2014)

In both these cases, a strategy of 'spatial incrementalism' – embedding controversial services in the local built environment in ways that are less visible – might be allowing the harm reduction model to be slowly and cautiously institutionalized within a relatively conservative context.

Conclusion

This paper discusses how space and (drug) policy are co-constituted in and through the work of numerous actors. It introduces notions of policy frontiers and constrained policy mobility into ongoing discussions of how best to conceptualize if, and how, policy models circulate. It also discusses the uneven, relational, political landscapes of drug harm reduction policy models across Greater Vancouver, with a particular focus on drug policy advocacy and implementation in Surrey, BC. We argue that the frontier politics that emerges when a mobile policy model encounters political and institutional barriers and resistance constitutes a policy frontier – a 'fuzzy geographic space' where outcomes are not predetermined and where policy change *may* occur, even if slowly, incrementally, or cautiously.

At the regional scale, in the context of our case study, but also at other scales, including the international, frontier politics (expressed through policy actors' everyday interactions, professional practice, and political negotiations) produces an uneven and dynamic policy assemblage. In the case of Greater Vancouver, various actors operating in and beyond the region shape its uneven regional harm reduction assemblage. Surrey is policed by a federal police force, operating, at the time of the research under an anti-harm reduction conservative federal government; Vancouver has a local police department generally supportive of harm reduction. Surrey lacks a strong history of progressive political activism, and local politicians with ties to conservative provincial and federal policy-makers, construct powerful imaginaries of a permissive Vancouver drug approach that is at odds with a more 'family-oriented' Surrey. These representations justify continued official adherence to enforcement- and abstinence-oriented approaches even as others in Surrey – from public health practitioners to harm reduction advocates – find opportunities to engage in what they characterize as more pragmatic approaches. Yet, these opposing forces, for and against harm reduction, should not be conceptualized as irreducible and oppositional elements of a dualism. Of course, they are in one sense – opponents and supporters of harm reduction are unlikely to be reconciled easily – but, at the same time, these forces can be usefully conceptualized as a relational dyad (McCann & Ward, 2015; Sayer, 1992). In relation they constitute a dynamic policy landscape which, through its relationality and dynamism, holds out the prospect for change.

The policy mobilities literature understands change as mutation: policies mutate as they move from place to place and they re-mould the places, institutions, and political regimes through which they travel. For Peck and Theodore (2015, p. 137), 'no policy is ever literally "transferred"':

> Instead, a more appropriate metaphor might be that of "transduction" ... referring to the process in which viral vectors introduce foreign DNA into a receiving cell, leading to genetic mutation. If policy models can be seen, correspondingly, to establish webs of viral connection, they do so through processes of always-imperfect translation that nevertheless result in transformative change and continuous adaptation.

"Imagined in this way," they continue, "policy mobility comes to resemble ... a moving landscape, or an evolving ecosystem." This argument resonates with our notion of a policy assemblage, but it is not to suggest, however, that policy change is a "natural" process. It is a social one in which social actors continually experiment to mould new models into their particular situations, often in contradiction to other ongoing experiments (Peck & Theodore, 2015).

The history of harm reduction activism, from its origins in Europe, to its current uneven spread across the world (Harm Reduction International, 2015) emphasizes that its advocates know that models from one place cannot be imported unchanged into another. Rather, the character of programmes like needle exchange, drug consumption rooms, etc. must be experimented with, advocated for, and moulded to fit local cultures of drug use, health care systems, regulatory regimes, political contexts, physical spaces, and 'drugscapes' (McCann & Temenos, 2015). This lesson applies even across urban regions. It is quite possible that what harm reduction looks like in one part of a region might be different from its character in another. It is a matter of mutation, not replication. Thus, if harm reduction were to gain a firmer foothold in Surrey, there is no necessary reason to believe that a 'Vancouver model' would emerge, despite the dominant political narrative in Surrey. By the same token, while certain commonalities connect the strategies used by harm reduction advocates in different places, the particular balance of these strategies – work within institutions at various scales, protest politics, civil disobedience, appeals to scientific evidence, emotional narratives, etc. – will also differ from place to place.

In every place, alternative policy models will encounter barriers, but, as we have argued, policy barriers, boundaries, or frontiers are not absolute or insurmountable. Rather, they are spaces of constraint and parts of dynamic (changing and changeable) assemblages. They constitute spaces in which alliances can be built, debate can occur, and experimentation can take place. In the case of drug policy, these policy frontiers are quite literally spaces of life and death.

Acknowledgements

We are grateful to those who agreed to participate in this study. Comments by Nick Blomley and Kendra Strauss greatly benefited the larger project from which this paper comes. We also thank Tom Baker and Cristina Temenos for insightful comments, as well as the two anonymous reviewers and Ronan Paddison for guidance on improving an earlier draft. We are grateful to Stewart Williams and Barney Warf for inviting us to submit to this special issue. The usual disclaimers apply.

Disclosure statement

No potential conflict of interest was reported by the authors.

Funding

This work was supported by the Social Sciences and Humanities Research Council of Canada, Royal Canadian Geographical Society, and the Association of American Geographers Urban Specialty Group.

Notes

1. Unfortunately, due to data quality concerns with the introduction of a voluntary survey in 2011, rather than a mandatory census, we use income data drawn from the 2006 Census of Canada.
2. Calculated by the authors using average annual caseloads from unpublished BC Ministry of Social Development and Social Innovation data obtained upon request from the Ministry.
3. We use the term 'drug user groups' although we recognize that defining people as 'drug users', as opposed to people who use drugs, can problematically essentialize them – defining them as if they are nothing but their relationship to psychoactive substances. Our intention here is simply to point out the focus of the groups in question.
4. In abstract terms, this is also a description of Vancouver's Four Pillars approach. In both cities, enforcement, prevention, treatment, and harm reduction are brought together and exist in tension. In concrete terms, however, the weight given to each and the tension among them are different from place to place.

References

Allen, J., & Cochrane, A. (2007). Beyond the territorial fix: Regional assemblages, politics and power. *Regional Studies*, *41*(9), 1161–1175.

Bacchi, C. (2009). *Analysing policy: What's the problem represented to be? French's Forest*. Frenchs Forest: Pearson.

Baker, T., Cook, I., McCann, E., Temenos, C., & Ward, K. (in press). Policies on the move. *Annals of the Association of American Geographers*.

Baker, T., & Ruming, K. (2014). Making "Global Sydney": Spatial imaginaries, worlding and strategic plans. *International Journal of Urban and Regional Research*, *39*(1), 62–78.

Ball, S. J. (1993). What is policy? Texts, trajectories and toolboxes. *Discourse: Studies in the Cultural Politics of Education*, *13*(2), 10–17.

Bernstein, S. E., & Bennett, D. (2013). Zoned out: "NIMBYism", addiction services and municipal governance in British Columbia. *The International Journal of Drug Policy*, *24*(6), e61–e65.

Boyd, S., & Carter, C. (2014). *Killer weed: Marijuana grow ops, media, and justice*. Toronto: University of Toronto Press.

Boyd, S., MacPherson, D., & Osborn, B. (2009). *Raise shit! Social action saving lives*. Halifax: Fernwood.

Carter, C. (2009). Making residential cannabis growing operations actionable: A critical policy analysis. *The International Journal of Drug Policy*, *20*(4), 371–376.

City of Surrey. (2007a). *Crime reduction strategy*. Retrieved March 4, 2015, from http://www.surrey.ca/files/Crime_Reduction_Strategy.pdf

City of Surrey. (2007b). *2007 state of the city address*. Retrieved March 4, 2015, from http://www.surrey.ca/city-government/3055.aspx

Clarke, N. (2012). Urban policy mobility, anti-politics, and histories of the transnational municipal movement. *Progress in Human Geography*, *36*(1), 25–43.

Dhillon, S. (2015, October 19). Dianne Watts, star Conservative candidate, wins in Surrey. *The Globe and Mail*. Retrieved November 22, 2015, from http://www.theglobeandmail.com/

Erickson, P. G., Riley, D. M., Cheung, Y. W., & O'Hare, P. (Eds.). (1997). *Harm reduction: A new direction for drug policies and programs*. Toronto: University of Toronto Press.

Flowerdew, R., & Martin, D. (Eds.). (2005). *Methods in human geography* (2nd ed.). Essex: Pearson Education.

Geddes, J. (2010). RCMP and the truth about safe injection sites. *Maclean's*. Retrieved March 4, 2015, from http://www.macleans.ca/news/canada/injecting-truth/

Gonzalez, S. (2011). Bilbao and Barcelona "in Motion": How urban regeneration "models" travel and mutate in the global flows of policy tourism. *Urban Studies*, *48*(7), 1397–1418.

Harm Reduction International. (2015). *The global state of harm reduction*. Retrieved September 1, 2015, from www.ihra.net/global-state-of-harm-reduction

Harrison, J., & Hoyler, M. (2014). Governing the new metropolis. *Urban Studies*, *51*(11), 2249–2266.

Jacobs, J. M. (2012). Urban geographies I: Still thinking cities relationally. *Progress in Human Geography*, 36(3), 412–422.

Jenion, G. (2010). *Beyond "what works" in reducing crime: The development of a municipal community safety strategy in British Columbia* (Unpublished PhD dissertation). School of Criminology, Simon Fraser University.

Jonas, A. E. G. (2012). City-regionalism: Questions of distribution and politics. *Progress in Human Geography*, *36*(6), 822–829.

Katic, G., & Fenn, S. (2014, September 26). In Surrey, "Harm Reduction" drug approaches a hard sell. *The Tyee*. Retrieved March 4, 2015, from http://thetyee.ca/News/2014/09/26/Surrey-Harm-Reduction-Drug/

Kaye, K. (2010). *Drug courts and the treatment of addiction: Therapeutic jurisprudence and neoliberal governance* (Unpublished PhD dissertation). Department of Social and Cultural Analysis, New York University.

Kaye, K. (2012). Rehabilitating the "drugs lifestyle": Criminal justice, social control, and the cultivation of agency. *Ethnography*, *14*(2), 207–232.

Kerr, T., & Wood, E. (2008). Misrepresentation of science undermines HIV prevention. *Canadian Medical Association Journal, 178*(7), 964.
The Leader. (2006, June 2). British model of policing being explored by Surrey. *The Leader*, p. 3.
The Leader. (2007a, January 19). Courting a U.S. system. *The Leader*, p. 1.
The Leader. (2007b, April 11). City hires anti-crime boss. *The Leader*, pp. 23–24.
Leitner, H., Peck, J., & Sheppard, E. (2007). Squaring up neoliberalism. In H. Leitner, J. Peck, & E. Sheppard (Eds.), *Contesting neoliberalism: Urban frontiers* (pp. 311–327). New York, NY: Guilford Press.
Lipsky, M. (1980). *Street-level bureaucracy*. New York, NY: Russell Sage.
Longhurst, A. (2015). *Policy frontiers: City-regional politics of poverty and drug policy mobility* (Unpublished MA thesis). Department of Geography, Simon Fraser University.
Luymes, G. (2008, April 24). Mayor joins fan club of upscale Whalley condos. *The Province*, p. 8.
McCann, E. (2008). Expertise, truth, and urban policy mobilities: Global circuits of knowledge in the development of Vancouver, Canada's "four pillar" drug strategy. *Environment and Planning A, 40*(4), 885–904.
McCann, E. (2011a). Points of reference: Knowledge of elsewhere in the politics of urban drug policy. In *Mobile urbanism: Cities and policymaking in the global age* (pp. 97–122). Minneapolis: University of Minnesota Press.
McCann, E. (2011b). Urban policy mobilities and global circuits of knowledge: Toward a research agenda urban policy mobilities and global circuits of knowledge. *Annals of the Association of American Geographers, 101*(1), 107–130.
McCann, E. (2011c). Veritable inventions: Cities, policies and assemblage. *Area, 43*(2), 143–147.
McCann, E. (2013). Policy boosterism, policy mobilities, and the extrospective city. *Urban Geography, 34* (1), 5–29.
McCann, E., Roy, A., & Ward, K. (2013). Assembling/worlding cities. *Urban Geography, 34*(5), 581–589.
McCann, E., & Temenos, C. (2015). Mobilizing drug consumption rooms: Inter-place networks and harm reduction drug policy. *Health & Place, 31*, 216–223.
McCann, E., & Ward, K. (2010). Relationality/territoriality: Toward a conceptualization of cities in the world. *Geoforum, 41*(2), 175–184.
McCann, E., & Ward, K. (Eds.). (2011). *Mobile urbanism: Cities and policymaking in the global age*. Minneapolis: University of Minnesota Press.
McCann, E., & Ward, K. (2012). Policy assemblages, mobilities and mutations: Toward a multidisciplinary conversation. *Political Studies Review, 10*(3), 325–332.
McCann, E., & Ward, K. (2015). Thinking through dualisms in urban policy mobilities. *International Journal of Urban & Regional Research, 39*(4), 828–830.
McMartin, P. (2003, January 30). Whalley represents the other drug strategy. *The Vancouver Sun*, B1.
Ministry of Health. (2005). *Harm reduction: A BC community guide*. Retrieved March 4, 2014, from http://www.health.gov.bc.ca/library/publications/year/2005/hrcommunityguide.pdf
Parliament of Canada. (2009, November 9). The standing senate committee on legal and constitutional affairs evidence. Retrieved March 4, 2015, from http://www.parl.gc.ca/Content/SEN/Committee/402/lega/47503-e.htm?comm_id=11&Language=E&Parl=40&Ses=2
Peck, J. (2002). Political economies of scale: Fast policy, interscalar relations, and neoliberal workfare. *Economic Geography, 78*(3), 331–360.
Peck, J., & Theodore, N. (2010a). Mobilizing policy: Models, methods, and mutations. *Geoforum, 41*(2), 169–174.
Peck, J., & Theodore, N. (2010b). Recombinant workfare, across the Americas: Transnationalizing "fast" social policy. *Geoforum, 41*(2), 195–208.
Peck, J., & Theodore, N. (Eds.). (2010c). Theme issue: Mobilizing policy. *Geoforum, 41*(2), 169–226.
Peck, J., & Theodore, N. (2012). Follow the policy: A distended case approach. *Environment and Planning A, 44*(1), 21–30.
Peck, J., & Theodore, N. (2015). *Fast policy: Experimental statecraft at the thresholds of neoliberalism*. Minneapolis: University of Minnesota Press.
Peck, J., & Tickell, A. (2002). Neoliberalizing space. *Antipode, 34*(3), 380–404.
Proudfoot, J. (2011). *The anxious enjoyment of poverty: Drug addiction, panhandling, and the spaces of psychoanalysis* (Unpublished PhD dissertation). Department of Geography, Simon Fraser University.
Proudfoot, J., & McCann, E. (2008). At street level: Bureaucratic practice in the management of urban neighborhood change. *Urban Geography, 29*(4), 348–370.

Reevely, D. (2002, December 30). Safe drug sites won't fly in Surrey, politicians say. *The Vancouver Sun*, p. A1.

Roy, A., & Ong, A. (Eds.). (2011). *Worlding cities: Asian experiments and the art of being global*. Malden, MA: Wiley-Blackwell.

Sayer, A. (1992). *Method in social science: A realist approach*. New York, NY: Routledge.

Shore, C., Wright, S., & Pero, D. (Eds.). (2011). *Policy worlds: Anthropology and the analysis of contemporary power*. New York, NY: Berghahn Books.

Statistics Canada. (2007). *Surrey, British Columbia. 2006 Community Profiles. 2006 Census* [Catalogue no. 92-591-XWE]. Retrieved November 22, 2015, from Statistics Canada: http://www12.statcan.ca/census-recensement/2006/dp-pd/prof/92-591/index.cfm?Lang=E

Temenos, C. (2014). Differential policy mobilities: Transnational advocacy and harm reduction drug policy (Unpublished PhD dissertation). Department of Geography, Simon Fraser University.

Temenos, C. (2015). Mobilizing drug policy activism: Conferences, convergence spaces, and ephemeral fixtures in social movement mobilization. *Space & Polity*. Advance online publication.

Temenos, C., & McCann, E. (2013). Geographies of policy mobilities. *Geography Compass*, *7*(5), 344–357.

Ward, K. (2006). 'Policies in motion', urban management and state restructuring: The trans-local expansion of business improvement districts. *International Journal of Urban and Regional Research*, *30*(1), 54–75.

Yeatman, A. (1998). Introduction. In A. Yeatman (Ed.), *Activism and the policy process* (pp. 1–15). St Leonards: Allen & Unwin.

Mobilizing drug policy activism: conferences, convergence spaces and ephemeral fixtures in social movement mobilization

Cristina Temenos

Humanities Center, Northeastern University, Boston, MA, USA

This paper explores the role of conferences as "convergence space": temporary events with lasting material effects. Drawing on three harm reduction conferences occurring between 2011 and 2012, I argue that conferences are both ephemeral fixtures in the landscape of policy activism, and are important nodes through which policy mobilization occurs. Conference spaces provide opportunities for ideas to be shared, produced and advocated. They serve as important sites for the construction of relationships that are required to form and maintain policy advocacy networks and harness political opportunity structures for drug policy reform.

1. Introduction

Contestation over the best way to regulate psychoactive substances is not new. The rules and regulations that have governed substances, from caffeine and sugar, to alcohol and tobacco, to cannabis and opium, are as myriad as the ways in which the substances are found and used. Socio-cultural norms have always dictated the prevailing attitudes towards psychoactive substances. Contemporary debates over the management of illicit drugs and the people who consume them are no exception. From 2006 until 2013, 40 US states introduced legislation to ease drug laws, including the legalization of the production, sale and consumption of cannabis in the states of Washington and Colorado (Desilver, 2014). In 2000, Portugal decriminalized all drugs for personal use, leading to what has widely been seen as a successful drug policy (Hughes & Stevens, 2012). In 2013 Uruguay became the first nation state to legalize the production and sale of cannabis. These policy trends are the culmination of ongoing efforts in the drug policy reform movement that focuses on: increasing access to health services for people marginalized through drug use; reducing violent crime surrounding the production and sale of illicit substances; decreasing governmental funds spent on the policing of psychoactive substances, their producers and consumers; and decreasing the overall social costs that the "war on drugs" approach has wrought on people across the globe.

Drug policy reform is a movement supported by diverse interest groups with diverse values and ideologies. Neoliberal think-tanks, public health advocates, religious movements, celebrities, business magnates and human rights activists have all called for reform of drug laws, from the UN

Single Convention on Controlled Substances all the way to municipal by-laws governing the possession of sterile syringes (Branson, 2012; Easton, 2004; Pugel, 2013; United Nations Office on Drugs and Crime, 2014). While the ways in which such diverse groups of policy activists learn from each other are equally numerous, the importance of face-to-face meetings as a social movement strategy is often seen as crucial to long-term success. They are important for the production and exchange of knowledge, as well as for building and maintaining inter-personal ties across localities (Davies, 2012; Della Porta & Andretta, 2002; Haug, 2013; McAdam & Paulsen, 1993; Routledge, 2003, 2009).

This paper explores the role of conferences as a particular type of face-to-face meeting, in order to better understand the ways that knowledge exchange and interpersonal experience come together to affect drug policy activism. Using data collected from mixed qualitative methods including: participant observation at three harm reduction conferences; media and documentary analysis of drug policies, policy debates and conference media coverage; and 73 in-depth interviews with conference organizers, attendees and activists, I focus specifically on harm reduction conferences within this movement because harm reduction is becoming more common at all levels of governance. Harm reduction is a set of "policies, programmes and practices that aim primarily to reduce the adverse health, social and economic consequences of the use of legal and illegal psychoactive drugs without necessarily reducing drug consumption" (International Harm Reduction Association, n.d.). It is accepted and present throughout UN and World Health Organization documents, and many city governments, such as Toronto, Frankfurt and New York have implemented harm reduction drug policies. While the medical community regards harm reduction as best practice (Marlatt & Witkiewitz, 2010; Ritter & Cameron, 2006; Strike et al., 2011), and harm reduction policies are generally successful when implemented (Marlatt & Witkiewitz, 2010; Percival, 2009), they remain highly contested. They are often pitted in direct opposition to the war on drugs, and criminalization approaches to illegal substances and the people who use them. As a result, harm reduction is also a global social movement that is focused on equitable access to health care, social justice and human rights. The conferences discussed here emerge from, and are important events in this social movement.

I argue that conferences are both important spaces for the social reproduction of advocacy movements through the production and dissemination of knowledge, and for the encounters that contribute to creating and strengthening relationships among people. Further, I argue that the physical infrastructures that affect the placing of conferences in turn implicate cities in the production of social movements and policy mobilization. Conferences are both ephemeral fixtures in the landscape of policy activism, and are important nodes through which policy mobilization occurs. Conference spaces provide opportunities for ideas to be shared, produced and advocated. They serve as important sites for the construction of relationships that are required to form and maintain policy advocacy networks and harness political opportunity structures for drug policy reform.

In the discussion that follows, I explore work on urban social movements and their attendant spatialites together with recent work on policy mobilities to illustrate the relational and mundane aspects of where policy gets conceived, advocated for and mobilized in particular, situated ways. My aim here is to focus on the *process*, rather than the effects of policy mobilization. The focus on processes involved in movement mobilization are understood as processes of assemblage, the deliberate drawing together and territorialization of "globally mobile resources, ideas, and knowledge" (McCann & Ward, 2012, p. 43). I will do so by drawing on examples from three harm reduction conferences occurring between 2011 and 2012. Harm Reduction Canada, held in Ottawa, Canada in 2011, and the 2012 Harm Reduction Coalition's (HRC) National Conference held in Portland, USA, were both national level conferences attracting international attendees. Harm Reduction Canada had about 150 attendees, and the HRC National Conference had over

800 (personal communication with conference organizer; http://harmreduction.org). The Euro-Harm Reduction Network conference, in Marseilles, France in 2011 was a regional conference that hosted about 170 attendees from Europe, North America, and the Middle East (personal communication with conference organizer).

The next section of this paper reviews recent relevant literatures on urban policy mobilities, urban social movements, assemblage and informational infrastructures. I then go on to look at empirical data on the role of conferences in the reproduction of social movements through their contribution to and maintenance of informational infrastructures. The subsequent section considers the relationship between conferences and physical urban infrastructures. The conclusion provides some insight into how these relationships contribute broadly to informational infrastructures, and specifically to drug policy reform.

2. Policy mobilities

Policy mobilities research has, from its inception, been about the movement of policy knowledge and technologies. Concerned with the ways in which policies are made up, moved around and reterritorialized in places elsewhere, policy mobilities research emerged from a discomfiture with static theorizations of policy transfer that produced narrow and hierarchical models of the policy process which neglected individual actors, agency, policy mutations and local contingencies (for a full critique, see McCann & Ward, 2013). Policy mobilities holds that the mobilization of policy is simultaneously in motion and fixed in place – whether it is being pieced together so as to be successfully implemented (or marketed) in a particular place or whether it is mutating as it travels – through multiple people and knowledge networks or informational infrastructures. This relationality is present when policy is *in the process* of being implemented, and changing as it is realized on the ground. Questions about the who, how and why of these processes make up the essential approach of trying to understand, more holistically, how policies are made, mobilized and mutated. This research is attentive to the micro-spaces of policy process, in the form of: embodied and local perspectives (Keil & Ali, 2011; McCann, 2008, Temenos & McCann, 2012), the "structuring fields" of policy mobilization (Cook & Ward, 2011, 2012; Peck & Theodore, 2010; Ward, 2006), policy tourism (Cook, Ward, & Ward, 2014; González, 2011), and the historical contingencies of policy learning and change (Clarke, 2012; Cook et al., 2014; Cook & Ward, 2011; Harris and Moore, 2013; Jacobs & Lees, 2013).

McCann (2008, 2011b) has charted the importation and transformation of drug policy from cities in Europe to Vancouver, Canada. This work highlights the local contingencies of policy model making, such as the public health crisis around HIV rates that was declared in Vancouver (see also Boyd, Macpherson, & Osborn, 2009; Wood et al., 2004) and which required an alternative policy solution to the then-current drug policy (McCann, 2008, 2011b). This work also pays attention to the situated histories of drug use and its management that preceded the model in cities in Europe, especially Frankfurt, Germany, the city that Vancouver's current drug policy primarily echoes (McCann, 2008). In understanding how urban drug policy is made mobile, McCann (2008, p. 9) identifies three primary elements: the learning strategies employed by local actors intent on instigating policy change; the role of experts in spreading policy ideas; and the labour of institutions and organizations that work to provide information and *spaces* that facilitate policy mobilization. It is this last element, these spaces of encounter, with which this paper is concerned.

Conferences as sites of learning and exchange have long held value for diverse communities such as; political conferences, academic conferences, business conventions, and I would add to this, activist conferences (Adey, 2006; Craggs & Mahony, 2014; Diani, 2000; DiPetro, Bretter, Rompf, & Godlewska, 2008; England & Ward, 2007; McLaren & Mills, 2008; Tanford,

Montgomery, & Nelson, 2012). Early work on policy mobilities has noted the importance of face-to-face communication in the form of conferences and policy tourism (González, 2011; McCann, 2008; Ward, 2006). Cook and Ward (2012) use ethnographic methods to explicate the ways a single conference becomes part of an informational infrastructure focused on importing a particular form of learning and operation, Business Improvement Districts, into cities in Sweden. Through this ethnographic focus on a conference they demonstrate the path-dependencies through which policy ideas travel. This work highlights the process of importing policy experts as architects of policies and programmes deemed successful elsewhere, and the value of conferences for localized individuals to educate them about best practice and benchmarking strategies of policy making and implementation.

Building on this work, my aim is to expand the understanding of informational infrastructures' roles in policy advocacy by charting a series of conferences and analysing how conferences build on each other, and how they build a movement for policy mobilization over time. Understanding how a series of harm reduction conferences sustain and build knowledge and momentum for a public health drug policy model is useful for several reasons. First it demonstrates the ongoing advocacy work done by multiple constellations of actors. Focusing on a series of event spaces helps to articulate the complex spatial vocabularies in and through which policies are made. Second, this focus helps us to chart the shift in attitudes and ideas about best practice approaches to drug policy, and by extension shifting understandings of governance practices, human rights and health over a period of time. Finally, analysing a series of conferences within a particular social movement aimed at policy change is important because it draws together different and particular geographies of drug policy by territorializing ephemeral practices and fragments of memory that shape the actions and thinking of policy makers and mid-level bureaucrats, those in powerful positions who make and enact policies that govern drug use and treatment. "Ideas and practices arrive from elsewhere or emerge in particular contexts in all sorts of ways – through forgotten conversations at meetings, long-distant reading of publications or reports, unpredictable friendship and collegial networks, as well as formal or informal association in which taken-for-granted understanding might be confirmed. It is important to consider," Robinson (2013, p. 9) argues, "that the infrastructure of policy transfer … is significantly immaterial" (see also Bunnell, 2015; Jacobs, 2012; Prince, 2012). This work renders visible the paths connecting topological spaces of policy-making and advocacy work.

3. Convergence space

Placing our understanding of conferences within the wider context of political opportunity structures helps to uncover the spatiality in policy activism. As discussed above, there are numerous examinations of the role of conferences, mass demonstrations and mega events as occurrences that work to catalyse social movements (Davies, 2012; Della Porta and Andretta, 2002; Diani, 2000; Routledge, 2003, 2009; Wainwright, Prudham, & Glassman, 2000). While much of this work interestingly engages the ways that these events function temporally within the history of a social movement, it is only recently that they have begun to be spatially conceptualized. "Place, space, territory, region, scale and networks", Miller (2013, p. 285) notes, "have each been placed front and centre by a variety of social movement scholars and each spatiality-specific approach has yielded valuable insights, yet there has been little progress toward a more integrative approach". Drawing on Jessop et al.'s (2008) theorizations of sociospatial relations, Miller (2013) and others have worked to move beyond the typological and nested scalar hierarchies that much of this work produces to extrapolate the co-scalar production of social movements and advocacy networks (Davies, 2012; Leitner, Sheppard, & Sziarto, 2008; Nicholls, 2009; Nicholls, Miller, & Beaumont, 2013).

In one such understanding, Routledge (2003, p. 346) puts forward the notion of a convergence space, which I draw upon here. Convergence spaces can be understood as dynamic systems: "constructed out of a complexity of interrelations and interactions across all spatial scales". Convergence spaces come into being for delimited times, so in this sense they are fleeting, or ephemeral. Yet they also have lasting effects because of their facilitation of encounter – people being able to meet and network, as well as to strengthen existing relationships – maintaining weak ties. Convergence space can be understood as relational space. It facilitates the production, exchange and legitimation of knowledge, by convening people from varying interest groups and resources in a particular place at a particular time, and at the same time, place-based ideologies and differences are negotiated within convergence spaces. Drawing on Massey (1994), Routledge (2003, p. 346) argues that places where "collective political rituals" like conferences are held, "become 'articulated moments' … in the enactment of global [social movements]". That is, convergence space constitutes the space of mobility within an advocacy movement. It allows the drawing together of people and resources to engage in knowledge production, exchange, planning and actions to address specific issues of contention, such as drug policy.

There are three attributes of convergence space: First, they are collections of diverse interest groups with shared values and/or goals. Convergence spaces comprise diverse social movements that articulate collective visions. Second, they allow for variegated forms of spatial interaction between individuals and groups, they bring people and groups into contact who might not otherwise meet. A convergence space is an assemblage, a deliberate drawing together of people, resources and ideas. Third, these "spaces facilitate multi-scalar political action by participant movements" (Routledge, 2003, p. 345). Convergence spaces make room for diverse social movement organizations to come together, and therefore facilitate ongoing spatialized relationships, imparting meaning on the ephemeral.

For example, it is not uncommon, when referring to annual or biannual gatherings that people will refer to them by place. "Were you in Seattle?" in the context of discussing North American social action, needs no explanation. The question clearly refers to the anti-globalization protests and other forms of collective action surrounding the World Trade Organization meetings in 1999. Similarly, harm reduction advocates refer to conferences by the city in which they were held: Toronto, Portland, Liverpool. The relational "articulated moment" of a convergence space facilitates movement mobilization and simultaneously disambiguates roles of places elsewhere within social movements, canonizing certain places as pivotal within a particular struggle. The relationality of conference space as convergence space allows for the place-based event to have lasting and far-reaching effects on a social movement, and its attendant mobilization geographically across space. As I will show below, they also facilitate social movements' ability to move forward to affect political change in specific places elsewhere. Expanding the notion of convergence space through an examination of conferences works towards also expanding our understanding of the spatio-temporal production of social movements as multi-scalar networks.

Similarly, recent work on urban social movements has engaged the notion of the productive city through understandings of relationality. Uitermark, Nicholls, and Loopmans (2012, p. 2) understand the city as

> a generative space of mobilizations … the frontline where states constantly create new governmental methods to protect and produce social and political order, including repression, surveillance, clientelism, corporatism, participatory and citizenship initiatives, etc. These techniques combine in different ways … [making cities] the places where new ways of regulating, ordering and controlling social life are invented.

I argue that the city's role in the making up of conference space as convergence space can be usefully understood as an "assembling agent" (McFarlane, 2009), contributing its particular, situated logics to a broader multiplicity of ideas in the making up of a movement, such as harm reduction, or drug policy reform. The urban, in this sense brings about particular mobilities that produce material effects in both policy and politics, as well as the technical underpinnings – the infrastructures that help to bolster social life.

The value in conceptualizing social movements through assemblage is the concepts' ability to deepen territorialized understandings of site-specific contingencies and their connections to other places. Assemblage is not used here in the Deluzian sense of the creation of flat ontologies, rather the opposite, its value is in helping to trance difficult, ephemeral events and the uneven geographies through which they are produced. In this sense assemblage is a methodological tool as much as a conceptual one. It highlights territorialized contingencies "in terms of… [assemblages'] histories, the labour required to produce them, and their inevitable capacity to exceed the connections between other groups or places in the movement" (McFarlane, 2009, p. 562, see also Davies, 2012). Here, the notion of convergence space is useful to understand not only why a particular event, such as a conference, is important in the life-span of a social movement.

It helps to situate such a fleeting event in the material histories of place. A convergence space acts to create a mooring point within an assemblage. Conceptualizing convergence space through assemblage highlights that these spaces are not simply a "resultant formation" (McFarlane, 2009, p. 562), they are also constitutive of particular configurations. These spaces mediate ongoing power dynamics, the labour and pre-established processes that work to facilitate social movements. People, resources and knowledge coalesce in specific constellations that operate through pre-defined networks and pathways. The previous processes of assembling these networks have in turn created a series of informational infrastructures, to which this next section turns.

4. Informational Infrastructures

As spaces through which knowledge around specific policy models are produced and transferred, informational infrastructures are not inherently territorial. Rather, they exist and operate through interpersonal networks linked through the socio-technical landscapes of policy work. Informational infrastructures can be defined as "institutions, organizations, and technologies, that frame and package knowledge about best policy practices, successful cities, and cutting-edge ideas for specific audiences" (Temenos & McCann, 2013, 805, see also McCann, 2008, 2011a; Cook & Ward, 2011). They can be understood as agentive, power-laden entities that are made up of at least four subsets of actors and institutions: states, educators, media, and professional and activist organizations (Temenos & McCann, 2013)[1]. Informational infrastructures serve to produce, present, propose and propel best practice policy models via conduits such as: research, publications, media, accreditation processes, policy tourism and of course conferences. Table 1, which is by no means comprehensive, highlights some of the major technologies, actors and processes of informational infrastructures that are operationalized by policy activists.

It is with this understanding, of conferences – as a convergence space, and as a part of the broader informational infrastructures of policy mobilization that we consider the specific processes of siting conferences, and how this placing has a lasting affect on both the city as well as the policy movement. Within health geography, there has been much work done on the siting of health services in cities (cf. Pierce, Martin, Greiner, and Scherr (2012)). However, work has not focused on the siting of health-related events and health social movements in the same way (for exceptions see Brown, 1997; Klawiter, 1999). Paying attention to the site selection of convergence spaces in the policy activism of public health drug policies, I argue, is important both for understanding the infrastructural form of the city, and for understanding how urban spaces of public health are constructed. Pierce et al. (2012, p. 1086) maintain that: "attention

Table 1: Informational Infrastructures.

Institutions	Actors, Technologies, Processes
States	All scales; State actors (politicians, bureaucrats, etc); State power of implementation; Legitimacy.
Educators	Educators & trainers formally educating policy actors; Legitimation/ certification practices; Power to frame knowledge.
Media	Repetition of narratives; Frame policies, actors, cities as 'good'/'bad'; Social media facilitates knowledge exchange between publics and institutions.
Professional & Activist Organizations	Frame, value, facilitate transfer of policy knowledge; Mobilize through: publications, websites, site visits, conferences.

to "politics" in research on health can help better answer questions about the locus of decision making that produces health landscapes and outcomes such as definitions of well-being and health in urban social life". This 'locus of decision making' is often black-boxed, and the processes by which decision-making occurs are rarely transparent, because, as Robinson (2013) notes, ideas are often formed through fragments of documents, fleeting conversations or remembered conference presentations. Thus there is rarely a clear place-based understanding of where policy comes from. Looking to conferences as convergence space however, these loci are rendered tangible. The places where those fragments, conversations and presentations were encountered come to the foreground. These impermanent gatherings facilitate knowledge exchange and influence decision-making processes. In focusing on conference space as convergence space attends "to practices and the multiple modalities through which power is executed" (Miller, 2013, p. 289, see also McFarlane, 2009). A government office where a policy is signed into law, for example, is then understood as relationally extended, assembled from other actions, meetings and places, rather than as an isolated and black-boxed locality where power "happens".

Cook and Ward (2012) note that informational infrastructures have grown in recent years because of an increase in activities and processes associated with making "good policy" – which makes it more likely that specific policy models will be made mobile and implemented in places elsewhere. They have also argued for a deeper understanding of the role of conferences as temporary, or time limited, events that draw people together, allowing for people with shared values and interests the opportunity for face-to-face communication and knowledge exchange. They are advocating for the consideration of the technical as political in policy making. This is echoed by Miller (2007, 2013), who advocates for a re-inscription of Foucauldian technologies of power into spatial understandings of social movements. Those spatial technologies that operate in a co-scalar sense, technologies making up convergence space, informational infrastructures and even urban form, work to bring about an assemblage within contentious spatial politics and sites of urban public health.

In the remainder of the paper I draw on these concepts to explore three harm reduction conferences to argue that conference spaces contribute to the ongoing production of informational infrastructures within the harm reduction movement. Serving as space for best-practice knowledge exchange, they also operate as political space where certain ideas, practices and technologies are re-inscribed through face-to-face encounter. Conferences as convergence space are both ephemeral fixtures in the landscape of policy activism, and are important nodes through which policy mobilization occurs. Conference spaces provide opportunities for ideas to be shared, produced and advocated for and they serve as important sites for the construction of relationships required to form and maintain policy advocacy networks and harness political opportunity structures for drug policy reform.

As noted above, this research entailed participant observation at three conferences on harm reduction drug policy in North America and Europe. The regional and national conferences attendance ranged from 150 to 800 attendees from local activists and service providers to international advocates and experts. They were held in Ottawa, Marseilles and Portland, respectively. Participant observation in attendance at the conferences was augmented by face-to-face and telephone interviews with conference organizers and attendees before, during and after the events. The paper now goes on to illustrate the role of conference space as convergence space through observation and analysis.

5. Spaces of learning and exchange

5.1 *Locating convergence space*

Harm reduction drug policies, such as those legalizing syringe exchange, are often contested on moral grounds by those who argue that they enable illegal activity (drug use), yet local public health officials often understand that harm reduction approaches to drug consumption contribute to healthier communities. Simultaneously, healthier communities contribute to remaking urban spaces by for example, reducing public drug consumption, in turn rendering the city more attractive to economic development interests. Conference organizers often took these local political debates into account when choosing the site of their conferences. Political alliances, or alternatively, clear conflict with city governments was something that organizers were acutely aware of, and affected their choice. In Marseilles, the conference organizer spoke of deliberately siting the conference there because the local government supported harm reduction, while the federal government was still sceptical of the approach. One respondent put it this way:

> Well you know, that [decision] was interesting, but we always try and go where there's conflict, so we can raise the profile locally … this year its Marseilles. If the French government sees all these people coming to their cities … well, that's a good thing. If they're seen as being a leader in this, well it only helps the mayor. (Interview, Conference Organizer, 2011)

In this sentiment, one can see a clear deliberation, focused on awareness raising and harnessing political opportunity structures to raise public and governmental awareness, using the convergence of people to extend the social movement locally. The respondent went on to explain that when governments see people travelling to conferences on harm reduction, it helps the social movement. Pro-business governments are more likely to act favourably towards harm reduction practices such as implementing needle exchange or drug consumption rooms.

In all three cases, interviews revealed a selection of the conference sites as both political, and practical. There is a balancing act, of siting the conference in a place that might do good – but also ensuring that the conference is a success. One organizer put it this way:

> … first we went to Oakland and there were thousands of people. Then we thought lets go to Cleveland – they have a needle exchange that's in trouble, let go there. Well, no one came! Who wants to go to Cleveland? So we had like 700 people there. So we weren't building on what we had started in Oakland. So we thought ok well we have to go to locations that people like. No help in Miami for local people, but there were tonnes of people there, because they loved Miami. Portland is somewhere where we have a lot of support from the health department, they're really invested … so it's a place that people want to go to because its trendy, Portlandia, you know? (Interview, Conference Organizer, 2012)

Building a yearly following of conference goers maintains weak ties – relationships garnered by shared goals and values, though not a shared identity – making the relationships and the movement stronger. Conferences constitute the sort of purposeful convergence space that, as Nicholls (2009, p. 85) notes, provide "favorable conditions for diverse activists to initiate and strengthen ties in areas of common interest. As these ties strengthen over time, they become important generators of rich social capital". In this case, in Oakland, the intent to create a localized political opportunity structure, using the conference as a tool to raise awareness and show support of the health service, created tensions between the ongoing effort to maintain and build transnational advocacy networks, and to intervene at an acutely local level.

Portland it seemed, was a happy medium. The county health department was characterized as supportive of harm reduction services, and for harm reduction practitioners from small and mid-sized cities, places where harm reduction was perceived to be under threat, and/or unsupported, having officials from the health department speak at the conference lead to many in-depth discussions about practical strategies to gain support from government and health agencies, as well as the wider public. The presence of supportive officials in Portland both maintained movement momentum and lead to small scale movement strategizing. Conference organizers were able to help leave "a legacy ... [of] something that's improved" (Interview, Conference Organizer, 2012) through the media attention and political engagement that the event helped to catalyse. As Uitermark et al. (2012, p. 2546) state: "Contention and movements emanate from cities but also stretch outwards as activists broker relations between local and their more geographically distant allies." In the case of the HRC National Conference, it was able to broker those relations in place by bringing activists, advocates, health care professionals, social service workers, and people who use drugs to Portland, while simultaneously bringing government officials, mid-level government bureaucrats, and local media to the conference. Cities then serve to anchor movements, such as harm reduction, while also increasing inter-urban connections between activists from elsewhere and local stakeholders. The city, whether it is Oakland, Portland or Marseilles, works to anchor memories of encounter around a territorialized point. This effect deepens the relationality of the event, the conference, by expanding its influence both topologically and intellectually within the broader social movement.

5.2 *Encounter and maintaining ties*

Conferences are mobilized in several ways. Not only do they bring people together, engendering an embodied mobility – discussed above – but conferences also facilitate the transfer of knowledge and the construction and maintenance of weak and strong ties. This translation is almost always the main purpose of any conference, be it activist or academic in nature (Craggs & Mahony, 2014). And it is the intent that the assembling of people and ideas, the creation of such a convergence space will contribute to the production of policy change through advocacy. Moving people shifts technical and ideological understandings of drug policy. For example, the HRC National Conference theme was "From Social Justice to Public Health." Meant to both highlight the grass roots history of harm reduction – the first needle exchanges were begun by people actively using drugs – and to simultaneously refocus attention to the way in which harm reduction had become a public health initiative, the conference theme itself connotes mobility over time. It does not merely mean change over time, rather it highlights the understanding that mobilities are historically situated and path-dependent. The drawing together of public health and social justice in the same theme also highlights the ongoing work to acknowledge collectivity, in terms of collective action as a social movement as well as collective practices such as peer-lead syringe exchange, in the Harm Reduction movement. Public health, a population level medical intervention is presented as a next step in the Harm Reduction movement, following from the social justice momentum that had previously animated the movement. Indeed the next HRC Conference theme, "Intersections & Crossroads: Doing Together What We Can't Do Apart," similarly evokes mobility. It also carries on the normative understanding of harm reduction as a collective practice and movement.

Collective action is often operationalized through transnational associative processes, looking to groups elsewhere who share similar values for political and resource support. "These connections are grounded in place- and face-to-face based moments of articulation" (Routledge, 2003, p. 344). The work of searching for alternatives, protocols and technical practices sometimes comes from an Internet search. However the value of encounter – physical meetings – was something that almost all of the people I spoke with emphasized. One conference organizer noted:

> You forget how much people get out of physical connections because we do so much online. People forget there is so much value in meeting face-to face ... we're more likely to follow things up once we've physically met them. Its difficult to get the momentum going only online, you need the face-to-face contact. I think it's really easy to ignore emails if you haven't met someone. (Interview, Conference Organizer, 2011)

The face-to-face meeting creates ties because the encounter is physical and embedded in a specific place. It enhances the experience through a sensory engagement of sights, sounds, smells and proximity. At the same time that conferences produce meaningful opportunities for face-to-face meetings, they also re-produce certain hierarchies within the social movement. Later in our interview, the same conference organizer discussed these tensions, which highlighted those able to engage in conference mobility:

> We aimed to offer people a platform to have discussions that were important to them. I think they appreciated the opportunity to have those contentious conversations. At the international levels, which is where people have the privilege to talk about it all the time, it's often policy people, and its us [professional advocates] having those conversations. So there was a lot of front line workers, and that went really well ... I'm hoping they went away with a sense of ownership. That was the main objective. (Interview, Conference Organizer, 2011)

There is both a hope and a concerted effort on the part of conference organizers to facilitate connections between professional policy activists and front line harm reduction practitioners, including people who use drugs and access harm reduction services. Harm reduction as a movement maintains a debate about its medicalization, and a concern that the movement has become too institutionalized. Drug user activists in particular, as well as many front line workers are vocal within discussions during conference sessions as well as outside of the formalized spaces, such as at a lunch break, or over a drink. Ensuring that there are the resources and space for such movement members to attend the conference was important for the organizers, a point I will return to below.

It is important to note that a conference acting as a space of encounter does not magically create connections, spur mobilization or change people's thinking. There is an ongoing massaging of ideas and meetings that occur in the orchestrated spaces that constitute convergence spaces such as conferences. Unstructured events, such as coffee breaks, and evening receptions are as important as the scheduled plenary sessions (Cook & Ward, 2012; Craggs & Mahony, 2014). In the evenings, there were several different events that were scheduled, such as the Canadian debut of a documentary, *Raw Opium*. While not a "mandatory" part of the conference, it was a highly promoted event where several conference keynote speakers were also scheduled to speak on a panel. Most of the audience that night was made up of conference goers. Conference participants had made plans before and after to go for meals or drinks. These informal meetings and gatherings were not merely a place to unwind after a long day of sessions, but also served as a space to reinforce and foster relationships among conference participants (Nicholls, 2009;

Routledge, 2003). It was here that many discussions between drug user activists and professional policy advocates were able to extend into longer, drawn-out debates. This opportunity allowed the extension of the conference space out of the convention centre and into the city. Further, it extending the influence of the conference as a fleeting event further into the informational infrastructure of harm reduction as a social movement.

Professional advocates were present at all of the conferences I attended. In many cases this group of people, which for example included the Drug Policy Program Coordinator at the Hungarian Civil Liberties Association, the Director of the Canadian Drug Policy Coalition, and board members of the International Network of People Who Use Drugs, were in attendance at several of the same conferences – as well as other meetings and events throughout the year. During conferences meetings were set, and the normally geographically dispersed group of activists were able to come together, renewing their ties. Often, their co-presence on panels contributed to a sense of camaraderie, connectedness and shared values throughout the room. Participants often joked with each other, and referred, in conference sessions to previous meetings and encounters with each other. The continuity of key figures within the movement appearing over time is another key component that functions to build the advocacy movement itself (Craggs & Mahony, 2014; Nicholls, 2009). The co-presence of policy activists in official conference sessions, together with informal meetings contributes to the formalization of knowledge transfer within harm reduction, as well as to the socio-spatiality of the informational infrastructure within the drug policy reform movement.

6. Conferences, path dependencies and physical infrastructures

Beyond building the informational infrastructures on which drug policy advocacy is predicated, attention to the physical infrastructures that enable conferences as successful convergence spaces is also a key consideration. Is the conference accessible? Location and accessibility was a major point of consideration in all three conferences, from both the city where the conference is held, to the conference hall itself. One conference organizer noted the importance of having activists and traditionally marginalized groups, in this case, people who use drugs, feel comfortable in the space.

> That's why we had it at the uni[versity], because people with records – people who live on the street – they don't want to walk into a conference hall. "Spruce room, what … is Spruce room?" They're not going to ask a security guard for directions. Campus – well there's still barriers and all, but at least it's a public space – supposedly … so it makes it better for them, you know? (Interview, Conference Organizer, 2011)

As McCann (2011, p. 120) observes, "decisions about how and where to hold meetings are strategic, offering benefits to the organizing institutions, the attendees, and the local hosts". This is important from the broader global, national or city scale, right down to the microspaces of a convention centre, hotel, university or public park. Another conference organizer spoke to the geographic location of conferences. Referring back to a now disbanded organization that ran a large international harm reduction conference, they complained: "They were always picking islands off of islands – you couldn't get there! Forget scholarships! And who can afford it? They had one token drug user" (Interview, Conference Organizer, 2011). This quote highlights the social justice nature of the conference, and the politics of including the people affected by drug policy in spaces and processes of knowledge production, the economics of attending the conference – the costs are often prohibitive – and even more so if they are not held in large urban centres that have planned economic strategies around attracting the business of conferences and mega events. The connection between the economic viability, conference sustainability and physical infrastructures came up with two of the three organizers. One noted that they chose locations based on: "East, West, Central [United States]" (Interview, Conference Organizer, 2012) specifically so that local harm reduction practitioners and local people who use drugs were able to garner the resources necessary to attend the conferences.

Additionally, each of the three conferences held pre-meetings specifically for drug user organizers. By providing a deliberate space occurring before the "main event", social movement organizations such as EuroHRN, attempted to ensure that they lived up to their political commitments, taking the mantra of drug user organizers, "Nothing about us without us," seriously. Meeting in advance of other policy advocates and harm reduction practitioners enabled drug user activists to take a meaningful leading role in shaping subsequent conference discussions around advocacy techniques and priority issues. The pre-conference in Marseilles for example was:

> … part of a wider recognition within the harm reduction movement that it is no longer possible for the global discussion on drug policy to continue without the full involvement of those most acutely affected i.e. people who use drugs. As such, this dual network building process has been a concrete example of the meaningful participation of people who use drugs in all policies and programmes that concern them. (Albers, 2012, p. 1)

Throughout the conference, self-identified drug user activists played a prominent part in the speakers' lists, panels and discussions. EuroHRN and many of the organizations for whom drug user activists worked also provided substantial scholarships to people who use drugs to be able to attend the conference. The prominent presence of people who use drugs at the event signified to both people who use drugs and the wider harm reduction community that: "There is every expectation that the two networks will maintain, build and strengthen ties by engaging in joint campaigns, that will both boost capacity and act as conduits for mutual learning and cooperation" (Albers, 2012, p. 1) The EuroHRN conference, coupled with the pre-conference meeting of the European Network of People Who Use Drugs is an example of the ways in which the conference served to build the informational infrastructure around the harm reduction movement, tapping into a co-production of convergence space. "Broadening the geographical and social base of a political insurgency necessarily introduces a wide range of *diverse* actors into the mix … While broadening the alliance provides activists with access to new resources and sources of legitimacy … " (Nicholls, 2009, 86 italics original) The two meetings, happening in tandem and drawing on the same physical infrastructures serve to build inter-personal relationships between people and to build trust among different social movement organizations.

6.1 *Extended relationality – material and ephemeral*

Mobilizing policy activism through convergence space both reterritorializes and extends it through personal mobility and over time. When convergence space is assembled into being in a city, there is, in the words of Mayer (2013, p. 183): "fresh momentum to the local movements, helping them overcome their fragmentation, and supporting their consolidation as well as their professionalization". Reterritorializing a global social movement such as harm reduction, in cities simultaneously contributes "to the transfer of repertoires associated with the work of transnationally oriented organizations, such as professional public relations work, conscious media orientation, and a flexible action repertoire utilizing pragmatic as well as militant action forms" (Mayer (2013, p. 183). Therefore the informational infrastructures, the public relations work and media orientations, for instance, are also deliberately spatialized. One organizer put it thus:

> Paris and Marseilles are kind of the two big focal points in terms of drug use. And both are kind of pioneers of harm reduction [in France]. The city of Marseille is a big supporter of harm reduction, and you could see that throughout the conference, with the municipal support and the fieldtrips. And they really want to open an injection room. The problem of course is that Sarkozy doesn't want to see injection rooms in France, however, if anywhere is going to do it, it will be Marseille. (Interview, Conference Organizer, 2011)

In this case, there is a sense of showcasing local success of harm reduction, and co-operation of transnational social movement and advocacy organizations with local government, with the intent of pushing back against an unfriendly national government. Holding the conference in Marseilles, the second largest city in France, rather than Paris, the largest and the capital, signals two strategic spatial tactics on the part of social movement organizations. Marseille, an industrial port city, has long had an association with the illegal drugs trade. It was a major node through which heroin was transported to North America from the 1950s to 1970s. The opening scenes of the 1971 film, *The French Connection* – loosely based around the smuggling ring – feature the narrow winding streets of the city, and zoom in to focus on the Mediterranean port, highlighting the movement of drugs through the city. Holding the conference in this city highlights a tension between the geographical imagination of Marseilles as a place of drug trade and hoping to help combat the stigma that this very reputation engenders. Second, there is the rationale that the conference impact will be amplified by calling it into being in a city that has the potential for achieving successful drug policy reform, and a city that is already advocating for increased harm reduction measures.

Indeed, as Miller (2013, 293) agues,

> Successful collective action – in most cases – involves building and shaping relationships not only among significant numbers of like minded activists, but also with apparatuses of states, corporations, or other powerful institution or groups in positions of authority in order to make meaningful claims upon them.

In the case of the EuroHRN conference, this was obvious from the venue, a municipal building in the downtown core. An examination of the welcome package provides further insight into the relationship between the state and EuroHRN. Beyond the conference schedule, the package contained an invitation from the city's deputy mayor; the welcome reception was hosted by the city. Rather than the usual pen and paper for taking notes, conference goers found the city's logo emblazoned on male and female condoms, a nod to the subject – harm reduction – of the conference. As well, the field trips, to needle exchanges and a local housing squat, were led by city employees.

Support and advocacy for harm reduction in the city of Marseilles was made evident through a continual branding process on the part of the city, and the frequent acknowledgements by EuroHRN conference organizers, of municipal support. This acknowledgement served two purposes. First EuroHRN helped bolster the image of the city government. Second, the knowledge of mutual support, the city's support for harm reduction, helped establish the feeling of community with harm reduction networks. This action, in turn, helped combat the isolation that is often felt among local social movements, and which is often cited as occurring among harm reduction practitioners (Pauly, 2008); something often mentioned in interviews. On another level, funding for the conference came from sponsorship of the European Commission, who also funded the international translation between French and English that was available in all of the conference plenaries. Financial and organizational support also came from the local municipal government of Marseille, and a local harm reduction organization, R'eduisones des Risques Lies a l'usages de Drouges (AFR). The conference served as a convergence space assembled through multi-level government support of harm reduction in a city advocating for intensified health services to treat some of its most marginalized populations.

7. Conclusion

Arguing that conferences play a role in building and sustaining political opportunity structures around drug policy reform, I have shown that they are important social movement strategies that help to maintain interpersonal and organizational ties. In the process of assembling a social movement around harm reduction and drug policy reform, conferences as convergence space also draw the city into this assemblage as topological fixture for movement mobilization. Physical urban infrastructures are enrolled in the production of a social movement, while having lasting effects that contribute to ongoing informational infrastructures among and within the cities where conferences occur. Conferences then, are important in building and maintaining informational infrastructures. They increase the relational work that is crucial for success within global social movements such as harm reduction, rendering cities such as Ottawa, Portland and Marseilles important to drug policy reform in cities like Regina, Austin or Bari.

The point of this paper is not to illustrate a specific corollary between a conference happening in one place and a clear policy shift in that place or elsewhere. Rather, my objective is to show that understanding how conferences are ephemeral fixtures, assemblages of transnational advocacy networks also helps us to understand the spatialities of policy mobilities and social movements, in the process uncovering the material and multiple territorializations that produce relational networks. By this, I mean that places elsewhere are not just held up as some ideal model, some geographic imaginary, but that some places serve as physical space where policy advocacy occurs. Indeed, sitting down to speak with conference organizers and participants about specific conferences, those in Ottawa, Portland and Marseilles, the conversation was never restricted to just those places. Every person I spoke with discussed each of these conferences in relation to others, in other places, and at times to each other. This indicates particular trajectories. Each of the conferences that are focused on here came, in part, from elsewhere, and in so doing are illustrative of how they build on both meaning and momentum. Conferences are implicated in social movements, and also cities are implicated in conferences. Therefore it is not only that conferences as convergence space are important to assembling social movements and policy activism, and that conferences are urban events, but also that understanding informational infrastructures through the lens of policy mobilities highlights the meanings, motives and processes by which infrastructures form and flow. Policy making "from below", advocacy for policy change, is an important empirical object through which to understand the spatial effects of mobilizing policy change, sometimes in ways which have the potential to resist dominant forms of urban neoliberalization.

Further interrogation of these convergence spaces has the potential to yield deeper and more nuanced insight into the role of conferences within the drug policy reform movement. This paper used three conferences occurring within a two-year period. During this time there were countless other conferences and meetings held that focused on drug policy reform. Two annual meetings of the United Nations Commission on Narcotic Drugs (CND), for example, happened over this time. This institutional space also acts as an important convergence space within not only the drug policy reform movement, but within broader networks that are concerned with the legal geographies of psychoactive substances. Within the context of drug policy reform, the CND often came up in my interviews with organizers and activists. One organizer and activist said of the CND:

> To change drug policy in this country you need to have the top cop and the top drug people. You need to have that relationship. So I discovered, I can meet these people if I go to Vienna the same time as

> they do ... Now I can pick up the phone and they'll take my call, because of the work I did in Vienna. (Interview, Conference Organizer, 2012)

The organizer went on to link attendance at CND meetings with the conference which was being organized, highlighting the importance of face-to-face interaction over time. An examination of convergence spaces over time can help to more fully understand the ways in which advocacy work is built up to effect real political change at various scales. The CND's constant location in Vienna, for example, acts as a guidepost in a policy process of international drug policy. It is both an important event for transnational and national drug policy makers, and the realm of international diplomacy (Craggs, 2014; Kuus, 2011), and it is an important convergence space for drug policy reform activists to meet each other, encounter those in powerful positions, and to engage in contentious social action (Craggs & Mahony, 2014; Wainwright et al., 2000).

Policy advocacy happens in many forms, and is always a part of the mobilization of specific policy models. This paper addresses a fundamental, grassroots form of policy activism by considering the place of harm reduction conferences in the informational infrastructures of advocacy and implementation of urban public health. Harm reduction as a social movement encompasses a tripartite identity of policy, practice and philosophy. Its identity is fluid and politically contested, while its status as a best-practice public health approach to providing health services has a strong evidence base.

If we are to understand mobility as "a social process operating through and constitutive of *social* space" (McCann, 2011, p. 117, italics original), rather than as "desocialized movement" (Cresswell, 2001, 14), then examining a series of conferences over time begins to territorialize the ephemeral spaces of policy making and knowledge exchange. This territorialization creates *ephemeral fixtures* in the landscape of policy activism, thus helping to further interrogate the ways in which policy is "arrived at" (Robinson, 2013, p. 1) and to make clear the recent and often obscured histories of particular assemblages In a world in which embodied mobility is often taken as fact, looking at who is able to be mobile, such as elite policy advocates, and how mobility is achieved, that is, though the support of social movement organizations or governments is a key question for the geographies of social movements. Further, examining the micro-spaces of where people are mobilized to, such as cities, universities, hotel ballrooms or needle exchange "fieldtrips", brings into focus the complex relationships of policy activism in general and drug policy reform efforts in particular.

Acknowledgements

I would like to thank those organizers, activists and others who took the time to speak with me for this work. I would also like to thank Eugene McCann, Byron Miller, Ian Cook, and Tyler McCreary for comments on an earlier draft. Thanks to Ronan Paddison, Stewart Williams, and Barney Warf for their editorial guidance. And to the two anonymous reviewers for their helpful comments. Responsibility for the argument is of course entirely my own.

Disclosure statement

No potential conflict of interest was reported by the author.

Note

1. These four subsets of actors are in no way considered static or hermetically sealed. There can be overlap and actors may change roles over time.

References

Adey, P. (2006). If mobility is everything then it is nothing: Towards a relational politics of (im)mobilities. *Mobilities*, *1*(1), 75.

Albers, E. (2012). *European network of people who use drugs project final report*. London: European Harm Reduction Network.

Boyd, S., Macpherson, D., & Osborn, B. (2009). *Raise shit! social action saving lives*. Fernwood: Halifax.

Branson, R. (2012). Its time to end the failed war on drugs. Retrieved from http://www.telegraph.co.uk/news/uknews/crime/9031855/Its-time-to-end-the-failed-war-on-drugs.html

Brown, M. P. (1997). *Replacing citizenship: AIDS activism and radical democracy*. New York: Guilford Press.

Bunnell, T. (2015). Antecedent cities and inter-referencing effects: Learning from and extending beyond critiques of neoloberalization. *Urban Studies*, *52*(11), 1983–2000.

Clarke, N. (2012). Urban policy mobility, anti-politics, and histories of the transnational municipal movement. *Progress in Human Geography*, *36*(1), 25–43.

Cook, I. R., & Ward, K. (2011). Trans-urban networks of learning, mega events and policy tourism: The case of Manchester's commonwealth and olympic games projects. *Urban Studies*, *48*(12), 2519–2535.

Cook, I. R., & Ward, K. (2012). Conferences, informational infrastructures and mobile policies: The process of getting Sweden "BID ready". *European Urban and Regional Studies*, *19*(2), 137–152.

Cook, I. R., Ward, S. V., & Ward, K. (2014). A springtime journey to the Soviet Union: Postwar planning and policy mobilities through the Iron Curtain. *International Journal of Urban and Regional Research*, *38*(3), 805–822.

Craggs, R. (2014). Postcolonial geographies, decolonization, and the performance of geopolitics at Commonwealth conferences. *Singapore Journal of Tropical Geography*, *35*, 39–55.

Craggs, R., & Mahony, M. (2014). The geographies of the conference: Knowledge, performance and protest. *Geography Compass*, *8*(6), 414–430.

Cresswell, T. (2001). Mobilities. special issue. *New Formation*, *43*, 7–157.

Davies, A. D. (2012). Assemblage and social movements: Tibet support groups and the spatialities of political organisation. *Transactions of the Institute of British Geographers*, *37*, 273–286.

Della Porta, D., & Andretta, M. (2002). Social movements and public administration: Spontaneous citizens' committees in florence. *International Journal of Urban and Regional Research*, *26*, 244–265.

Desilver, D. (2014). Feds may be rethinking drug war but states have been leading the way. Retrieved from http://www.pewresearch.org/fact-tank/2014/04/02/feds-may-be-rethinking-the-drug-war-but-states-have-been-leading-the-way/

Diani, M. (2000). Social movement networks virtual and real. *Information, Communication & Society*, *3*(3), 386–401.

DiPetro, R. B., Bretter, D., Rompf, P., & Godlewska, M. (2008). An exploratory study of differences among meeting and exhibition planners in their destination selection criteria. *Journal of Convention and Event Tourism*, *9*, 258–276.

Easton, S. (2004). *Marijuana growth in British Columbia*. Vancouver: The Fraser Institute.

England, K., & Ward, K. (Ed.). (2007). *Neoliberalization: States, networks, peoples*. Oxford: Blackwell.

González, S. (2011). Bilbao and Barcelona in motion. How urban regeneration "models" travel and mutate in the global flows of policy tourism. *Urban Studies*, *48*(7), 1397–1418.

Harm Reduction Coalition. Retrieved April 12, 2014, from http://harmreduction.org/our-work/national-conference/

Harris, A., & Moore, S. (2013). Planning histories and practices of circulating urban knowledge. *International Journal of Urban and Regional Research*, *37*(5), 1499–1509.

Haug, C. (2013). Organizing spaces: Meeting arenas as a social movement infrastructure between organization, network, and institution. *Organization Studies*, *34*(5–6), 705–732.

Hughes, C. E., & Stevens, A. (2012). A resounding success or a disastrous failure: Re-examining the interpretation of evidence on the Portuguese decriminalisation of illicit drugs. *Drug and Alcohol Review*, *31*, 101–113.

International Harm Reduction Association. (n.d.). What is harm reduction? Retrieved April 1, 2014, from http://www.ihra.net/what-is-harm-reduction

Jacobs, J. M. (2012). Urban geographies I still thinking cities relationally. *Progress in Human Geography*, *36* (3), 412–422.

Jacobs, J. M., & Lees, L. (2013). Defensible space on the move: revisiting the urban geography of Alice Coleman. *International Journal of Urban and Regional Research*, *37*(5), 1559–1583.

Jessop, B., Brenner, N., & Jones, M. (2008). Theorizing sociospatial relations. *Environment and Planning D: Society and Space*, *26*(3), 389–401.

Keil, R., & Ali, H. (2011). The urban political pathology of emerging infection disease in the age of the global city. In E. McCann & K. Ward (Eds.), *Mobile urbanism: Cities and policy making in the global age* (pp. 123–146). Minneapolis: Minnesota Press.

Klawiter, M. (1999). Racing for the cure, walking women, and toxic touring: Mapping cultures of action within the bay area terrain of breast cancer. *Social Problems*, *46*, 104–126.

Kuus, M. (2011). Policy and geopolitics: Bounding Europe in Europe. *Annals of the Association of American Geographers*, *101*(5), 1140–1155.

Leitner, H., Sheppard, E., & Sziarto, M. (2008). The spatialities of contentious politics. *Transactions of the Institute for British Geographers*, *33*, 157–172.

Marlatt, G. A., & Witkiewitz, K. (2010). Update on harm-reduction policy and intervention research. *Annual Review of Clinical Psychology*, *6*, 591–606.

Massey, D. B. (1994). *Space, place, and gender*. Minneapolis: University of Minnesota Press.

Mayer, M. (2013). Multiscalar mobilization for the just city: New spatial politics of urban movements. In W. Nicholls, B. Miller, & J. Beaumont (Eds.), *Spaces of contention: Spatialities and social movements* (pp. 163–198). Ashgate: London.

McAdam, D., & Paulsen, R. (1993). Specifying the relationship between social ties and activism. *American Journal of Sociology*, *99*(3), 640–667.

McCann, E. (2008). Expertise, truth, and urban policy mobilities: Global circuits of knowledge in the development of Vancouver, Canada's "four pillar" drug strategy. *Environment and Planning A*, *40*(4), 885–904.

McCann, E. (2011a). Urban policy mobilities and global circuits of knowledge: Toward a research agenda. *Annals of the Association of American Geographers*, *101*(1), 107–130.

McCann, E. (2011b). "Points of reference: Knowledge of elsewhere in the politics of urban drug policy". In E. McCann & K. Ward (Eds.), *Assembling urbanism: Mobilizing knowledge & shaping cities in a global context* (pp. 97–122). Minneapolis: University of Minnesota Press.

McCann, E., & Ward, K. (2012). Assembling urbanism: following policies and "studying through" the sites and situations of policy making. *Environment and Planning A*, *44*, 42–51.

McCann, E., & Ward, K. (2013). A multi-disciplinary approach to policy transfer research: geographies, assemblages, mobilities and mutations. *Policy Studies*, *34*(1), 2–18.

McFarlane, C. (2009). Translocal assemblages: space, power and social movements. *Geoforum*, *40*(4), 561–567.

McLaren, P. G., & Mills, A. J. (2008). "I'd like to thank the academy": An analysis of the awards discourse at the Atlantic Schools of Business conference. *Canadian Journal of Administrative Sciences/Revue Canadienne des Sciences de l'Administration*, *25*, 307–316.

Miller, B. (2007). Modes of governance, modes of resistance. In Peck Leitner & Sheppard (Eds.), *Contesting neoliberalism* (pp. 223–249). New York: Guilford Press.

Miller, B. (2013). Spatialities of mobilization: building and breaking relationships. In W. Nicholls, B. Miller, & J. Beaumont (Eds.), *Spaces of contention: Spatialities and social movements* (pp. 285–298). Ashgate: London.

Nicholls, W. (2009). Place, networks, space: theorising the geographies of social movements. *Transactions of the Institute of British Geographers*, *34*(1), 78–93.

Nicholls, W., Miller, B., & Beaumont, J. (2013). *Spaces of contention: Spatialities and social movements*. Ashgate: London.

Pauly, B. B. (2008). Shifting moral values to enhance access to health care: Harm reduction as a context for ethical nursing practice. *International Journal of Drug Policy*, *19*(3), 195–204.

Peck, J., & Theodore, N. (2010). Mobilizing policy: Models, methods, and mutations. *Geoforum*, *41*(2), 169–174.

Percival, G. (2009). Exploring the influence of local policy networks on the implementation of drug policy reform: The case of California's substance abuse and crime prevention act. *Journal of Public Administration Research and Theory*, *19*(4), 795–815.

Pierce, J., Martin, D. G., Greiner, A., Scherr, A. (2012). Urban politics and mental health: An agenda for health geographic research. *Annals of the Association of American Geographers*, *102*(5), 1084–1092.

Prince, R. (2012). Metaphors of policy mobility: Fluid spaces of "creativity" policy. *Geografiska Annaler Series B, Human Geography*, *94*, 317–331.

Pugel, J. (August 14, 2013) Why I'm lobbying to repeal the federal ban on needle exchange funding. *The Stranger.* Retrieved from http://slog.thestranger.com/slog/archives/2013/08/14/this-police-chief-says-lift-federal-ban-on-needle-exchange-funding

Ritter, A., & Cameron, J. (2006). A review of the efficacy and effectiveness of harm reduction strategies for alcohol, tobacco and illicit drugs. *Drug and alcohol review*, *25*(6), 611–624.
Robinson, J. (2013). "Arriving at" urban policies/the urban: Traces of elsewhere in making city futures. In O. Söderström, et al. (Eds.), *Critical mobilities* (pp. 1–28). Lausanne: EPFL and Routledge.
Routledge, P. (2003). Convergence space: Process geographies of grassroots globalization networks. *Transactions of the Institute of British Geographers*, *28*(3), 333–349.
Routledge, P. (2009). Transnational resistance: Global justice networks and spaces of convergence. *Geography Compass*, *3*, 1881–1901.
Strike, C., Watson, T. M., Lavigne, P., Hopkins, S., Shore, R., Young, D., & Millson, P. (2011). Guidelines for better harm reduction: Evaluating implementation of best practice recommendations for needle and syringe programs (NSPs). *International Journal of Drug Policy*, *22*(1), 34–40.
Tanford, S., Montgomery, R. Nelson, K. (2012). Factors that influence attendance, satisfaction, and loyalty for conventions. *Journal of Convention & Event Tourism*, *13*(4), 290–318.
Temenos, C., & McCann, E. (2012). The local politics of policy mobility: learning, persuasion, and the production of a municipal sustainability fix. *Environment and Planning A*, *44*, 1389–1406.
Temenos, C., & McCann, E. (2013). Policies. In P. Adey, D. Bissell, K. Hannam, P. Merriman, & M. Sheller (Eds.), *The routledge handbook of mobilities* (pp. 575–584). New York: Routledge.
Uitermark, J., Nicholls, W., & Loopmans, M. (2012). Cities and social movements: Theorizing beyond the right to the city. *Environment and Planning A*, *44*(11), 2546–2554.
United Nations Office on Drugs and Crime. (2014). Fifty-seventh session of the Commission on Narcotic Drugs high-level segment, *57*(1). 1–15.
Wainwright, J., Prudham, S., & Glassman, J. (2000). The battles in seattle: Microgeographies of resistance and the challenge of building alternative futures. *Environment and Planning D: Society and Space*, *18*, 5–13.
Ward, K. (2006). "Policies in motion", urban management and state restructuring: The trans-local expansion of business improvement districts. *International Journal of Urban and Regional Research*, *30*, 54–75.
Wood, E., Kerr, T., Small, W., Li, K., Marsh, D. C., Montaner, J. S., & Tyndall, M. W. (2004). Changes in public order after the opening of a medically supervised safer injecting facility for illicit injection drug users. *Canadian Medical Association Journal*, *171*(7), 731–734.

Conclusions

Barney Warf[a] and Stewart Williams[b]

[a]Department of Geography and Atmospheric Science, University of Kansas, Lawrence, USA; [b]School of Land and Food, University of Tasmania, Hobart, Australia

Psychoactive drugs have long been a companion to most if not all human societies. Medicinal drugs and recreational ones alike have been used to shape health and consciousness for better or worse in essentially every historical moment and geographical locale. Both plant-based drugs and more recent synthetic creations have received tremendous scrutiny in the modern world, notably from the media, academics, government agencies and policy officials. As the chapters in this book demonstrate, drugs are far more than simply a set of biochemical stimulants. Rather, they are deeply embedded in varying historical contexts, cultural norms and legal practices. Moreover, drugs are also profoundly spatial: the production, transportation, exchange and consumption of drugs of various sorts speak volumes about local differences in social values, beliefs and practices concerning drugs, let alone how the state monitors and regulates their use.

States have attempted to control drugs for centuries, often on grounds of protecting public health and morality. This phenomenon offers a clear example of Foucauldian biopolitics, of how the state produces "proper" subjects and delegitimizes others (Bergschmidt, 2004; Keane, 2009). Because the regulation and prohibition of drugs affect different groups in varying ways, drug policy is profoundly uneven in its social impacts. Moreover, because drugs are deeply geographical—arising from and resulting in highly variegated landscapes in regard to their creation and use—the regulation of drugs is a geopolitical process. Geographical analyses of drugs have grown to include how multiple scales, ranging from that of the individual actor to that of the world economy, are deeply intertwined.

The chapters in this book examined drugs in a wide variety of contexts and from a variety of conceptual perspectives. The book thus falls within a longer tradition of studying drugs geographically (DeVerteuil and Wilton, 2009; Rengert, 1996; Steinberg et al., 2004; Taylor et al., 2013; Thomas et al., 2008; Williams, 2014, 2016; Wilton and Moreno, 2012). In this book, Chris Duvall's examination of African cannabis signifies its importance despite being ignored by agricultural development circles. Attempts to restrict it have caused a loss of income for countless small farmers and inhibited the economic viability of numerous small rural communities. In his analysis of so-called narco-states, Pierre-Arnaud Chouvy escapes the "territorial trap" of the nation-state that has long underpinned most analyses of international drug flows, pointing instead to the assemblages and networks that cross borders with ease. In Emine Evered and Kyle Evered's depiction of Turkish alcohol culture, a tradition that predates the Ottoman Empire is seen now to face mounting challenges from Islamists. In Ireland, as Julien Mercille illustrates, alcohol consumption has been reshaped by neoliberal policies concerning trade, taxes and privatization operating at the global, European and national scales; the chapter offers a multi-scalar analysis that serves as a useful template for spatially informed analyses in other contexts. Stephen Parkin's ethnographic analysis of intravenous drug use in Britain focuses on the role of drug-related litter and its implications for public space. Legal geographies, public health and biopolitics converge in Stewart Williams' chapter on Sydney's Medically Supervised Injecting Centre, which reveals that drug use is the result of lines of power that effortlessly cross long-established spatial hierarchies. Using Surrey, British Columbia, as a case study, Andrew Longhurst and Eugene McCann trace the contours of harm reduction initiatives and the "frontier politics" that swirl around attempts at its implementation. Finally, Cristina Temenos turns to drug policy conferences, examined as ephemeral moments on the drug landscape that often have lasting effects.

With topics grounded in Africa and Turkey, Australia and Britain, Ireland and British Columbia, these chapters draw on a variety of local and national contexts to tease out the complex, often bewildering, intersections among drugs, drug use, drug laws and drug geographies. The lines of thought that run throughout these chapters both reveal much about contemporary modes of geographic analysis and offer routes for the effective analysis of drugs and other issues in other times and places. In all of these chapters, for example, once-solid, taken-for-granted categories (e.g., that of drugs or the nation-state) have been rejected in favor of more fluid definitions, networks and topologies. In all of them, again, the power to make and enforce drug policy shines through clearly, shaping both the microgeographies of daily life as well as the urban and regional landscapes of drug production and consumption. Long-standing dichotomies such as local/global, place/space, cultural/economic, matter/meaning and individual/social, however, offer few insights into this set of issues. Rather, the chapters convey a sense of geographies constituted through flows and movements, multiplicities and rhizomes, actor-networks and assemblages and power-geometries and relational places, with an understanding of space and spatiality as highly plastic and mutable that underscores complexity, ephemerality and fluidity.

The shifting landscapes of drug production and consumption are the uneven, often unintended, outcomes of the power and agency of, as well as the relationships among, multiple actors, human and nonhuman alike. These actors include the drugs themselves in assorted forms (e.g., compare cannabis leaf and resin with synthetic versions such as Kronic, and powder cocaine with its far more addictive, smokable derivative, crack cocaine), the producers (e.g., cannabis and coca growers responsible for various levels of output; and meth labs that might be set up on an industrial scale or small enough to fit inside a car as a mobile operation), the dealers and intermediaries (including internationally organized gangs as well as street-corner pushers) and the consumers (ranging from casual cocaine users found at parties to those addicts with life-threatening habits). Then there are the corporations (e.g., in pharmaceuticals manufacture), the state, media, nonprofit agencies and community organizations and activist groups. Collectively, their interactions range from the highly localized encounters in and of neighborhoods (e.g., as dangerous ghettoes where police fear to patrol or as places of sanctuary providing harm reduction services) through to such well-organized international arrangements as those behind the smuggling of heroin and opium from Afghanistan or Southeast Asia into Europe and North America (e.g., once including the CIA) and those that enabled vast quantities of cocaine to be shipped into the United States (e.g., by the infamous Medellin cartel under Colombian kingpin Pablo Escobar). The complex spatialities that result from these interactions are contingent, unstable and highly variable across time and space. Like other types of geographies, those concerning drugs exhibit a "fibrous, thread-like, wiry, stringy, ropy, capillary character that is never captured by the notions of levels, layers, territories, spheres, categories, structures, or systems" (Paasi, 2004, p. 541). With these conclusions in mind, then, the geographies of drugs and drug use serve as a useful window into wider conceptualizations of how social relations, individual behaviors, power, the state and discourses are simultaneously determinant. Finally, because the boundaries between legal and illegal drugs fluctuate over time, they generate ever-changing geographies of production and consumption through both circulation and arrests.

Why do states bother to regulate drugs? In focusing on notions of the biopolitical, it is easy to be distracted from the very real dangers that some drugs do present. In the United States, for example, illegal drugs kill roughly 40,000 people annually, one every 13 minutes but still a far cry from the hundreds of thousands who die from cigarettes and alcohol (Office of National Drug Control Policy, 2014). Addiction to heroin, methamphetamines and painkillers has ruined the lives of countless others, including children, especially in impoverished inner city and rural areas. "Hard" drugs thus present a clear and present public health hazard, and attempts to rein them in are not unreasonable. Dismissing all drug policies on the grounds that they constitute state oppression is a naïve and counterproductive discursive strategy. For this reason, libertarian interpretations that advocate freedom to use all drugs are misguided. Attempts to curtail drug use tend to focus on the production rather than consumption of drugs. Drug policies can range dramatically from the cruel and irrational to the benign and harmless; an example of the latter is the famous DARE (Drug Abuse Resistance Education) program popular in many American schools that educated children about drugs, only to lead to higher rates of usage among well-informed consumers (Marlow and Rhodes, 1994).

Drug policies are closely entwined with relations of ethnicity, age, class, gender and place, thus affecting peoples and social groups differentially. Not surprisingly, it is invariably the socially marginalized who are inevitably the most adversely affected. For example, in the United States, the "war on drugs" initiated by President Richard Nixon in the 1970s inflicted vast waves of damage on countless millions of people, from coca farmers in Bolivia to inner city youth in America's cities. Targeting minorities with surgical precision, it led to the incarceration of millions, the arrests of many more, and untold numbers of damaged lives, primarily of young men of color. The United States, with 5 percent of the world's population, today has 25 percent of its prisoners, the highest incarceration rate in the world; one out of ten black males is either in jail or on probation. This mass incarceration has even been likened to the infamous Jim Crow laws of the South (Alexander, 2010), which so greatly restricted the political and daily lives of African-Americans. The racially uneven impacts of drug policies include the lighter sentences for cocaine, used more by whites, than crack smokable cocaine, used by blacks. So great has the devastation of this project been that many observers have concluded that the war on drugs has been worse than any damage created by drugs themselves (Baum, 1996; Carpenter, 2003; Gray, 2012). Few countries allow drugs to be produced and consumed free of state interference (although Uruguay comes close).

An important means to appreciate the spatiality of drugs is through the lens of embodiment. The body—what Longhurst (1994) memorably called "the geography closest in"—was central to Foucault's notion of biopolitics with its interest in security, territory and population. Rather than abstract processes, social relations are seen as embodied in individuals who, in turn, are always deeply embedded in networks. While bodies typically appear as "natural," they are in fact social constructions deeply inscribed with multiple meanings, "embodiments" of class, gender, ethnic and other relations. The body is the primary vehicle through which prevailing economic and political institutions inscribe the self, producing a bundle of signs that encodes, reproduces and contests hegemonic notions of identity, order and discipline, morality and ethics, sensuality and sexuality. Bodies, once taken for granted as given and now firmly embedded in their cultural milieu, have become instrumental to human geography (Nast and Pile, 1998). Both drug use and the regulation of drugs involve the literal embodiment of state regulation, which all too often is focused like a gun on young, male, nonwhite bodies. Drug use may be seen as an assemblage of bodies, drugs and urban spaces (Malins, 2004). The regulation of drugs is thus inescapably the regulation of bodies. In this light, the spatiality of drugs has much in common with the literature on the geography of policing space (Herbert, 1996, 2010), and, more broadly, geographies of crime.

Another prominent feature of drugs is the discourses that swirl around them (Gootenberg, 2009). From attempts to portray cannabis as a "colored people's drug" in the 1920s and 1930s to Nancy Reagan's famous and simplistic "Just Say No" exhortation, the symbolic and linguistic meanings pertaining to drugs have been an inevitable feature of their production and use. Other examples include discourses of control, danger and pleasure. Some discourses are even more damaging than the drugs themselves, demonizing users, particularly nonwhites, as subhuman. Such representations abound during "moral panics," when drugs are seen as a threat to the prevailing social order (Goode and Ben-Yehuda, 1994). Given that drugs are simultaneously political, economic, cultural and social in nature, it is helpful to view them in light of cultural political economy, an approach that seeks to bridge the divide between traditional Marxist perspectives and poststructuralist concerns with identity politics, discourse and political performance (Gibson and Kong, 2005; Jessop and Oosterlynck, 2008; Jessop and Sum, 2001).

The intersections of drugs, policy, bodies, discourse and place can be readily seen in the context of American cannabis laws. In the 1930s, as Congress moved steadily toward making cannabis (commonly then also referred to as marijuana) illegal, the discourses invoked against it selectively deployed racialized and gendered discourses in deliberately inaccurate ways, often invoking racist imagery. The infamous movie *Reefer Madness* (1936), now a cult classic, depicted marijuana destroying the lives of adolescents, leading to murder, rape and criminal insanity, and concluded that it was more dangerous than heroin or opium. Marijuana posters typically portrayed a helpless, white female being seduced or overpowered by a Satan-like figure, usually dark skinned. Such tropes also popped up in Nixon's "War on Drugs," which was, and still is, of course, a war on drug users, primarily minorities (Elwood, 1994; Nunn, 2002; Provine, 2007).

Nonetheless, in the United States, cannabis legalization has recently made great gains in popularity. A 2016 Gallup poll indicated that 60 percent of the public favors removing legal restrictions (Swift, 2016). Medical marijuana has made great strides, and is legal in the majority of US states, where many people use it to treat the symptoms of glaucoma, chemotherapy, arthritis, neurological disorders and other ailments. Meanwhile, recreational marijuana—already legal in Alaska, Washington, Oregon and Colorado—became legal in an additional four states following the US election of November 2016 (California, Nevada, Massachusetts and Maine). Those that have legalized recreational marijuana, notably Colorado, have witnessed a boom in tax revenues and tourism. Even so, cannabis remains a Schedule I drug under the US federal government's Controlled Substances Act, on a par with heroin and lysergic acid diethylamide (LSD), although there has never been a medically confirmed case of death from cannabis. Without a more realistic classification, scientific research on cannabis—careful, double-blind studies, rather than anecdotes—is impossible. Annually, roughly 800,000 Americans are arrested for cannabis possession, or 86 per hour, more than for all violent crimes combined (Wegman, 2014). Clearly, legal policies toward drugs are often not grounded in scientific evidence but serve political interests that benefit from their regulation. Not surprisingly, for example, some of the strongest opposition to marijuana legalization has come from the prison guards' union, which has the most to lose should the drug become legal in much of the country. Such comments underscore the fact that drug policy is fundamentally about power and vested interests, and that political rather than scientific criteria often reign foremost in the making of drug laws.

So what are we to make of the relations between drugs, law, people, place and the state? Few easy generalizations can be made for those tend to degenerate into simplistic stereotypes that overlook the complexities and nuances of drug use and policy. Drugs are profoundly social and political objects, and to view them in any other way is to succumb to a false, asocial interpretation that rips them from their legal and cultural contexts. State policies take almost as many forms as drugs themselves, and range in scope, intent and effectiveness. The exertion of state jurisdiction over drugs and drug users is an exercise in power, often with appalling consequences. And finally, drugs are multi-scalar phenomena, tying producers, traffickers, dealers and users together (along with legislators and regulators) in webs that sometimes cross continents. For this reason, the consequences of actions concerning drugs—their production and consumption, regulation and control—and the rhetorics that inevitably accompany them can reverberate over vast distances. Neoliberal drug policies do not simply incarcerate people in developing countries, but reach back across a myriad of linkages to affect landscapes and livelihoods in Afghanistan, Peru, Mexico and elsewhere. Thus drugs are a concise manifestation of globalization in all its profound complexity and gory realty. Reasonable, nuanced views of drug policy would therefore be well advised to take these facets into account.

References

Alexander, M. (2010). *The new Jim Crow: Mass incarceration in the age of colorblindness*. New York, NY: New Press.

Baum, D. (1996). *Smoke and mirrors: The war on drugs and the politics of failure*. Waltham, MD: Little, Brown.

Bergschmidt, V. (2004). Pleasure, power and dangerous substances: Applying Foucault to the study of 'heroin dependence' in Germany. *Anthropology and Medicine*, 11, 59–73.

Carpenter, T. (2003). *Bad neighbor policy: Washington's futile war on drugs in Latin America*. Basingstoke, UK: Palgrave MacMillan.

DeVerteuil, G., and R. Wilton. (2009). The geographies of intoxicants: From production and consumption to regulation, treatment and prevention. *Geography Compass*, 3, 478–494.

Elwood, W. (1994). *Rhetoric in the war on drugs*. Westport, CT: Praeger.

Gibson, C., and L. Kong. (2005). Cultural economy, a critical review. *Progress in Human Geography*, 29, 541–561.

Goode, E., and N. Ben-Yehuda. (1994). Moral panics: Culture, politics and social construction. *American Review of Sociology*, 20, 149–171.

Gootenberg, P. (2009). Talking about the flow: Drugs, borders, and the discourse of drug control. *Cultural Critique*, 71, 13–46.

Gray, J. (2012). *Why our drug laws have failed and what we can do about it* (2nd ed.). Philadelphia, PA: Temple University Press.

Herbert, S. (1996). The normative ordering of police territoriality: Making and marking space with the Los Angeles Police Department. *Annals of the Association of American Geographers*, 86(3), 567–582.

Herbert, S. (2010). Territoriality and the police. *Professional Geographer*, 49(1), 86–94.

Jessop, B., and S. Oosterlynck. (2008). Cultural political economy: On making the cultural turn without falling into soft economic sociology. *Geoforum*, 39(3), 1155–1169.

Jessop, B., and N-L. Sum. (2001). Pre-disciplinary and post-disciplinary perspectives in political economy. *New Political Economy*, 6(1), 89–101.

Keane, H. (2009). Foucault on methadone: Beyond biopower. *International Journal of Drug Policy*, 20, 450–452.

Longhurst, R. (1994). The geography closest in - the body... the politics of pregnability. *Geographical Research*, 32(2), 214–223.

Malins, P. (2004). Body–space assemblages and folds: Theorizing the relationship between injecting drug user bodies and urban space. *Continuum: Journal of Media & Cultural Studies*, 18(4), 483–495.

Marlow, K., and S. Rhodes. 1994. Study: DARE teaches kids about drugs but doesn't prevent use. *Chicago Tribune* (November 6).

Nast, H., and S. Pile. (Eds.). (1998). *Places through the body*. London and New York: Routledge.
Nunn, K. (2002). Race, crime and the pool of surplus criminality: Or why the "War on Drugs" was a war on Blacks. *Gender, Race and Justice*, 6, 381–445.
Office of National Drug Control Policy. (2014). Consequences of illegal drug use in America. https://www.whitehouse.gov/sites/default/files/ondcp/Fact_Sheets/consequences_of_illicit_drug_use_-_fact_sheet_april_2014.pdf
Paasi, A. (2004). Place and region: Looking through the prism of scale. *Progress in Human Geography*, 28, 536–546.
Provine, D. (2007). *Unequal under law: Race in the war on drugs*. Chicago, IL: University of Chicago Press.
Rengert, G. (1996). *The geography of illegal drugs*. Boulder, CO: West View Press.
Steinberg, M., Hobbs, J., and Mathewson, K. (Eds). (2004). *Dangerous harvest: Drug plants and the transformation of indigenous landscapes*. Oxford: Oxford University Press.
Swift, A. (2016). Support for legal marijuana use up to 60% in U.S. http://www.gallup.com/poll/196550/support-legal-marijuana.aspx
Taylor, J. S., C. Jasparro, and K. Mattson. (2013). Geographers and drugs: A survey of the literature. *Geographical Review*, 103, 415–430.
Thomas, Y., D. Richardson, and I. Cheung. (Eds.). (2008). *Geography and drug addiction*. Dordrecht, the Netherlands: Springer.
Wegman, J. (2014). The injustice of marijuana arrests. *New York Times* (July 28). http://www.nytimes.com/2014/07/29/opinion/high-time-the-injustice-of-marijuana-arrests.html?_r=0
Williams, S. (2014). *Geography of drugs. Oxford annotated bibliographies*. New York, NY: Oxford University Press (online publication).
Williams, S. (2016). Situating drugs and drug use geographically: From place to space and back again. *International Journal of Drug Policy*, 33, 1–5.
Wilton, R., and C. Moreno. (2012). Critical geographies of drugs and alcohol. *Social & Cultural Geography*, 13, 99–108.

Index

Note: **Boldface** page numbers refer to figures and tables. Page numbers followed with "n" refer to footnotes.